ALASKA

FODOR'S MODERN GUIDES

are compiled, researched, and edited by an international team of travel writers, field correspondents, and editors. The series, which now almost covers the globe, was founded by Eugene Fodor.

OFFICES

New York & London

Editorial Staff for ALASKA 1981

Editor: CYNTHIA NELSON

Area Editor: NORMA SPRING

Editorial Associate: BETH IOGHA

Editorial Assistant: CASTLEWOOD

Illustrations: SANDRA LANG

Maps and City Plans: DYNO LOWENSTEIN

FODOR'S
ALASKA
1981

FODOR'S MODERN GUIDES, INC.
Distributed by
DAVID McKAY COMPANY, INC.
New York

**All the following Guides are current (most of them also in
the Hodder and Stoughton British edition).**

CURRENT FODOR'S COUNTRY AND AREA TITLES:

AUSTRALIA, NEW ZEALAND AND SOUTH PACIFIC	INDIA
AUSTRIA	IRELAND
BAJA CALIFORNIA	ISRAEL
BELGIUM AND LUXEMBOURG	ITALY
BERMUDA	JAPAN AND KOREA
BRAZIL	JORDAN AND HOLY LAND
CANADA	MEXICO
CARIBBEAN AND BAHAMAS	NORTH AFRICA
CENTRAL AMERICA	PEOPLE'S REPUBLIC OF CHINA
EASTERN EUROPE	PORTUGAL
EGYPT	SCANDINAVIA
EUROPE	SOUTH AMERICA
FRANCE	SOUTHEAST ASIA
GERMANY	SOVIET UNION
GREAT BRITAIN	SPAIN
GREECE	SWITZERLAND
HOLLAND	TURKEY
	YUGOSLAVIA

CITY GUIDES:

LONDON	ROME
PARIS	WASHINGTON, D.C.

FODOR'S BUDGET SERIES:

BUDGET EUROPE	BUDGET GERMANY
BUDGET TRAVEL IN AMERICA	BUDGET ITALY
BUDGET CARIBBEAN	BUDGET MEXICO
BUDGET BRITAIN	BUDGET SPAIN
BUDGET FRANCE	BUDGET JAPAN

USA GUIDES:

USA (in one volume)	NEW YORK
CALIFORNIA	NEW ENGLAND
COLORADO	FLORIDA
HAWAII	MIDWEST
FAR WEST	OUTDOORS AMERICA
ALASKA	PENNSYLVANIA
SOUTHWEST	SUNBELT LEISURE GUIDE
SOUTH	

SPECIAL INTEREST SERIES:
CIVIL WAR SITES

CONTENTS

CONTENTS

ALASKA

Bigger than Life Size

BY
NORMA SPRING

A Seattle-based freelance writer, Mrs. Spring's books include Alaska,
Pioneer State *and* Alaska, the Complete Travel Book. *She is also the
author of numerous newspaper and magazine articles on Alaska, as
well as round-the-world travel, including a book on travel in the
U.S.S.R.,* Roaming Russia, Siberia, and Middle Asia, *illustrated with
color and black-and-white photographs by husband Bob.*

Ask an Alaskan enthusiast what's so "great" about the Great Land
in the northwest corner of our continent, and stand back for an
earful. Just the name "Alaska" is enough to trigger a torrent of prose
(or poetry) comparable to the unleashing of the state's mighty rivers
during the annual spring ice breakup.

You may be sorry you asked, unless you are serious about wanting

1

to know, and you are planning to travel to Alaska. First come the generalities: the soul-satisfying wilderness where birds, animals, and sea life are confronted on their home grounds; the rugged natural beauty of the land—fresh, unspoiled as yet; lots of elbow room for recreation, with skiing, hiking, climbing, snowmobiling, fishing, hunting, beachcombing, river rafting, rock-hounding, and bird-watching, for starters.

Next, some specific, Alaskan superlatives: the most western state—than Hawaii, even; most northern tip of the United States (Point Barrow); most shoreline (34,000 miles); most time zones (four); longest days (in summer); longest nights (in winter); highest point on the North American continent (Mount McKinley, 20,320 feet); and a land area bigger than Texas (2½ times). Moreover, those 586,412 square miles allow about 1½ square miles for every resident. The still-sparse population numbers over 400,000.

Truthfully, the enthusiasm is justified. In this book, we'll mention some of the things that make Alaska a unique and fascinating travel destination: the nature of the land, what it's like to travel there—including cost—and the nature of the people.

The First Visitors

Alaska, over the centuries, can be compared to a sleeping giant, periodically aroused by those who would like to share the treasures hoarded in vast virgin forests, mountains, and seas. Scientists estimate that the first visitors came 25,000 to 35,000 years ago, probably following their food supply—meat on the hoof and paw—which was heading for then-greener pastures. While it lasted, about 3,000 years, animals and people used a land bridge across the Bering Sea which connected the Asian and North American continents. When it was drowned again by the melting of ice-age glaciers, seafarers continued to paddle across.

In waves of different ethnic backgrounds, some early "tourists" stayed to settle, making up the basic aboriginals of Alaska: the Indians in the milder coastal regions of southeast Alaska and the interior; the Aleuts in the Aleutian Island chain; and the Eskimos in the Arctic. Other tribes migrated southward to people the rest of the continent.

Russian America

The Russians, close neighbors on the west, came to call in the eighteenth century. They met native Aleuts as they island-hopped along the volcanic island chain. In 1741, they sighted the mainland. The Aleuts had been calling Alaska a similar-sounding name meaning "the great land." The Russians chose to claim and colonize their discovery as "Russian America" for the rest of the eighteenth and over half of the nineteenth century.

Their first settlement was on Kodiak Island in the Gulf of Alaska, but in a few years, Governor Baranof moved the capital to Sitka. It was more on the traveled path, had a milder climate, and was more sheltered.

Trade flourished west to Hawaii and down the western coast to Fort Ross, California. The Russians built ships with the abundant Sitka spruce. Sitka-cast iron bells for missions and ice for San Francisco bars were part of the southbound cargo. Northbound ships brought back food for the colonies. Furs were in demand in the courts of Europe and Asia, especially the lovely, soft seal fur. Russian fur traders had found the annual breeding rookeries in the Pribilof Islands, tiny dots in the Bering Sea, and they harvested the fur seal almost to extinction.

History Repeats Itself

The Russian colonies in "Russian America," far removed from their capital (then St. Petersburg), were proving too expensive to maintain. Russia preferred to relinquish its holdings to the United States rather than to the more aggressive British and Spanish, both busily exploring and trading along the Northwest coast. Negotiating with William H. Seward, U.S. Secretary of State, the Russians came up with a bargain offer.

In 1867, after much debate in Congress, the United States reluctantly paid 2½¢ an acre for this "white elephant," far removed from the heart of the U.S. For most of the next century, the treasures stored in "Uncle Sam's attic" lay unnoticed, except for sporadic golden bonanzas. Sensational at the time, these were inclined to peter out, or else were controversial, or hard to reach.

The circa-1900 flurry of gold rushes drew thousands, but relatively few stayed on. The panicky recognition that Alaska's position was strategic for national defense in World War II brought in military installations and people and Federal Government-based economy. Searches for metals and other vital raw materials caused off-again, on-again excitement. The development of the oil discoveries on the North Slope had to wait for the green light in the form of Native Land Claim settlements, and proven ecology-protection measures.

Achievement of statehood (49th star) was sensational, but mainly in Alaska. For several years thereafter, people from "outside" (everywhere else but Alaska) were still asking how to get there from the United States, wondering if English was spoken, and what kind of foreign postage was required.

The 1964 earthquake hit the most densely-populated area, Anchorage, hard. In 1967, the year that Alaskans held a year-long party to celebrate the Centennial of Purchase, floods inundated Fairbanks, second largest city. These catastrophes helped to pinpoint Alaska on the map. Based on necessity, disaster triggered a wave of new buildings and modernization.

But the events which started Alaska's latest boom—heard round the world—were the settlement of the Native Land Claims and the building of the oil pipeline. There are yet many problems to be resolved, among them tax structures, use of land, and whether to build more roads into underdeveloped areas. But Alaskans are optimists. They believe the prosperity with them now will continue—around the corner, maybe forever. The potentials are tremendous, and free enterprise flourishes in newly-formed Native Corporations. Somewhat stumbling, these corporations are dedicated to administer their lands and the income from them for the good of all the natives.

In the Arctic, for example, tourism appears to be a natural. The Eskimos are hospitable by nature and are accustomed to entertaining transient visitors. Over the years they've practiced on explorers, adventurers, Arctic researchers, and the military. They are investing their dollars in the "creature comforts" they think visitors need, like modern hotels; and for themselves, in housing, stores, and utilities.

While the natives head into the future but still have a foot in the past, it is a fascinating time to visit Eskimo towns Kotzebue and Barrow. You'll see new ways vs. old, and combinations of both. Skin boats have outboard motors. Women carve up seal meat and prepare sealskin storage pokes using the ancient, efficient ooloo, a sharp, curved "woman's knife." If you peek into a natural deep freezer dug out of permafrost you may see TV dinners stashed along with whale meat, fish, caribou, seal, and walrus.

The Alaskans

Alaskans today are a convivial mix of native (about a sixth of the population) Eskimos, Indians, and Aleuts; born-in Alaskans and immigrants from all over the continental "South-48" states and Hawaii; and descendants of foreign explorers and settlers, including Russians.

To visit some natives on their home (ancestral) grounds, the only way to get there is to fly: to the Pribilof islands, home of the Aleuts, and to Arctic Eskimo towns. Nome, turn-of-the-century gold-rush city, is now the home of the King Island Eskimos, who used to live on a large rocky island in the Bering Sea.

It's possible to arrange a visit to smaller, more remote villages around the coast and along the Yukon and Kuskokwim Rivers by bush planes on their daily rounds. If you want to stay longer, the pilot usually knows someone who would be willing to take in a guest for overnight, or a few days. You pay for lodging, and can either bring your own food or pay a little more and take pot-luck with the family.

Athabascan Indians live in the interior; the Tlingits live along the southeast seacoast. Thanks to the mild climate and the bounty of forest and sea, the Tlingits lived an affluent life. They had time to be sociable and to develop their arts, especially woodcarving.

The art of carving tall totem poles is being perpetuated. North and south of Ketchikan are stands of authentically reproduced totems. The Sitka National Historical Park has totems outside the Visitors' Center, and carved housepoles inside. Near the head of Lynn Canal, at Port Chilkoot, the Alaskan Indian Arts program has been studying, preserving, and reproducing Tlingit Indian arts and crafts from totem carving to Indian dancing.

Human Nature

There are no noticeable language or racial barriers among the still-small population of stubborn, independent, hardworking residents. With spirits (and they are sometimes full of them) fiercely loyal, and with great pride in their state, Alaskans have some qualities in common. You'll note their vigor and their youth (average age mid-twenties) and that they seem well educated.

Alaskans are individualists. Probably having lots of elbow room has something to do with it. They revel in their wide open spaces and freedom for infinite outdoor recreation. There are debates, and a reckoning coming up, on how much land should be saved and how much used. The acreage set aside in national parks, forests, monuments, and game refuges is more than in all the other 49 states combined, and 99 percent of the state is undeveloped, so far.

Alaskans fish and hunt for subsistence, for food in the locker, and a boost to the family budget. Whole families work together at what needs doing, especially during the long, light summer months. They are experts at work, often handling more than one job at a time. If they seem to work hard, you should see them play! The calendar is full of games and festivals celebrating everything from ice worms

(Cordova in February) to whales (Point Hope in June). Almost any excuse puts them in a festive mood.

The original sourdough miners, those who panned during the gold rush, have (hopefully) found their eternal golden reward. It's been over 80 years since that big bonanza. There are still original Alaskan homesteaders, though proving up by building a cabin and living off the land hasn't been allowed for years. After being in Alaska during the war, soldiers and many others were drawn back.

The *real* Alaskans now are the ones who live there, sticking it out through boom and bust, forever enthusiastic about their raw, rarely mild, sometimes violent land. They accept the unexpected and cope with what they have to. The happiest visitors adopt their philosophy.

Alaskans know it takes time to get around and savor their big state. Moreover, everything written or rumored has probably been true at some time or place. The key is to stay flexible. Take possible (inevitable) delays or change of plans with an open mind. They may not necessarily refer to disaster, but the saying among Alaskans is that if something *can* happen, it will.

If there is something you want to know, never be afraid to ask. Alaskans will point you toward their favorite things: a colorful bar, museum, children's zoo, local entertainment, or the top rock group currently playing in town.

Sorting Out the Geography

The grand-scale peninsula jutting into two great oceans and two seas has multiple personalities and many faces. Geographically, there are several Alaskas; glaciers, snow, ice, and permafrost are balanced by smoking volcanoes, desert sand, grassy plains, and rainforest jungles. Though some areas grow trees thick as fur on a husky pup, there are infinite stretches of tundra, from the Russian meaning "where the trees are not."

The weather is dry, and the weather is dank, with record rainfalls and fog in some areas. An outdoor thermometer on a bank in Fairbanks, in the interior, can register minus 60 degrees in winter and soar to 98 above in summer. The seasons are unequal: long dark winters, offset by short light summers. Fall and spring are fleeting, pronounced, and beautiful. These contrasts are contained in Alaska's six varied geographical regions that shape up into a big dipper, which is the state's chosen symbol and the inspiration for its flag.

A young native, Benny Benson, designed the flag that won a school contest sponsored by the American Legion in 1926. He had good reasons for choosing the Big Dipper's 7 stars and the North Star in gold, against a deep blue background: "The blue field is for the Alaska sky and the forget-me-not, Alaska's state flower. The North Star is for the future State of Alaska, the most northerly of the Union. The Dipper is for the Great Bear—symbolizing strength."

Think of the Dipper tilted so its handle stretches down from the bowl south and east. Southeast Alaska, also called the "Panhandle," is a substantial string of lush green, timbered islands plus a narrow coastal strip, separated from Canada by mountains. No connecting conventional highways here. Between the archipelago and mainland Alaska winds the famous Inside Passage water route to Alaska, well-used even before its gold rush heyday at the turn of the century. Indians, explorers, traders, and adventurers plied it in the past. Today's "Marine Highway" traffic includes freighters, yachts, barges, ferries, and cruise ships.

The rest of the Alaskas are contained in the cup. The bulkiest Alaska is the interior, a vast basin bordered on the east by Canada and defined by giant mountain ranges and mighty rivers. Here, and bordering the Gulf of Alaska area, including the Kenai Peninusla, are most of Alaska's still-scanty roads, including the end of the Alaska Highway in Fairbanks. About one-fifth of the state is accessible by road.

More Alaskas, set off by natural barriers, stretch around the coastal fringes, washed by the Pacific and Arctic Oceans and the Bering and Chukchi Seas. No roads lead to western, southwestern, and Arctic Alaska. They are served by planes, bush size to jet. Some of the best of Alaska adventuring lies in the far out places.

The "Grand Tour," or How to See it All

A "grand circle route" has evolved with the development and improvement of transportation and roads. It's expandable and reversible, and as personal as you want to make it, depending on your style of travel. Roughly, if you go one way by land (Alaska Highway), you return by water (Inside Passage) several thousand miles and days, or weeks, later. Or vice versa. In between, when you come to the end of marine and land routes, you take a plane. No roads lead to the fringes of Alaska: the Arctic Coast, Far West Alaska, and out onto the Alaska Peninsula and the Aleutian Island Chain.

Cruise ships and tour operators offer combination land/sea/air tours for varying lengths of time and assorted prices. They follow this circular route in general, spelling out the variations and embellishments. They usually allow opportunities to add optional tours, preferably when you sign up for the basic tour.

If you are a do-it-yourself, independent traveler, there is nowhere better to practice than in Alaska. You won't be lonesome as you travel the circuit route! Camping or trailering, you'll meet other families, retired couples, and young people, sharing strategically-placed and scenic campgrounds.

A flexible schedule allows you to stop and blend into the community for a few days of sightseeing or fishing. Fish are big, especially among the deep passages of the Southeast Panhandle Islands. There are fishing derbies galore throughout most of the year. Visitors with the desire and a license (one-day $5; 10 days, $15; a year, $30) are welcome to compete for substantial cash and merchandise prizes.

Another great do-it-yourself sport is following roads to their endings. Only a few miles out of cities and town, and you are in wilderness. Even on main roads, you are likely to see wild animals amble across. Warning signs are posted for moose.

South of Anchorage, the Kenai Peninsula's Sterling Highway gives up at Homer, at the tip of Homer Spit, a 5-mile-long finger of land jutting into fjord-like Kachemak Bay. The extraordinarily beautiful balance of mountains, sea, islands, and coastline has attracted a colony of artists.

Much of the lively summer scene takes place on the Spit and in the surrounding salt chuck. Camping, beachcombing, fishing, crabbing, clamming, and bird- and sea-life watching are all spectacular among Kachemak Bay's islands, fjords, glaciers, and even volcanoes. A working fish boat provides tour and ferry service to campgrounds and settlements across the bay.

The Richardson Highway terminates in oil-busy Valdez, southern Alaska's pipeline terminal. It traverses some of Alaska's most gorgeous scenery, winding down a narrow canyon that was first a gold rush trail, then a wagon road, and now a paved highway to the interior, paralleled by the pipeline.

Road endings are usually gateways to other areas. In this case, a ferry crosses spectacular Prince William Sound noted for bird- and sea-life and Columbia Glacier (one of the largest) to Whittier. From here, a railway portage connects with the highway to Anchorage.

The Alaska Highway is still an achievement that appeals to pioneer spirits. Everyone should sometime drive (or go by motorcoach) at least one way, partly for perspective. The "Alcan," historic and monumental Canada-U.S. joint venture during World War II, was pushed through mountain and muskeg in a few months. It set a record for building military highways.

Out of the Past

A particular delight of sightseeing in almost overwhelmingly large Alaska is taking to varied, sometimes ingenious, or historic modes of transportation as needed, or just for fun or photos. From Skagway, at the north end of the Inside Passage, cruisers can switch to the White Pass and Yukon Route. This amazing narrow-gauge railroad was engineered through almost impossible rock cliffs and mountains before 1900. It eased the way to the Klondike gold fields, replacing the miners' killing treks carrying tons of supplies to the top of the pass.

Today, converted from steam to diesel, the W. P. & Y. R. Railroad is still a working train, carrying ore, supplies, cars, and passengers between the seacoast and the interior. Remnants remain of the pre-railroad, backbreaking "trail of '98." To the top of the Pass and back has long been a popular excursion. Many still choose this nostalgic route to Whitehorse rather than driving the new Carcross Highway. Ferry travelers can ride the rails and ship their vehicle on through to join the Alaska Highway at Whitehorse.

Out of Fairbanks is another delightful sample of early-day transportation, a riverboat. The sternwheeler *Discovery* churns up the Chena River, reminiscent of the days when the Yukon was the "marine highway" to the Klondike. The 4-hour trip along part of the route is a nostalgic paddle into Fairbanks' golden past. The captain and hostesses, often local students from the University of Alaska, describe and point out many phases of far north life: vintage and modern log homes, trapper's camp, dog teams, float planes, and rich gold streams.

Just for contrast, there's a very popular mode of transportation forty miles down Turnagain Arm from Anchorage. Would you believe a chair-lift? At Mount Alyeska, Alaska's largest year-round see and ski resort, Alaskans and visitors take a leisurely ride up 2,000 feet to grand picture-taking viewpoints. The sundeck overlooks mountain-bordered reaches that Captain Cook named. He thought there was a through passsage to Prince William Sound, but found the way blocked by mountains and the magnificent Portage Glacier. So he had to "Turn again" (and go back).

From Dog Teams to Jets

Getting to the Pribilofs today points up the amazing development of air transportation in the last 30 years. It's a 2,000-mile round trip from Anchorage over massive snowy peaks of the Alaska Peninsula, tapering down to the rocky sea-level islands of the Aleutian Range. This was the supply route for U.S. forces during World War II, when Japan tried to use the islands as stepping-stones to invasion via Alaska.

A veteran bush pilot, Bob Reeve, pioneered the flights, and his Reeve Aleutian Airways is still the "only way to fly" out the Chain. His planes, mostly prop jets, are bigger and better now. Otherwise, it's the same informal delivery operation.

Space is blocked off as needed for freight, and there are usually 30-some seats left over for passengers. Aleuts, like other natives living in far-out places, became members of jet sets before auto clubs. Some passengers will be government workers, many in wildlife jobs. The others heading for St. Paul Island may be on a tour, bent on watching seals and birds and taking pictures in the accessible rookeries, and getting acquainted with the town's friendly residents, about 500 descendants of Aleut-Russians. Two hundred years ago, the Russians transplanted Aleuts here to harvest fur seals. They are still in business. The herds are now restored to full strength, about 1¼ million, due to careful management.

The pilot and crew obviously enjoy being "tour guides." They point out old lava flows, some still-smoking volcanic peaks, rusting debris and Quonset huts left at Cold Bay base after the war, and sea life. During the 200-mile Bering Sea leg, there may be a pod of playful whales.

Five islets make up the Pribilof group. St. Paul, the headquarters, is a green, treeless oasis, with rippling belts of lush grass contrasting with red volcanic soil.

Other Than Jets

Besides commercial jets, there are many small air services listed in cities and towns. Small planes are fine for picture-taking and sightseeing in the bush country, and the pilots are some of the most skillful. As they say, "There are old pilots and bold pilots, but no old bold pilots."

A record number of Alaskans own and fly planes. Note the number of small planes lining Anchorage's Hood Lake next to the

International Airport. Out of town, you may see a plane parked next to the house. Because of the distances and limited number of highways, air travel is necessary, and popular.

You'll see some sled dogs, unemployed in summer, staked out in Eskimo towns while the pups roam and scrounge freely. You'll also see snow machines, motorbikes, cars, trucks, and tour buses, freighted in by Hercules jets. With the accent on saving energy, "working" dog teams may come back in full force. Meanwhile, dog sleds are still considered most practical for patrolling beats like McKinley Park in winter, and fine looking teams are groomed for myriad sled-dog races. Everyone turns out for the World Chammpionship Sled Dog Races during the February Anchorage Fur Rendezvous. The grueling 1,000-mile Inditarod Trail Race is a classic. Starting from near Anchorage and ending in Nome, it commemorates an early mail route mercy-run when diphtheria serum was rushed by relays to isolated, stricken Nome in 1925.

And in the Future

Now that the controversial Alaska pipeline is completed, some see the working "haul" road as a new travel-corridor to the far north. As an extension of the Alaska Highway, it would add additional recreational road-miles.

The North Slope could become a major tourist attraction, perhaps even an Arctic museum. Those who have already been there, as workers or visitors, have been impressed with the number and variety of birds nesting in ice-melt lakes among the permafrost mounds called "pingos." The caribou have continued to migrate. Along with pump stations, gathering lines, drill pads, wells and "Christmas trees" (capped wells) are the research sites, evidence of the effort put into preserving the Arctic's fragile ecology.

And there are barely-touched destinations to explore around the coastal fringes: islands like Shishmaref, historic World War II sites out in the Aleutian Island Chain, and the Bristol Bay fishing banks.

Coastal western Alaska boasts a "Window on the East" as intriguing as Russian Peter the Great's "Window on the West," near Leningrad. Flightseeing planes go within the very shadow of Siberia. Though poles apart in politics, the mainlands of the U.S.S.R. and the U.S. are separated by 55 miles at the narrowest point in the Bering Sea. Every once in a while someone talks of rebuilding that land-bridge, or constructing an underwater tube. Think of the tourism possibilities! Except for the problem of bridging the Atlantic, and some complexities of connecting roads across the continents, it could be the start of a "Trans-World Highway."

Travel promotion experts and marketing specialists are kept busy trying to predict the trends. Surveys show that travel north continues to increase and that Mt. McKinley National Park is still the top tourist attraction. They've determined that the "typical tourist" is somewhat younger now, and inclined to be independent. Fine, all-inclusive package tours, attractive in scope and price, continue to draw individuals and groups, including many senior citizens. This means increasing the food and lodging facilities and expanding the travel possibilities—the places a traveler can reach and those that appeal to special interests.

Some main pattern changes have to do with season and length of stay. Innovators in the travel industry see Alaska as more than a summer-only destination. They are fashioning attractive tours and happenings for every season, even the dead of winter.

Because of improved travel, especially by air, and competitive (cheaper) fares, the trend is toward shorter and more frequent trips to the Great Land. Visitors with only a few days for vacation can jet to and explore one area at a time. Fly/Drive packages are popular, and short-term trips now reach once-remote areas. "Mini-tours" fly from Seattle to Glacier Bay in summer to cruise and overnight up-bay. The price (from under $500 for a 3-day, 2-night tour) for a look at one of Southeast Alaska's main attractions seems most reasonable, considering the amount of transportation included.

Anchorage and Fairbanks are already world air-crossroads with a rapidly-developing cultural climate and potential wealth to support fine arts. They may be on the way to take their place among the world's great cities. Future travelers may flock there to enjoy the very best music, art, drama, and sports.

If this introduction has titillated your adventuresome spirit, read on. The general Facts at Your Fingertips section and the more specific Practical Information, plus the Exploring sections, will help you to decide your style of travel in Alaska and will point you in some right directions.

FACTS AT YOUR FINGERTIPS

WHEN TO GO. Henry Gannett, wandering map-maker, *circa* 1900, endeared himself to Alaskans forever by advising: ". . . if you are young, stay away until you grow older . . ." He opined that Alaska's natural beauty overshadowed any world counterpart to the point that "all other scenery becomes flat and insipid. It is not well to dull one's capacity for such enjoyment by seeing the finest first."

Actually, today's answer should be "now" or "as soon as possible," while there are still nostalgic touches from the past, and contrasts brought on by the old cultures adapting to the jet-age present, as they plan for a bright future.

Summer is the most popular time for visiting Alaska. This is the longest and lightest season in the far north. It spans about two and one-half months, roughly from mid-June (the year's longest day is June 21st) until toward the end of August. By the middle of June, even residents in the far north have usually contended with "break-up," the time when frozen ground thaws on the surface. As for summer, it lasts until the leaves, nipped by frost at night and starting to turn color, herald fall—which could be anytime after mid-August.

Many of today's visitors, however, are developing a taste for "offseasoning" with their tours, and for a lower cost. In the Arctic, the tundra and restless seas have their own particular splendor, whether ice-locked in winter under the midday moon, or blooming and sparkling in summer under the midnight sun. There is charm in the fleeting spring, and also in "Septober." Then the low-growing tundra plants turn red and gold and bright with berries, and the evergreen forests are enriched with the yellow-golds of deciduous birch and aspen.

FALL FUN IN ALASKA

After the light and busy summer, Alaskans resume such favorite and vital activities as hunting and fishing, and not just for sport—a moose in the locker is money in the bank. Bear, deer, birds, fish, and food such as berries to be had for the gathering, are both tasty and a boost to family budgets. And Alaskans also take time to hike, canoe, tackle rivers by Kayak and raft, and otherwise explore and enjoy their vast wilderness state.

Those who vacation in Alaska during early autumn can share in some special fall bonuses. Above the brilliant foliage, skies may be unbelievably blue, and the mountains and glaciers, always sensational, may be enhanced by fresh dustings of snow.

If you are serious about "going Alaskan," you can travel more in-dependently than a summer tourist, rubbing shoulders out of doors with Alaskans and even camping out. Daytime temperatures can still be delightful, though evenings get progressively nippier. Dress properly and take the morning skim of ice on the water bucket in stride. The bugs will have given up and so will the majority of campers. There'll be space in the campgrounds

13

and in the motels and hotels for those who prefer a roof. An extra bonus is the lower price on tours, transportation, and accommodations.

Alaskans rarely pass up an opportunity to celebrate Alaska's history. Fall's most important date was set over a century ago at Sitka, on the west side of big Baranof Island, in the northern part of the Southeast Panhandle. On October 18, 1867, Russia transferred all its holdings in "Russian America" to the United States. The ceremony took place overlooking Sitka's beautiful, busy, island-dotted harbor. On Alaska Day the townspeople, in period dress (including some vintage Russian-American soldier uniforms), climb Castle Hill for the ceremonies. The festivities in Sitka last for three days and feature contests, a parade, a pageant, and a costume ball.

Fall is also fine in Anchorage, hub of Alaska's highway system and headquarters for trips to the fish- and game-filled Kenai Peninsula, McKinley National Park, Valdez and the Prince William Sound area, and the Matanuska Valley. All will be sporting golden fall colors. If you get to Palmer during the ten days before Labor Day, you'll find everyone going all out for the annual State Fair, where they display vegetables of amazing size grown under the midnight sun.

As for regions like Kotzebue, above the Arctic Circle, early fall visitors will find the Eskimos winding up their preparation of winter food delicacies. If you are interested, someone is likely to show you what they have stashed away in their natural freezer, a deep hole dug into the permanently frozen ground—perhaps caribou, or reindeer, fish, seal, walrus, or whale meat, along with succulent Arctic berries still being picked and preserved.

Alaskans slide smoothly from fall into the holidays, celebrated with fervor even in the smallest villages. But they are just a prelude to the fun and games of winter: dogsled races, snowmobile competitions, winter carnivals. People play in the snow as long as it lasts.

FUN IN WINTER?

It's not news that the birds and the bikini set head south for winter. But how about flying north for an out-of-the-ordinary winter vacation spiced with that special Alaskan off-seasoning?

During those short summers with the long, sunlit days, everyone works hard greeting visitors, minding their own business—often more than one—and making hay for the long nights ahead. Alaskans look forward to winter, when they feel they have earned the right to unwind and play, with gusto. And the hardy residents are masters at coming up with guaranteed antidotes for "cabin fever" or other winter doldrums.

Big-city Anchorage on the Gulf Coast of South Central Alaska has a lively winter social season. You can have a ball here, especially if you come for the annual Fur Rendezvous, the "Rondy." They hold a bang-up Miner's and Trapper's Costume Ball during the action-packed 10-day celebration. Competitors in the famous World Championship Sled Dog Races come from as far away as the east coast to challenge Alaska bush-village mushers for thousands of dollars in prize money. There are round-the-clock events, and even a fur auction, which started it all in the first place.

In and around Anchorage there are at least ten recreation areas for cross-country and rope-tow skiing. There is ice skating in some 15 rinks, wide open spaces for snowmobiling, and ice fishing in lakes reached by snowshoes. Mount Alyeska, the most developed ski area, is only 40 miles from Anchorage along mountain-rimmed Turnagain Arm. The skiing never really stops there. People from all over the world take advantage of ski-packages and have all the snow they can handle around the lodge in season. Multiple rope tows and chairlifts hoist enthusiasts to higher elevations offering spectacular vistas. The rest of the year diehard skiers fly up to glacier snow.

You'll find cross-country and ski-slope companions in communities wherever there is snow and the terrain to support the action. Eaglecrest, in the state's capital, Juneau, is one of the newest ski developments, with a day lodge and lifts. Though located in milder Southeast Alaska, winter skiers can count on snow at Eaglecrest elevations when it is raining (frequently) at sea-level Juneau.

Enthusiastic visitors also will want to sample Fairbanks at its wintry best. In this second-largest Alaska city, situated in the Interior, the summer-to-winter spread of temperature can be an amazing 150°. Even though in winter the thermometer may drop far below zero, however, this hardly fazes the residents. It is home of the farthest-north University of Alaska, and both students and residents are lively and competitive. They salute the North's classic form of transportation with Women's, Men's, and Junior North American Dog Sled Championship races.

The classic of these competitions, however, is the Iditarod Dog Sled Race in March. Covering over a thousand miles, it starts at Knik, near Anchorage. When it will end, with the winning team trotting down Nome's Front Street along the frozen Bering Sea, is anyone's bet (and they do). But visitors don't have to mush to get there. From Anchorage, the winter jet flight over snow-covered tundra and large meandering rivers is spectacular. Locked in winter ice, the rivers look like broad white highways.

Winter tours are offered February through May. They include some smooth dog sledding past pressure ridges frozen in fantastic shapes in the Bering Sea. When the tomcod are running you're welcome to try ice fishing along with the Eskimos. Warm parkas and other insulated clothing and boots are issued to guests when needed for playing outdoors. Indoors, both visitors and the King Island Eskimos welcome the diversion of Native craft demonstrations: ivory carving, skin sewing, and Eskimo dancing and singing. Visitors are invited to join in, too.

Some swear there's no place like Nome to celebrate New Year's Eve. In Bering Sea Time, it's the last zone in the world to reach midnight. But watch out for those mid-winter nights on the town. While bar-hopping and elbow-bending in the notorious Front Street saloons, it's hard to know when to call it a night, because it hardly ever gets light in mid-winter.

If you have the time and the inclination, don't give up on sailing to Alaska, just because the luxury cruise ships have gone south for the winter. Though Arctic seas freeze, the milder, protected Inside Passage remains open. The big, sturdy Alaska State super-ferries make their runs, on a reduced schedule and at reduced prices. The scenery along this route can be awesome, with loads of fresh snow on the mountains and seaside glaciers. They say the fishing is good even in winter in the ice-free saltwater lapping at port towns from Ketchikan to Sitka.

Throughout the state, communities line up a full, action-packed winter schedule for themselves, and Alaskans are quick to recognize kindred souls from "outside." Cheechakos (newcomers) are urged to join in the fun and games. For sure, anyone who participates in these winter happenings will be exposed to Alaska's warmest side—its people.

 PLANNING YOUR TRIP. If you don't want to bother with reservations on your own, a travel agent won't cost you a cent, except for specific charges like telegrams. He gets his fee from the hotel or carrier he books for you. A travel agent can also be of help for those who prefer to take their vacations on a "package tour"—thus keeping your own planning to a minimum. If you prefer the convenience of standardized accommodations, remember that the various hotel and motel chains publish free directories of their members that enable you to plan and reserve everything ahead of time.

If you plan your own itinerary, keep ever in mind the size of this largest state, and the changeable nature of the land which can lead to unexpected shifts and/or delays in travel plans. Here are some helpful hints. Weigh the amount of time you have, add a day or more for delays due to unforeseeable (not necessarily disagreeable) circumstances, and give thought to some sidetrips. Then compute the mileage from your map, assess your finances, and match it all up with the available transportation.

The State of Alaska and members of the travel industry issue stacks of informational material, including maps which pinpoint attractions, list historical sites, parks, etc. City chambers of commerce are also good sources of information. Specific addresses are given under *Practical Information* at the end of the Exploring chapters.

Plan to board the pets, discontinue paper and milk deliveries, and tell your local police and fire departments when you'll be leaving and when you expect to return. Ask a kindly neighbor to keep an eye on your house; fully protect your swimming pool against intruders. Have a neighbor keep your mail, or have it held at the post office. Consider having your telephone temporarily disconnected if you plan to be away more than a few weeks. Look into the purchase of trip insurance (including baggage), and make certain your auto, fire, and other insurance policies are up-to-date. Today most people who travel use credit cards for important expenses such as gas, repairs, lodgings and some meals. Consider converting the greater portion of your trip money into traveler's checks. Arrange to have your lawn mowed at the usual times, and leave that kindly neighbor your itinerary (insofar as is possible), car license number, and a key to your home (and tell police and firemen he has it). Since some hotel and motel chains give discounts (10%–25%) to senior citizens, be sure to have some sort of identification along if you qualify. Usually NARP or NRTA membership is best. (See below at the end of the hotels and motels section.)

PACKING. *What to take, what to wear.* Make a packing list for each member of the family. Then check off items as you pack them. It will save time, reduce confusion. Almost any item you may need will be available in Alaskan stores and supermarkets, but the price will be higher. Always carry an extra pair of glasses, including sunglasses, particularly if they're prescription ones. A travel iron is always a good tote-along, as are some transparent plastic film bags (small and large) for wet suits, socks, etc. They are also excellent for packing shoes, cosmetics, and other easily damaged items. Don't minimize the importance of bringing sunglasses and lotion, too. Contrary to the early-day polar image of Alaska, that midnight sun burns bright and long—in summer. In winter, the sun-and-snow combination can be brilliant. An Alaskan tan, or burn, can be achieved in short order when you spend time out-of-doors.

As for insect repellent, you'll do well to keep some handy. Even the most avid Alaska boosters admit to periodic plagues of mosquitoes, "no-see-um's" i.e. and gnats in the "bush" (which comes right up to city thresholds). The mosquitoes peak after breakup, breeding in the soggy land through June, tapering off in July and August. Though the land is fairly insect-free by September and through the winter, fishermen and other wilderness fans should carry a bug bomb and wipe-on repellent the rest of the year.

In addition to the essentials such as a camera and plenty of film, some extras that could be useful are binoculars for spotting shy animals across the tundra and Dall sheep and mountain goats in high rocky mountain pastures, a compass, and a magnifying glass to help read fine-print maps. If you fly, remember that despite signs to the contrary, airport security X-ray machines do in fact damage your films in about 17 percent of the cases. Have them inspected by hand.

All members of the family should have sturdy shoes with nonslip soles. Keep them handy in the back of the car. You never know when you may want to stop and clamber along a rocky trail to some site. Carry the family rain gear in a separate bag, in the back of the car (so no one will have to get out and hunt for it in a downpour en route).

Women will probably want to stick to one or two basic colors for their holiday wardrobes, so that they can manage with one set of accessories. If possible, include one knit or jersey dress or a pants suit. For dress-up evenings, take along a few "basic" dresses you can vary with a simple change of accessories. That way you can dress up or down to suit the occasion.

Speaking of dressing down, "naturism" or nudism has barely taken hold in Alaska and will probably never spread to the extent it has in such sunny states as Florida, California, and Hawaii. This is most likely due to climate; other reasons could include the aforementioned insects. However, bring a swimsuit. Many hotels have pools and health clubs. Communities have their own swimming pools, plus beaches in many recreational areas. There are saunas in surprising places—at Kachemak Bay Lodge on China Poot Bay across from the Homer Spit on the Kenai Peninsula; in Wien Air's Angler's Paradise, located so you can plunge right into icy Nonvianuk Lake. But Alaska is so big and so sparsely populated, it's safe to wager that anyone with a back-to-nature yearning will not have to go far to find a suitable spot to disrobe—while keeping an eye out for bears, and for flightseers in small planes or helicopters.

Don't Be Formal. Alaskans take people at face value, and if it's bearded it's in good company, along with governor, legislator, or professional. Everything is very casual, including dress.

Whatever style you travel, travel light (even on tours, when baggage transfers are usually included). You may have to tote your own bags. Quick drycleaning, laundry service, and laundromats are in all larger cities and most small ones.

The accent is on comfort. In summer, the snow and ice will be only part of the scenery, in glaciers or on mountain peaks. Generally, the climate will be mild and pleasant. Bring something warmer for cooler evenings, a sweater or jacket, but you won't need Arctic gear. A warm parka comes with the Arctic tours, for the duration, if needed. But even in the Arctic, in summer, you'll have to dig down a few inches to find permafrost, and the ice pack will be lurking far out at sea.

Easily-stowed rain gear and a pair of foldaway rain boots are a good idea, especially for sightseeing in moister southeast Alaska. Wear comfortable shoes. The amount of walking you do will be limited only by your stamina.

What Will It Cost?

Alaskans are resigned to the tariff, fortified by "cost-of-living" increased salaries. The Division of Tourism is as anxious to change the "high price tag" label, as it is to refute the "all-snow-and-ice" image left over from Purchase debates in Congress over a century ago.

The truth is, it does cost more, up to a fourth—or even more—than similar travel in the South-48. It depends on the length of the supply line, mainly. A hamburger costs more in the Arctic than in Southeast Alaska, for example. It's likely to be a "brazierburger" from the Dairy Queen chain that stretches from Ketchikan to Kotzebue.

With the pipeline-construction flurry subsiding, some items, like lodging, are bound to improve in cost, availability, and service. Some sleeping choices are camping out; reserving a remote fly-in wilderness Forest Service cabin ($5 a party a night, air fare extra); wilderness resorts; motels, motor inns, trailer parks; or hotels. Some of them are highrise and high priced, may be $50 to $60 a night, double, and more. The quality will be fine, and some are "Alaska Deluxe." Few, however, may fit the Super Deluxe and Deluxe categories described under "Hotel and Motel Categories" later in this chapter.

Eating possibilities are limited, even nonexistent, in some small villages, and infinite in the larger cities. You can purchase snacks to dinner makings from supermarkets, and there are chain eateries from the "Colonel" to "Mr. Salt," penthouse restaurants in hotels, and specialty restaurants featuring international dishes.

Sooner or later, however, you will wind up eating in a restaurant, and even here there are a number of things you can do to cut costs. 1) Always stop at the cash register and look over the menu *before* you sit down. 2) Have a few standard items like coffee, fruit juice, dessert, side dishes, to test the price range. 3) Look around to see what other people are actually receiving. Are the portions big or small? How much of the meal is padded with coleslaw? Is there more than one piece of tomato in the salad? How generous, or stingy, is the supply of bread and butter? 4) Order a complete dinner; a la carte *always* adds up to more. 5) If there is a salad bar, or any kind of smorgasbord arrangement, you can fill up there and save on dessert and extras. 6) Ask about smaller portions, at reduced prices, for children. More and more places are providing them now. 7) Go to a Chinese restaurant and order *one less* main dish than the number of people in your group. You'll still come away pleasantly full. 8) Ask for the Day's Special, House Special, Chef's Special, or whatever it's called. Chances are that it will be better and more abundant than the other things on the menu. 9) Remember that in better restaurants lunch may be more of a bargain than dinner. 10) Many of the same fast food chains of the "south-48" are now established in Alaska, and they offer good value for your money.

If you like a drink before dinner or bed, bring your own bottle. Most hotels and motels supply ice free or for very little, but the markup on alcoholic beverages in restaurants, bars, lounges and dining rooms is enormous, and in some states peculiar laws apply regarding alcohol consumption. And in any case, a good domestic dry white wine makes a fine aperitif and can be far cheaper than a cocktail. Confine your public drinking to the "happy hours" advertised by many Alaskan bars, and save. The price is drastically lowered on some drinks. However, learn the local drinking laws; they vary throughout the state.

Another travel tip: plan ahead and buy ahead. Your flight from home can be calculated on "tour-basing fares," a great saving over point-to-point prices— perhaps, 30 to 60%. Buying an overall package tour and adding, ahead of time, optional tours out of main cities is a thrifty way to see a lot of Alaska in a limited time. Meals usually are not included on prepaid package tours, but it is good to know the basic cost, what it includes, and that it is inflation-proof for the duration of the trip.

Timing is important, too. Instead of aiming for Alaska's busy midsummer days, think "thrift season." During early spring and autumn, prices may be 10 or 15% lower, with no skimping on what the tour offers. Those who travel at these times often get more individual treatment, as may those who arrive in winter, when native hosts are less busy.

Actually, dollar for dollar, prices in Alaska compare favorably with those around the world. Regardless of how they travel, and considering what Alaska has to offer, most people return home feeling they have gotten a lot for their money.

 HOW TO GET THERE. The only way you *can't* get there is by train. Although there are trains *in* Alaska, there are no trains *to* Alaska. The nearest stations are in Seattle, Washington—served by Amtrak—and in

Vancouver, B.C., west coast terminal for the Canadian Pacific and the Canadian National railroads. But no matter, the remaining choices are many, by land, by sea, and by air. Getting to and traveling around Alaska is dealt with in the Practical Information section.

In general, the Southeast Panhandle's myriad islands and extensive coastline are approached only by sea and air. Only Haines and Skagway, at the upper end of the Inside Passage, have overland access routes to the Interior and north. The other towns and cities are connected only by the Southeast "Marine Highway" and by plane. There are no overland connecting highways.

Interior and Gulf of Alaska regions, with Anchorage and Fairbanks as the hubs, contain most of the highway system. Many points are also served by air, and some of them by the Southwest Marine Highway system.

Except for freighters and barges making deliveries during the limited period in summer when the seas are unfrozen and friendly, areas around the Fringes of Alaska are reached only by bush plane and jet.

Driving in Alaska is probably more unpredictable and challenging than in any other part of the nation. For example, don't leave food lying around in your parked car. The *bear,* one of the strongest of mammals, has been known to tear a car apart looking for tidbits. Another animal, the huge *moose,* is being reported quite frequently as a driving hazard, especially along the *Alaska Highway.* These animals, although in the East notoriously shy of people, have become sufficiently confident and inquisitive to stray onto the less traveled highways of the Northwest. A moose usually measures an ungainly seven feet from its hooves to its humped shoulders and weighs between 1,000 pounds and a ton. The best thing to do if you come across one while driving is to stop your car and wait. If the moose doesn't move off by itself, which it will nine times out of ten, try honking your horn.

A second hazard to watch for along the Alaska Highway, especially in summer, is *flying gravel.* Rubber matting can protect the gas tank. A bug screen will help keep gravel off the windshield. Use clear, hard plastic guards to cover your headlights. Don't cover them with cardboard or plywood because you'll need your lights often, even in daytime, when dust is thrown up by cars passing in both directions. Windshield washers are a help. Remember too, if you enter Alaska by way of the Alaska Highway, that the Canadian parts of the highway through which you must travel are for the most part unpaved. The speed limit is 50 mph in Canada and 55 mph in Alaska, except where posted otherwise. However, loose gravel is hazardous, and freeze and thaw also affect paving. Wise drivers assess conditions and usually stay under the limit, sometimes well under it.

If you get stuck on any kind of road be careful about pulling off on the shoulder; it could be soft. In summer it stays light late, and though traffic is also light, Alaska is full of Good Samaritans. It's part of the code to stop and query if someone appears to be in trouble. If they can't help you on the spot, they'll send aid from the nearest point, which could be miles away. In winter there are checkpoints for keeping track of motorists, and roads are patrolled.

PULLING A TRAILER

If you plan to pull a *trailer*—boat or house—on your holiday trip, and have never before done so, don't just hook up and set out. You need a whole new set of driving skills—starting, stopping, cornering, passing, *being* passed, and, most tricky of all, backing. Reading about it will help a little, but not much. Try to practice in an open field, but if this is not possible, take your maiden trip in light traffic. A few useful hints: In starting and stopping, do everything more slowly and gradually than you would normally; in cornering, swing wider than usual since the trailer won't follow exactly the rear wheels of the towing car. Too sharp a right turn will put your trailer wheels over the curb. Too sharp a left turn will squash a car waiting to let you make the turn. In passing, remember you're longer than usual. Allow more safe distance ahead to pull back into the right lane. A slight bit of extra steering will help if you're *being* passed by a large truck or bus. In these situations, the trailer is inclined to sway from air currents. Don't make it worse by slowing down. It's better to speed up slightly. In backing, the basic technique is to turn the steering wheel opposite to the way you would want the car to go if you were driving it alone. From there on, it's practice, practice, practice. Most states have special safety regulations for trailers, and these change frequently. If you plan to operate your trailer in several states, check with your motor club, the police, or the state motor vehicle department about the rules. Also talk it over with the dealer from whom you buy or lease your trailer. Generally, speed limits for cars hauling trailers are lower, parking of trailers (and automobiles) is prohibited on expressways and freeways, and tunnels often ban trailers equipped with cooking units which use propane gas.

In Alaska, be prepared for having to drive yourself off and on the ferries and railroad flat cars.

HOTEL AND MOTEL CATEGORIES

Hotels and motels in all the Fodor guidebooks to the U.S.A. are divided into five categories, arranged primarily by price but also taking into consideration the degree of comfort, the amount of service, and the atmosphere which will surround you in the establishment of your choice. Occasionally, an establishment with *deluxe* prices will offer only first-class service or atmosphere, and so we will list it as expensive. On the other hand, a hotel which charges only *moderate* prices may offer superior comfort and service, so we will list it as expensive. Our ratings are flexible and subject to change. We should also point out that many fine hotels and motels had to be omitted for lack of space.

Although the names of the various hotel and motel categories are standard throughout this series, the prices listed under each category may vary from area to area. This variance is meant to reflect local price standards, and take into account that what might be considered a *moderate* price in a large urban area might be quite *expensive* in a rural region. In every case, however, the dollar ranges for each category are clearly stated before each listing of establishments.

For categories in the different parts of Alaska, however, see appropriate chapter in the following portions of this book.

Super deluxe: This category is reserved for only a few hotels. In addition to giving the visitor all the amenities discussed under the deluxe category (below), the super deluxe hotel has a special atmosphere of glamor, good taste, and dignity. Its history will inevitably be full of many anecdotes, and it will probably be a favored meeting spot of local society. In short, super deluxe means the tops.

Deluxe: The minimum facilities must include bath and shower in all rooms, valet and laundry service, suites available, a well-appointed restaurant and a bar (where local law permits), room service, TV and telephone in room, air conditioning and heat (unless locale makes one or the other unnecessary), pleasing decor, and an atmosphere of luxury, calm, and elegance. There should be ample and personalized service. In a deluxe *motel,* there may be less service rendered by employees and more by automatic machines (such as refrigerators and ice-making machines in your room), but there should be a minimum of do-it-yourself in a truly deluxe establishment.

Expensive: All rooms must have bath or shower, valet and laundry service, restaurant and bar (local law permitting), at least some room service, TV and telephone in room, attractive furnishings, heat and air conditioning (locale not precluding). Although decor may be as good as that in deluxe establishments, hotels and motels in this category are frequently designed for commercial travelers or for families in a hurry and are somewhat impersonal in terms of service. As for *motels* in this category, valet and laundry service will probably be lacking; the units will be outstanding primarily for the convenient location and functional character, not for their attractive or comfortable qualities.

(Note: We often list top-notch ultra-modern hotels in this category, in spite of the fact that they have rates as high as deluxe hotels and motels. We do this because certain elements are missing in these hotels—usually, the missing element is service. In spite of automated devices such as ice-cube-making machines and message-signaling buzzers, service in these hotels is not up to the standard by which we judge deluxe establishments. Room service is incredibly slow in some of these places, and the entire atmosphere is often one of expediency over comfort, economy of manpower and overhead taking precedence over attention to the desires of guests.)

Moderate: Each room should have an attached bath or shower, there should be a restaurant *or* coffee shop, TV available, telephone in room, heat and air conditioning (locale not precluding), relatively convenient location, clean and comfortable rooms, and public rooms. *Motels* in this category may not have attached bath or shower, may not have a restaurant or coffee shop (though one is usually nearby), and, of course, may have no public rooms to speak of.

Inexpensive: Nearby bath or shower, telephone available, clean rooms are the minimum.

Free parking is assumed at all motels and motor hotels; you must pay for parking at most city hotels, though certain establishments have free parking, frequently for occupants of higher-than-minimum-rate rooms. *Baby sitter* lists are always available in good hotels and motels, and *cribs* for the children are always on hand—sometimes at no cost, but more frequently at a cost of $1 or $2 per night. The cost of a *cot* in your room, supplementing the beds, will also be around $3 per night, but moving an *extra single bed* into a room will cost from $7 in better hotels and motels.

Senior citizens may in some cases receive special discounts on lodgings and in restaurants—it doesn't hurt to ask. Holiday Inns give a 10% discount year-round to members of the NRTA (write to National Retired Teachers Association, Membership Division, 701 North Montgomery St., Ojai, California 93023) and the AARP (write to American Association of Retired Persons, Membership Division, 215 Long Beach Blvd., Long Beach, California 90802). The ITT Sheraton chain gives 25% off (call 800-325-3535) to members of the AARP, the NRTA, the National Association of Retired Persons, The Catholic Golden Age of United Societies of U.S.A., and the Old Age Security Pensioners of Canada. A price break for senior visitors may come in unexpected places. In the window of the *Fairbanks Inn Beauty Shop*, for example, a sign stated that Senior Citizen shampoos and sets were only $9 versus the usual $12 price. Take your I.D. along to Alaska.

The closest thing America has to Europe's bed-and-breakfast is the private houses that go by the various names of tourist home, guest home, or guest house. These are often large, still fairly elegant old homes in quiet residential or semiresidential parts of larger towns or along secondary roads and the main streets of small towns and resorts. Styles and standards vary widely, of course; generally private baths are less common and rates are pleasingly low. In many small towns such guest houses are excellent examples of the best a region has to offer of its own special atmosphere. Each one will be different, so that their advantage is precisely the opposite of that "no surprise" uniformity which motel chains pride themselves on. Few, if any, guest houses have heated pools, wall-to-wall carpeting, or exposed styrofoam-wooden beams in the bar. Few if any even have bars. What you do get, in addition to economy, is the personal flavor of a family atmosphere in a private home. In popular tourist areas, state or local tourist information offices or chambers of commerce usually have lists of homes that let out spare rooms to paying guests, and such a listing usually means that the places on it have been inspected and meet some reliable standard of cleanliness, comfort, and reasonable pricing. A nationwide *Guide to Guest Houses and Tourist Homes USA* is available from Tourist House Associates of America, Inc., P.O. Box 335-A, Greentown, Pennsylvania 18426.

In larger towns and cities a good bet for clean, plain, reliable lodging is a YMCA or YWCA. These buildings are usually centrally located, and their rates tend to run to less than half of those of hotels. Nonmembers are welcome, but may pay slightly more than members. A few very large Ys may have accommodations for couples but usually sexes are segregated. Decor is spartan and the cafeteria fare plain and wholesome, but a definite advantage is the use of the building's pool, gym, reading room, information services, and other facilities. For a directory, write to National Council of the YMCA, 291 Broadway, New York, N.Y. 10007; and the National Board of the YWCA, 600 Lexington Avenue, New York, N.Y. 10022.

DINING OUT. For evening meals, the best advice is to make reservations in advance whenever possible. Most hotels and farm vacation places have set dining hours. For motel stayers, life is simpler if the motel has a restaurant. If it hasn't, try and stay at one that is near a restaurant.

Few places in Alaska are very fussy about customers' dress, but you'll see signs requiring shoes and shirts. For women, pants and pants suits are now almost universally acceptable. For men, tie and jacket remains the standard, but turtleneck sweaters are becoming more and more common. Shorts are almost always frowned on for both men and women. Standards of dress are becoming more relaxed, so a neatly dressed customer will usually experience no problem. If in doubt about accepted dress at a particular establishment, call ahead.

Roadside stands, turnpike restaurants, and cafeterias have no fixed standards of dress.

If you're traveling with children, you may want to find out if a restaurant has a children's menu and commensurate prices (many do).

When figuring the tip on your check, base it on the total charges for the meal, not on the grand total, if that total includes a state sales tax. Don't tip on tax.

RESTAURANT CATEGORIES

Restaurants are divided into price categories as follows: *deluxe, expensive, moderate,* and *inexpensive.* Restaurant meals will cost more in Alaska, and as a general rule, expect restaurants in metropolitan areas to be higher in price, although many restaurants that feature foreign cuisine are often surprisingly inexpensive. We should also point out that limitations of space make it impossible to include every establishment. We have, therefore, included those which we consider the best within each price range.

Although the names of the various restaurant categories are standard throughout this series, the prices listed under each category may vary from area to area. This variation is meant to reflect local price standards, and take into account that what might be considered a *moderate* price in a large urban area might be quite *expensive* in a rural region. In every case, however, the dollar ranges for each category are clearly stated before each listing of establishments.

Deluxe: Many a fine restaurant around the country falls into this category. It will have its own well-deserved reputation for excellence, perhaps a house specialty or two for which it is famous, and an atmosphere of elegance or unique decor. It will have a good wine list where the law permits, and will be considered the best in town by the inhabitants. It will have a clean kitchen and attentive staff.

Expensive: In addition to the expected dishes, it will offer one or two house specialties, wine list, and cocktails (where law permits), air conditioning (unless locale makes it unnecessary), a general reputation for very good food and an adequate staff, an elegant decor, and appropriately dressed clientele.

Moderate: Cocktails and/or beer where law permits, air conditioning (when needed), clean kitchen, adequate staff, better-than-average service. General reputation for good, wholesome food.

Inexpensive: The bargain place in town, it is clean, even if plain. It will have when necessary air conditioning, tables (not a counter), and clean kitchen and will attempt to provide adequate service.

Chains: There are now several chains of restaurants, some of them nationwide, that offer reliable eating at excellent budget prices. Look for them as you travel, and check local telephone directories in cities where you stop.

FACTS AND FIGURES. The name of the 49th state came from a similar-sounding Aleut word meaning "great land of white to the east." The forget-me-not is the state flower; the Sitka spruce, the state tree; king salmon, the state fish; and the willow ptarmigan, the state bird. The state has adopted an official song, "Alaska's Flag." The state motto is "North to the Future." Juneau, in southeast Alaska, is the state capital. Alaskans voted to move it to a site in the interior, near the town of Willow, between Anchorage and Fairbanks, but reluctance to allocate funds for building and moving has so far prevented the project from getting underway.

Alaska ranks as the nation's biggest state—it is one-fifth the total size of the continental United States—with an area of 586,412 square miles, and a population estimated at over 400,000, living in four time zones. It is a big country in every sense: glaciers, fjords, forests, rivers, mountains, among them 20,320-foot Mount McKinley, highest on the North American continent. The Yukon is the longest river, with 1,400 of its almost 2,000 miles flowing through Alaska. The Malaspina, near Yakutat in Southeast Alaska, is the largest of 5,000 glaciers. There are more than three million lakes, each spreading over 20 acres. Lake Iliamna in Southwest Alaska is America's second largest freshwater lake. The state has abundant natural resources, including oil and natural gas, timber, valuable minerals, fish and game. Industries based on these, plus growing tourism, are the foundation of the burgeoning economy.

BUSINESS HOURS AND LOCAL TIME. Business hours for banks, shops, offices, cinemas, etc., are pretty much the same as for the rest of the country, except that those somehow related to tourism may be open longer in the summer. They celebrate the usual holidays on schedule, plus some special Alaskan ones: Admission (Statehood) Day, January 3; Seward's Day, March 26; and Alaska Day (the Purchase), on October 18.

TIPPING. Tipping is supposed to be a personal thing, your way of expressing your appreciation of someone who has taken pleasure and pride in giving you attentive, efficient, and personal service. Because standards of personal service in the United States are highly uneven, you should, when you get genuinely good service, feel secure in rewarding it, and when you feel that the service you got was slovenly, indifferent, or surly, don't hesitate to show this by the size, or withholding, of your tip. Remember that in many places the help are paid very little and depend on tips for the better part of their income. This is supposed to give them incentive to serve you well.

In Alaska, on a tour, it is often specified that tips are included, and on cruises it may be stated that "tips are not required." People often go out of their way to help visitors, obviously with no thought of a tip. On excursions where the motorcoach driver and/or tour guide has been exceptionally informative and helpful (and they usually are), the passengers may be inclined to take up a kitty, or to tip individually. Otherwise, use your good judgment and try not to insult a new-found "friend" who was just being hospitable and helpful as a matter of course. The following, as anywhere, may be helpful guidelines. These days, the going rate on *restaurant* service is 15% on the amount *before* taxes. Tipping at counters is not universal, but many people leave $0.25 on anything up to $1, and 10% on anything over that. For *bellboys,* 25¢ per bag is usual. However, if you load him down with all manner of bags, hatboxes, cameras, coats, etc., you might consider giving an extra quarter or two. In many places the help rely on tips for a goodly portion of their income. For one-night stays in most *hotels* and *motels* you leave nothing. If you stay longer, at the end of your stay leave the maid $1–$1.25 per day, or $5 per person per week for multiple occupancy. If you are staying at an *American Plan* hostelry (meals included) $1.50 per day per person for the waiter or waitress is considered sufficient, and is left at the end of your stay. However, if you have been surrounded by an army of servants (one bringing relishes, another rolls, etc.), add a few extra dollars and give the lump sum to the captain or *maitre d'hotel* when you leave, asking him to allocate it.

For the many other services you may encounter in a big hotel or resort, figure roughly as follows: doorman, 25¢ for taxi handling, 50¢ for help with baggage; bellhop, 25¢ per bag, more if you load him down with extras; parking attendant 50¢; bartender, 15%; room service, 10–15% of that bill; laundry or valet service, 15%; pool attendant, 50¢ per day; snackbar waiter at pool, beach, or golf club, 50¢ per person for food and 15% of the beverage check; locker attendant, 50¢ per person per day, or $2.50 per week; masseurs and masseuses, 20%; golf caddies, $1–per bag, or 15% of the greens fee for an 18-hole course, or $3 on a free course; barbers, 50¢; shoeshine attendants, 25¢; hairdressers, $1; manicurists, 50¢.

Transportation: Give 25¢ for any taxi fare under $1 and 15% for any above. Limousine service, 20%. Car rental agencies, nothing. Bus porters are tipped 25¢ per bag, drivers nothing. On charters and package tours, conductors and drivers usually get $5–$10 per day from the group as a whole, but be sure to ask whether this has already been figured into the package cost. On short local sightseeing runs, the driver-guide may get 25¢ per person, more if you think he has been especially helpful or personable. Airport bus drivers, nothing. Redcaps, in resort areas, 35¢ per suitcase, elsewhere, 25¢. Tipping at curbside check-in is unofficial, but same as above. On the plane, no tipping.

Railroads suggest you leave 10–15% per meal for dining car waiters, but the steward who seats you is not tipped. Sleeping-car porters get about $1 per person per night. The 25¢ or 35¢ you pay a railway station baggage porter is not a tip but the set fee that he must hand in at the end of the day along with the ticket stubs he has used. Therefore his tip is anything you give him above that, 25–50¢ per bag, depending on how heavy your luggage is.

 HINTS TO HANDICAPPED TRAVELERS. One of the newest, and largest, groups to enter the travel scene is the handicapped, literally millions of people who are in fact physically able to travel and who do so enthusiastically when they know that they can move about in safety and comfort. Generally their tours parallel those of the non-handicapped traveler, but at a more leisurely pace, and with all the logistics carefully checked out in advance. Two important sources of information in this field are: l) the book, *Access to the World: A Travel Guide for the Handicapped* by Louise Weiss, published by Chatham Square Press, Inc., 401 Broadway, New York, N.Y. 10013. This book covers travel by air, ship, train, bus, car and recreational vehicle; hotels and motels; travel agents and tour operators; destinations; access guides; health and medical problems; and travel organizations. 2) The *Travel Information Center,* Moss Rehabilitation Hospital, 12th Street and Tabor Road, Philadelphia, Penn. 19141. 3) *Easter Seal Society for Crippled Children and Adults,* Director of Education and Information Service, 2023 West Ogden Avenue, Chicago, Illinois 60612. The President's Committee on Employment of the Handicapped, Washington, D.C. 20210, has issued a list for handicapped travelers that tells where to write for guidebooks to nearly 100 U.S. cities. The Committee also has a guide to Highway Rest Area Facilities that are designed to be accessible to the handicapped. For a list of tour operators who arrange travel for the handicapped, write to *Society for the Advancement of Travel for the Handicapped,* 26 Court St., Brooklyn, N.Y. 11242.

In addition, two publications which give valuable information about motels, hotels, and restaurants (rating them, telling about steps, table heights, door widths, etc.) are *Where Turning Wheels Stop,* published by Paralyzed Veterans of America, 3636 16th St., N.W., Washington, D.C. 20010, and *The Wheelchair Traveler,* by Douglass R. Annand, Ball Hill Road, Milford, N.H. 03055. Many of the nation's national parks have special facilities for the handicapped. These are described in *National Park Guide for the Handicapped,* available from the U.S. Government Printing Office, Washington, D.C. 20402. TWA publishes a free 12-page pamphlet entitled *Consumer Information about Air Travel for the Handicapped* to explain available various arrangements and how to get them.

Visitor information centers in many Alaskan cities, and some small towns, will help the handicapped, whether the problem is sight, hearing, age, mobility, or just language. In Anchorage they are developing aids for the deaf and blind, and have a "language bank" for non-English speakers from a number of foreign countries.

The *Evergreen Travel Service* near Seattle has long been interested in travel for the handicapped. They claim that it is harder to imagine a cheerier, tougher bunch, and organize and expedite individual and group travel to Alaska, among other destinations in the world. For information, write Betty Hoffman or her son Jack at Evergreen Travel Service, Inc., 19505-L 44th Ave. West, Lynnwood, WA 98036.

SOUTHEAST ALASKA

Few Roads Lead to the Panhandle

The best place for island-hopping in Alaska is in the Southeast Panhandle region, where an almost-drowned mountain range makes up the Alexander Archipelago. It parallels a strip of the United States Northwest coast, set off from Canada by mountains that are well over a mile and a half high. This narrow mainland strip, plus the mountain-top island chain, make up Alaska's five-hundred-mile-long "Panhandle." Actually it's a dipper handle which extends south and east from the main body of the peninsula state. The cup holds the other diverse areas of Alaska: the Gulf and Interior, and the far northern and far western coastal fringes.

Thinking in terms of a Grand Circle Tour of Alaska, the time-proven sea approach is a winner. On the other hand, if you choose to reverse the Circle, the same marine- and mountainscapes and multiple evergreen islands of the Southeast Panhandle add up to a Grand Finale—they are the very essence of Alaska.

Either way, much of the scene, on a grand scale and gorgeous, continues to remain much as it was when earlier visitors admired it—canoe-paddling Indians, explorers of assorted nationalities in sailing ships, gold rushers who crowded onto almost anything that would float, and a wave of hardy tourists who came to sightsee the Great Land by steamship, before 1900.

For today's travelers, the choice is town-hopping with Alaska Airlines jets or by local air taxi services; port-calling via Alaska State Ferries or private boat; and by cruise ship. Sailing under many flags, a flotilla of cruise ships summer in Southeast Alaska waters, granting shore leaves to their passengers in assorted ports.

The towns along the Inside Passage are all different, each with its distinctive flavor, from first port Ketchikan, dedicated to fish and wood chips, to Sitka, with a Russian dressing. Place names—of towns and of myriad waterways—give clues to earlier visitors, who left their mark around Southeast Alaska. There's little mistaking nationalities among such labels as Baranof, Kupreanof, Prince of Wales, Petersburg. Klawock and Ketchikan are derived from similar-sounding Indian names.

Alaska Ahoy!

Like the birds and the humpback whales, cruise ships migrate annually from their winter cruising grounds to summer in far north Alaska. Their common destination is Glacier Bay, about 50 miles northwest of capital city Juneau, and their reason for heading there is a feast. Pods of whales go to feed on the rich plankton flourishing in the many coves and inlets of Glacier Bay National Monument, released from its icy wraps only half a century ago. The cruise ships take passengers to Glacier Bay via the Inside Passage to treat them to some of Alaska's grandest marine and mountain scenery and glimpses of its prolific wildlife.

There are plenty of rugged ways to see big, beautiful Alaska, but cruising isn't one of them. Today's "floating resorts" have all the comforts of home and then some. The spacious luxury liners are a far cry from the motley craft the feverish gold seekers clambered onto, and even from the steamships of the cruising-to-Alaska boom, during the 1890s.

Cruising is a style of travel that could be addictive, as well as fattening. Chefs definitely cater to the inner man and woman. Specialties at breakfast, lunch, dinner (and in between, such as at a midnight buffet) are likely to reflect the ship's country of origin. On Sitmar's Italian-style *Fairsea*, for example, don't pass up the pasta, served with a choice of many sauces—every bit, including the dough, prepared aboard.

Chefs serve their national dishes as well as Southeast Alaska's superb seafood: tiny shrimp, scallops, king crab, King salmon, halibut—and you can be sure that sometime during the voyage the dessert spectacular will be a flaming Baked Alaska. Moreover, artist-chefs can't resist sculpturing table decorations from large chunks of crystal-clear ice, calved by glaciers and snagged in nets by the ship's crew.

Lush green panoramas of timbered islands and mountain slopes leading up to formidable snowy peaks; fjords, glaciers, small fishing and logging towns; and lively bird and sea life lose nothing for being viewed in comfort from a deck chair or through a picture-window in the lounge. It's unusually smooth sailing in sheltered waters. The myriad islands on one hand and the towering peaks on the other are protection for this roomy passage "inside." And Alaska cruising can mean almost round-the-clock daylight for watching the shifting spectacular scenery and visiting super-friendly little ports where English is spoken.

The big question maiden voyagers ask is "Which ship shall I choose?" There is no pat answer. Each has its own personality and all have their particular charms. "Old salts," knowing they can count on the amenities they became accustomed to on a previous cruise, are inclined to stick with the same ship wherever she sails.

Picking by size from among the possibilities, Sitmar's 25,000-ton *Fairsea,* sailing from San Francisco, could be a winner. Scholars might choose the Orient Oversea's *S.S. Universe,* or the *Lindblad Explorer,* geared to education and nature. The world travelers include the *Royal Vikings* from San Francisco/Los Angeles, and Holland America's *Statendam,* roundtripping from Vancouver, B.C., Canada; the *Rotterdam,* from San Francisco. In 1981, Norwegian American Cruises will begin a series of five 14-day Alaska/Canada sailings on the *Sagafjord,* leaving from San Francisco.

Television's "Love Boat," Princess Cruises' 20,000-ton *Pacific Princess* shares the Alaska route with her twin, the *Island Princess,* and their smaller sister, the *Sun Princess.* They sail from Vancouver, B.C., for Princess Tours. Another Princess—no relative—sails for the Canadian Pacific Railroad: the *Princess Patricia.* A Russian newcomer, reminiscent of Alaska's past, the modern Soviet cruise ship *Odessa* was granted limited port calls in the Southeast during the summer of 1980. Aboard you could attend classes in Russian dancing, language and balalaika, buy Russian furs and handicrafts in the ship's shop, and be entertained by a Russian folkloric revue.

The cost of cruising now? Though there are lower prices available and they may be advertised, the happiest cruisers will probably be those who budget $125 to $150 a day per person, the price for a comfortable cabin on leading cruise ships.

Shipboard Life

During the 7- or 8-day roundtrip cruise (or 3 or 4 days one way), it's sailor's choice whether to relax and do nothing, or to join in the fun and games. Daily bulletins give the world news and what's in store for the day aboard ship. There'll be choice food and entertainment that varies with the ship. To offset the three squares and all those enticing extra snacks, there might be an exercise class in the lounge, a workout in the gym, a sauna, or that old favorite, several laps around the promenade deck while watching the passing scene. It may be a pod of whales, a small Indian village with totem poles, fishing boats, porpoises, or mountain vistas. The bridge will alert you. There are movies, bars, card tournaments, bingo, casino games, a library, duty-free shops, singles get-together—you name it. For example, instruction in rock painting was offered one summer by an art-minded cruise director on the *Prinsendam*. He encouraged passengers to pick up a smooth "pet rock" while ashore, and held an impromptu art class for those interested. Some painted local scenes. A winner was a humpbacked whale, on a rock so-shaped that it took just a few brush strokes to complete it.

Entertainment in ship lounges is by top professional talent—singers, dancers, musicians—from varied backgrounds, including the crew in a "special" sometime along the way. Informal talks and slide shows on upcoming ports-of-call inform visitors about the Indian–Russian–explorer–fur trader–fisherman–gold seeker background of this vast Panhandle region. That's when they prepare you for the weather, too, in places like Ketchikan. That lush greenery is a clue that rain may be a part of the experience. Follow the lead of the residents. Dress for rain and ignore it.

Shoreleave

Stops are at just the right intervals for stretching sea legs. In some ports the ship docks right downtown. In others, launches transport passengers to land. There is time for a city tour (the best way to become orientated), for more browsing, for shopping, or to take part in an activity like flightseeing or fishing.

They say the fishing is superb because of the points and narrow passes among the islands: large masses of migrating salmon must squeeze through and around them. Avid fisherman-cruisers have been known to buy a special one-day, non-resident fishing license ($5 at sporting goods stores), beetle off to a remote mountain lake, or spend a few hours King salmon fishing in the saltchuck. Alaskans use small planes like taxis for reaching fishing "hot spots." At Ketchikan, they claim the title "Salmon Capital of the World," as well as "First City of Alaska," by right of being the first port-of-call for planes and ships.

No Roads Lead to Ketchikan

A little over 15 years ago, Ketchikan and other similarly-isolated Panhandle towns came as close to being connected by a "road" as they are likely to, with the inauguration of the state's extensive Marine Highway System. It was an instant hit with Alaskans, who have been happily riding and singing "The Ferryboat Song" ever since.

Though there is periodic talk of a connecting combination ferry and over-island highway, it's not likely to happen very soon (if at all). The barriers are formidable for road-building in the usual sense, paved or unpaved.

Ketchikan is perched on a large mountainous island underneath 3,000-foot Deer Mountain. The island's name is a jaw-breaker, Revillagigedo, named by English mariner George Vancouver who was exploring the Inside Passage in 1793. He often named things for his crew and friends, in this case the Viceroy of Mexico.

Locals say Ketchikan's name was inspired by the local Indians, who were referring to a nearby waterfall that reminded them of an eagle with its wings spread out. However, it's apt for the appearance of the town as well. Imagine that you have hiked the 5-mile trail to the top of Deer Mountain and are looking out over the town and surrounding area. Ketchikan appears squeezed onto a narrow shelf. Actually, it's more like an overhang, considering that much of the 3-mile-long waterfront section is built out over the water. The docks are on pilings, and with no place to grow but north and south from its center, the town has a spread-eagle shape.

The jetport is only a short local ferry ride across Tongass Narrows.

From its dock, a few miles of local roads lead north and south to the city center and to surrounding recreational and work areas.

Until the new airport site was leveled, the airport was located on neighboring Annette Island, the nearest spot with enough level space. The "ferry" then was a Grumman Goose amphibian plane that took about 20 minutes to transfer passengers from jets to the city center. It was an impressive introduction, as the "bird" splashed down in the water and bellied up to the dock. Though the Gooses are gone now, there is still plenty of waterfront action, with ships coming and going and small float planes and air taxis skimming off and swishing down like big insects.

It's obvious that Ketchikan's skyline hasn't been static. Some highrises mark the two up-and-coming shopping centers at both ends of town. The large pulp mill is a standout, and there are schools, including a community college, small boat harbors, parks, and many attractive homes valiantly climbing the steep backdrop.

Ketchikan's Past

A capsulized history of Ketchikan starts with the Indian fishing camp at the mouth of Ketchikan Creek, long before white miners and fishermen came to settle in 1885. Shortly before 1900, however, the new town's future was brightened by gold discoveries, and the establishment of a cannery and sawmill. Fishing industries peaked in the 1930s, but declined in the 1940s. The thick, rapidly growing forests triggered the growth of the timber industry, more sawmills, and the mill of the Ketchikan Pulp Company (visitors welcome). Today, timber and tourism are mainstays.

One facet of tourism involves both trees and Indians, the art of totem carving. In Ketchikan you won't have to look far to see these "monuments in cedar." Some are downtown near the docks. More are within walking distance, at the Totem Heritage Cultural Center. This was started as a Bicentennial project for preserving the Tlingit and Haida poles from nearby Indian villages. You'll find authentic information here on the types of totems: Heraldic, depicting social standing; Memorial, usually for a dead chief; and Mortuary, with a section for ashes; devastating Ridicule, or "shame poles" for putting down an enemy; Potlatch poles for festivals; and—most common and important—House Poles, used in constructing community tribal houses.

At Totem Bight, on a point north of Ketchikan, overlooking

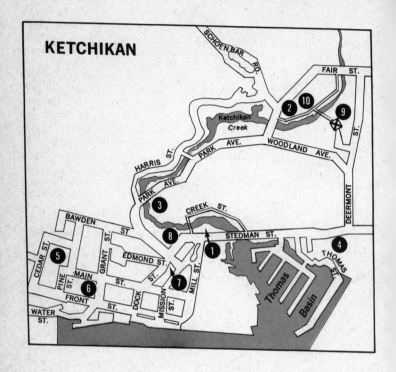

KETCHIKAN

Points of Interest

1) Chief Johnson Totem
2) Deer Mountain Hatchery
3) Fish Ladder-Salmon Carving
4) Ketchikan Mural
5) Kyan Totem
6) State Office Bldg.
7) St. John's Episcopal Church
8) Tongass Historical Society
   Museum
9) Totem Heritage Center
10) World's Largest Gold Nugget

Tongass Narrows, a stand of authentically reproduced totem poles guards a fine hand-crafted tribal house. It is a 16-minute drive and a short walk through the forest from the parking lot to the totem park.

Saxman Totem Park is about 2 miles south of Ketchikan at the Indian village of Saxman, named for a missionary who helped the Tlingit Indians who moved there before 1900. Natives can "read" the poles depicting birds, animals, and water dwellers. They (or a tour guide) can also identify the big chiefs portrayed including Abraham Lincoln, whose tall-hatted features are quite identifiable. He was honored for abolishing slavery in the U.S., which included the newly-acquired Territory of Alaska. Until then, the souvenirs that warfaring tribes had been bringing home were often people, to serve as slaves.

In case you wonder why the President is cut off at the knees, they say it is because the grateful Indians were working from a postcard photo, and that's where it ended. The time-rotted original of the Lincoln totem is encased in glass in the state museum at Juneau.

Ketchikan ranks fourth in Alaska city size. Population is almost 9,000; over 13,000 counting the surrounding communities it serves, mostly based on fishing and logging. Many small villages are definitely leaning toward tourism, such as Klawock, Metlakatla, Hydaburg, and Craig, on neighbor islands reached by smaller ferries, and smaller planes.

Local tours by the Ketchikan Sightseeing Co. will see that you don't miss anything, in a 2- to 3-hour orientation. There's lots of atmosphere and exercise hiking the steep streets that give way to wooden staircases leading to homes, and in one case to two small log buildings put there in memory of Fort Tongass, which guarded the area briefly, but was located elsewhere. There is interesting browsing in the Centennial Building, home of the Tongass Historical Society Museum. The Deer Mountain Hatchery in City Park offers year-round viewing of prized King and coho salmon reared for release in Ketchikan Creek. On the far side, wooden Creek St., on pilings, marks what's left of a notorious part of town, including some of the infamous "houses."

From town, you won't go far in either direction before running out of road. The North Tongass Highway starts at Chief Johnson's totem pole, set in the heart of town in 1901. It ends about 18 miles later at Settler's Cove Campground. The South Tongass road ends at a power plant. Side roads soon terminate at campgrounds and trail beginnings, viewpoints, lakes, boat launching ramps, or private property.

If you switch to sea and air transportation, sightseeing possibilities in the Ketchikan area are expanded. The active Visitors Bureau or the Chamber of Commerce steers visitors toward what's going on. For example, visitors are welcome to fish in the April to mid-July salmon derby, where the winners are usually well over 50 pounds and the prizes add up to thousands of dollars.

Visitors with longer time to spend can reserve one of more than 50 Forest Service cabins in the Ketchikan area (only $5 a night per party). Some are accessible by hiking, or boat; most are fly-ins. There are also more luxurious accommodations.

Nearby Behm Canal is one of Southeast's fishing hot spots. You can drive to Clover Pass Resort, 15 paved miles north of Ketchikan, a headquarters for the salmon derby. Hopeful fishermen strike out from here for hooking fighting King salmon. Yes Bay is 45 miles to the northwest, and besides fishing, features hiking, beachcombing and birdwatching (see *Wilderness Resorts*).

Bell Island, just off Behm Canal, is noted for its "fish and soak." The resort sits on hot springs appreciated by Indians and later commercial fishermen for their relaxing, therapeutic powers, as well as a chance for a good hot bath. Now sport fishermen go there for some of the best King salmon fishing in Alaska, from May until well into fall, plus fighting steelhead that run up a cold stream rushing past the row of guest cabins. Families of fishermen are kept happy soaking in the private tubs or swimming in the hot spring-fed Olympic-sized swimming pool, dropping a line off the docks, or nature watching (see *Spas*).

Some cruise ships include Wrangell and Petersburg in their itinerary, but most visitors arrive by ferry or plane.

Wrangell

Next up the line is Wrangell (rang'gull), also on an island near the mouth of the Stikine (stick-een') River, but not a cliffhanger like Ketchikan. It's a waterfront town, though with a different emphasis. Here, it's the shipping point for timber processed in the town's big sawmills, a port for logging tugs, and for Japanese lumber ships.

The town might well have developed a split personality, having been exposed to motley influences over the years: soldiers, Indians, fur and gold seekers, fishermen, loggers, rivermen. With a past that goes back to the Russians, Wrangell existed under three successive flags, first Russian, then British, and finally American, accompanied by as many name changes.

First it was called Redoubt Saint Dionysius. Next the British named it Fort Stikine. Then the Americans settled for the simpler name Wrangell, almost the same as the name the Russians had given to the whole island, when they named it for an early governor, Baron von Wrangel.

Don't count on much road travel while in Wrangell. Besides the two-mile loop to the airport, there is only the Zimovia Highway. It passes through town from the ferry dock and gives up at Pat's Creek campground, just over 11 miles. In between there is a short trail off the highway that goes to woodsy Rainbow Falls.

The Stikine River, however, shows possibilities of again becoming a "marine highway." In the past, the Stikine gave access to interior gold fields and was important as a mining supply route. History may be repeated, with copper the prize. Meanwhile, the Stikine has been discovered by river runners, who traverse part of its length in assorted craft. They get around its impassable Grand Canyon by making an air portage to Telegraph Creek, then running the rest of the 160 miles to Wrangell.

If you dig the archaic, be sure to look along the beach for petroglyphs, carvings on the rocks believed to have been doodled long ago by Indians waiting out hunting and fishing sessions. One is near

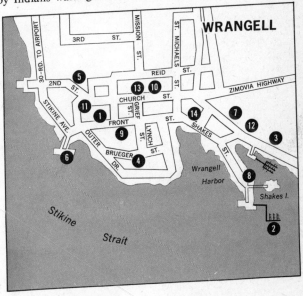

Points of Interest

1) Art Center
2) Boat Harbor
3) Chief Shakes Gravesite
4) City Hall—Totem
5) City Museum
6) Cruiseship Dock
7) Episcopal Church
8) Marine Bar (Fort Dionysius)
9) Petroglyph—Natl. Bank of Alaska
10) Presbyterian Church
11) Post Office
12) Raven Totem
13) St. Hose of Lima (Catholic)
14) Totem—Kicksadi

the ferry terminal; more are reached by a boardwalk trail taking off from the Airport Road.

More recent Indian art—many fine totem poles—decorate the streets, and a choice collection is on an island just offshore, reached by a foot-bridge. Little mid-harbor Chief Shakes Island honors the Indian chief with a replica of his community house under the watchful eyes of superbly-carved totem faces. Inside the house are more examples of Indian art, and some of their working tools.

Petersburg

Getting to Petersburg is an experience, whether you take the "high road" or the "low road." Alaska Airlines claims the "shortest jet flight in the world" from takeoff at Wrangell to put down at Petersburg. The schedule allows 20 minutes, but it's usually more like eleven. At eye level, the Marine Highway route squeaks through Wrangell Narrows, full of markers and other aids to help navigate the reefs and currents in the ticklish 23-mile stretch between Kupreanof and Mitkof Islands. It is sensationally narrow in places.

At first sight of Petersburg you might think that you are in the old country. Neat and cheery white Scandinavian-style houses and store-fronts, decked with bright-colored swirls of leaf and flower designs, and a sizeable fishing fleet adorn the waterfront.

The healthy-looking people will sport fishing garb, most likely from hip boots to Norwegian knits. If you happen to land there near the 17th of May, they may be wearing old-country costumes and dancing schottisches on the docks. You may even hear Norwegian spoken. But don't worry about a language barrier; visitors can get by very well with "Skol!" Every year on the weekend closest to "Syttende Mai" these descendants of Norwegian fishermen, who settled Peter Buschmann's town in 1897, go all out to celebrate Norwegian Independence Day and the fame of their halibut. Though the town is devoted to fish of all kinds, scaly and shell, it's best known for having the world's largest home-based halibut fleet.

It seems that everything has a fish flavor. Eat some, for sure, in the restaurants, or if you are there during the Festival, take in a local "fish feed." And don't miss the museum. In front is a large bronze sculpture, called "Fisk," (fish) in honor of them all. Inside you'll see a couple of big ones that didn't get away, stuffed and lying in state. The biggest is a King salmon, the record-breaker, weighing in at 126½ pounds.

The flatter, sea level terrain in the vicinity has created some sloughs. One of them is a photographers' delight. Because of the tides, the houses bordering Hammer's Slough are built on stilts. Along with warehouses and boats reflected in the still water, they make a picture-worthy scene.

You can drive a couple of miles to Sandy Beach picnic and recreation area. Drive the 34-mile Mitkof Highway for campgrounds, a fish ladder at Falls Creek, and the Crystal Lake Fish Hatchery. Near the end of the highway is the Stikine River Delta; at low tide the mud flats are exposed.

Petersburg's biggest attraction, literally, is about 25 miles east of town. The LeConte Glacier is the continent's southernmost tidewater glacier. It's very active, "calving" ice chunks so big that they are far from melted down by the time they reach the main channels. Flightseeing charters, or day tours on the steel-hulled catamaran *Blue Star* are popular, with sightings of whales, porpoises and seals almost guaranteed.

Tlingit/Russian Sitka

For centuries before the Russians came at the turn of the 18th

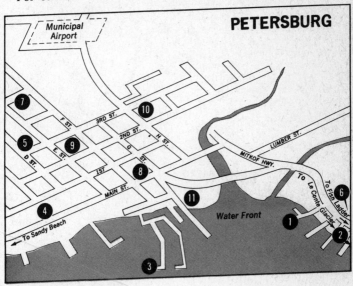

Points of Interet

1) Alaska Island Air Charter
2) Beachcomber Inn
3) Blue Star Cruises
4) Buschmann Historic Marker
5) Catholic Church
6) King Salmon Hotel
7) Lutheran Church
8) Mitkof Hotel
9) Museum and "Fisk"
10) Presbyterian Church
11) Visitor Parking

century, Sitka had been the ancestral home of the Tlingit Indian nation. Isolated on the far west side of their large island, they cherished their affluent life, living off the land and sea. And the living was easy, with plenty of game in the forests and a wealth of seafood. It was small wonder that the Indians took a dim view of Russian intrusion.

For photos, atmosphere, and orientation, the best spot is up some steps to the top of "Castle Hill." This promontory in downtown Sitka was the site of many major historical happenings. The "castle" of first Governor Alexander Baranof is long gone now, of course. What's left are some venerable cannon, a number with Russian markings. They point west to the Pacific Ocean past the lovely island-flecked harbor and Mt. Edgecumbe, an extinct volcano that looks like a mini Fujiyama.

Note the only other furnishing—a flagpole. Every October 18, everyone gathers around it, many wearing period costumes, the men with beards and the ladies with bonnets. Then they reenact the same ceremonies, lowering the Russian Double Eagle flag and raising the American flag that in 1867 marked the transfer of Russian America to the United States. Congress promptly renamed the new territory "Alaska."

Governor Baranof, guiding light for the settlement of Sitka, second capital of Russian America, left his name and mark. Sitka's island is named Baranof, and it is situated in the northern part of the large Alexander Archipelago. The Governor coveted the Sitka site for some of the same reasons the Tlingits did: beauty of setting, milder climate, and the forests. However, the Russians needed the wood for building craft larger than war canoes. Their ships traded far west to Hawaii and the Orient, and south along the west coast as far as Fort Ross, California. Baranof was well aware of the convenience of Sitka's location. Eventually the city grew and became so lively that it was called the "Paris of the Pacific." But not without a notable setback.

The *first* settlement site a few miles north of Sitka today was called Fort Archangel Michael. It was established in 1799 and was destroyed by the Tlingits in 1802. "I shall return," vowed Baranof, and did, in 1804, bent on building his next capital on the Tlingit's choice village property. The final "Battle for Alaska" began with the attack on their stronghold atop the hill. It ended at the Tlingit fort a few miles down the beach. Defeated, the Indians fled to the other side of the island and stayed there for the next twenty years. The battle site is now the 54-acre Sitka National Historical Park.

Sitka's Indian side is well represented here, beginning with totem poles in front of the building and along a shady lane that leads to the old fort site. Inside the attractive Visitor Center, The Battle is replayed in audio-visual, and there is a magnificent display of original totemic art. In the Indian Cultural Workshop rooms, artisans revive old crafts from wood carving to the difficult, almost lost, art of Chilkat blanket weaving.

At the nearby Sheldon Jackson College campus, the museum collection started by this early day missionary and educator also displays prized items, both Russian and Indian, including a detailed diorama of the original Indian Village. In the Centennial Building, there is also an accurate model of "New Archangel," as the Russians called the colony they built on the ruins of Indian Sitka. It shows where the Russians built boats, milled flour, cast bells for California missions, and cut ice from Swan Lake to ship to gold rush-booming San Francisco bars.

Near the replica of the blockhouse you can visit a crumbling old cemetery where a Russian princess is buried. She is said to have cried as she stood beside her husband, Governor Maksoutoff, during the transfer ceremonies.

For almost ten years, Sitka's town jewel, St. Michael's Cathedral, dating from 1844, was missing. Russian built with onion dome and carrot spire, the building burned in 1966, leaving a heart-breaking void smack in the middle of the main street. During the fire, everyone turned out. Through superhuman effort (maybe a miracle), most of the religious objects that could be carried, or that weren't fastened down, were saved.

St. Michael's Bishop Gregory was born in Kiev. He has a special affinity for the charming church. The ceremonies making him the first bishop of Sitka and Alaska to be consecrated in the Alaska diocese were celebrated in the replica of the church, even before it was completely rebuilt.

The Bishop stewards the lovely old treasures with TLC. Among them are ornate gospel books, including one from Fort Ross, chalices, crucifixes, some much-used wedding crowns, and an altar cloth said to have been worked by Princess Maksoutoff herself. There are many priceless icons, religious portraits in oil with only faces and hands exposed, the rest covered with ornate silver and gold-wrought frames. The Sitka Madonna icon was presented to the church by Russian American Company workers.

From Castle Hill, the newer landmarks are obvious, such as modern hotels that contrast with the distinctive vintage buildings, and the John O'Connell Bridge. It connects Sitka's island with Japonski

Island, where the Mt. Edgecumbe Alaska Native boarding high school, hospital and jet airport are located.

Before the bridge, a small ferry carried everyone back and forth for a few cents. All luggage and freight went to town abroad army "ducks," the amphibian craft developed during World War II. No one denies the convenience of the graceful-looking bridge, but visitor-wise the little ferry was a gem. Rubbing shoulders and talking with residents while crossing the harbor and admiring Sitka's marvelous setting made a captivating introduction. And it was a great unwinder after the jet speed arrival at the airport.

Over the years, Sitka's fortune has fluctuated with fishing and seafood processing plants, a Japanese-owned pulp mill, and Federal Government agencies. Just as the residents were adapting to sea invasion by the State Ferries, and a growing number of cruise ships, they were propelled into the jet set. Alaska Airlines inaugurated the Sitka air gateway to Alaska in 1967. Altogether, this has led to a fast-developing new industry, tourism, and in one way or another most of the residents are involved.

At any rate, stop in at the Sitka Visitor Bureau and Greater Sitka Chamber of Commerce offices in the Centennial Building on Harbor Drive. They'll know if the peppy New Archangel Russian Dancers are performing, if the annual Salmon Derby is in progress, and if there is a festival or celebration going on, such as the Fourth of July Logging Championship competitions. And they'll start you on the right foot for your own walking tour, or direct you to a guided tour by bus, which visits town highlights and points of interest a few miles out of town.

Juneau, the Capital

Although the state capital is on the mainland, getting there by road is out of the question. Access is only by sea and air. This more northernly part of the Panhandle continues to be set off by mountain barriers, including a formidable expanse of ice and snow, the Juneau Icefield. Lurking just beyond the mountains towering over the city, the approximately 4,000 square mile icefield is the source of all the glaciers in the area, including the Mendenhall Glacier, about 13 miles from downtown Juneau.

Besides being a main visitor attraction, the Mendenhall has been a good neighbor, obligingly retreating over some years now, making room for Juneau to expand into the suburbs. Less than 50 years ago, the glacier covered the rocks on which the Visitor Center now stands. Now the area formerly covered by the glacier is taken over by a jet

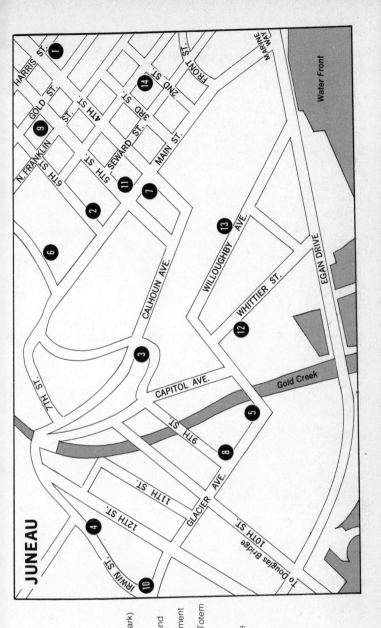

JUNEAU

Points of Interest

1) Bergman Hotel (landmark)
2) Four Story Totem
3) Governor Mansion
4) Grave of Joe Juneau and
   Dick Harris
5) Harris & Juneau Monument
6) House of Wickersham
7) Memorial Library and Totem
8) Native Crafts Exhibit
   (Federal Bldg.)
9) Old Russian Church
10) Plaque to Chief Kowee
11) State Capitol Bldg.
12) State Museum
13) State Office Bldg.
14) Visitors' Center

airport, a modern shopping center, homes built on some very fine view property, and camp and picnic grounds. No one seems particularly worried about the rumor that a cooler weather cycle which could cause the glacier to start advancing again may be due.

You can drive up and look the glacier in its mile-and-a-half wide, 100- to 200-foot high face. It is reflected in Mendenhall Lake, formed by melting ice, beginning about 1900. The displays in the Visitor Center tell about the plant and animal life supported in this recreational area. It's open 9 to 9 daily in summer; on weekends the rest of the year.

Hiking trails take off from the center and also many other places in and around Juneau. The overall look of Juneau is somewhat sophisticated now. Its skyline is augmented by modern government buildings, the Capitol, the State Office Building, and the State Court Building. The tallest is the Federal Building. But the walking map will also lead you to some surprises, remainders from earlier days. The Governor's Mansion is Colonial-style, its tall, smooth supporting pillars on the porch contrasting with nearby Indian totem poles. At Fifth and Gold streets, the tiny onion-domed St. Nicholas Russian Orthodox Church, dating from 1894, is a standout, though surrounded by other buildings now. It's not far from the landmark hotel, the Baranof. A new pride of Juneau is the award-winning Marine Park along the busy waterfront. It's a great place to meet the locals, and there may be swinging entertainment, such as the "Natural Gas Jazz Bank" livening up the 4th of July.

The Alaska State Museum in the subport area houses excellent Indian and Eskimo displays, rocks and minerals, and mounted wildlife specimens. Ramps instead of stairs, a boon to the handicapped, lead to upper levels. High on a slanty street overlooking Juneau is a small house-museum. James Wickersham, a judge, historian, and collector of Alaskan treasures lived here early in the century. Now, his niece, Ruth Allman, is hostess and narrator. She displays his artifacts and memorabilia, and tops the visit with her special "Flaming Sourdough Treat." Tickets and reservations are needed (tel. 586-1251) to put your name in her sourdough pot.

A ghost of Juneau's golden past haunts the slopes of Mount Roberts. Some ruins of buildings of the Alaska-Juneau Mine that produced over $80 million in gold before it was closed in 1944 are reminders that, before government, gold was a bigger business. Rich strikes by Joe Juneau and Dick Harris were made here in 1880, before the mad rushes elsewhere. The stampede that followed their discoveries settled Juneau, the first "Alaska" town, following the Purchase. Across the Douglas Bridge and south from Sandy Beach, there are remains of the Treadwell Mine. Old pilings along the shore and rusting machinery in the woods give little hint now that here was a mine even bigger than the A–J.

By 1900, there was agitation to move the capital from Sitka to booming Juneau. The reason? Sitka was considered too isolated and far off the beaten track to be the seat of government. Legislators argued that the capital should be nearer the population center. In 1906, the deed was done.

Ironically, Juneau is now facing the same dilemma. In 1974 the vote favored moving the capital from Juneau's 20,000 population area to a spot between the state's two largest cities. In 1976, voters approved a site near Willow, deemed within easier reach of over half of the state's residents, but starting from wilderness. Since, there have been some second thoughts.

Estimates from the drawing board indicate that a lot of pipeline revenue might be consumed by rebuilding from scratch and by moving costs; the money might be used to better advantage. Then, too, many have a genuine appreciation for Juneau's capital attributes, located as it is amid Southeast Alaska's great recreational opportunities. At this writing, no one is laying any bets on the outcome.

Glacier Bay

Two hundred years ago, no visitors saw Glacier Bay. It was only a dent in an icy shoreline. Over the next hundred years, due to a warming trend and some earthquakes, the ice rivers melted, forming Glacier Bay as they retreated with amazing speed up their fjord-like inlets. Nature's healing touch followed, repairing the scars of the glacier-scoured shores by covering them with lush rain forests that attracted abundant wildlife. The unusual icy wilderness also attracted naturalist John Muir, in 1879. He was fascinated by the flora, fauna and sea life. The Indians called the area "Thunder Bay," because of the sound effects caused by the "calving" of glaciers dropping huge ice chunks into the bay.

Muir's namesake glacier has now retreated miles farther up the bay, from the small cabin next to its face, where the naturalist lived while taking his notes.

Glacier Bay National Monument, where nature has stored her great collection of tidewater glaciers, continues to attract nature lovers, wildlife watchers, and fishermen. Cruise ships bring their passengers up the Bay for closeups of glacier grandeur, the highlight of an Inside Passage voyage. Charter boats are available that explore the Bay and also other photo-worthy waters such as Tracy Arm. "On your own-ers" can contact the Monument Headquarters for essential information on camping and recreation in the monument. Tour groups visit via Alaska Airlines scheduled flights from Juneau that take only 12 minutes to Gustavus Airport. From there it's ten miles by bus through mossy forest to overnight in Glacier Bay Lodge. Next morning, the lodge cruise boat *Thunder Bay* takes them to the glaciers. Or if they hanker to sleep next to a glacier, they can overnight far up-Bay on the lodge's mini-cruise liner, the *Glacier Bay Explorer*.

Gracious Living in the Ice Age

The adventure of snuggling up for a night in the "Ice Age" while within sight and sound of a grand-scale glacier was innovated in 1979. It has to be the epitome of wining and dining in an unusual place. The *Explorer* leaves the Glacier Bay Lodge dock after lunch. By dinner time, the ship is cruising a deep fjord that was once solid ice, heading for a rendezvous with glaciers—perhaps Margerie or her neighbor, Grand Pacific, both active calvers; perhaps nosing around Johns Hopkins Inlet, usually ice-choked by its active glacier. Safe anchorage for the night may be near Lamplugh or Reid Glaciers. Here you can walk on the beach and observe a surprising variety of small plants re-invading the recently (comparatively speaking) scoured terrain.

This party-sized luxury cruise ship has 32 twin-bedded staterooms with private facilities, a Glacier Vista Lounge, and a dining room with picture windows. Naturally the most popular entertainment aboard is glacier watching. Just outside the windows, the tumbling icy-blue face of a glacier and the towering Fairweather mountain range behind is truly a wide-screen spectacular. Some stay up all night, camera ready to snap an ice fall in the glow of the midnight sun. Those who retire to their staterooms know when a big chunk topples, however. First there is a rumble from the 150- to 200-foot glacierface; then there is the splashdown, followed by gentle lulling swells.

Unlike along the rest of the sheltered Inside Passage, sightseeing in Glacier Bay is a fairly recent phenomenon. The area was inundated by a "Little Ice Age" that started about 4,000 years ago, and ended about the middle of the eighteenth century. The ice sheet has been shrinking at a fast rate only over the past century. Capt. George Vancouver sailed by an icy shoreline in 1794. A hundred years later, naturalist John Muir was able to canoe 40 miles up a deep fjord-like bay left by the melting glaciers. Today ships can sail 40 miles beyond the campsite where Muir's namesake glacier once peered in his cabin window. Now Muir Glacier and others have retreated far up their inlets, leaving miles of waterways for birds, seals, whales, porpoises—and adventuresome visitors.

As the lush rainforests disappear and the vegetation dwindles, the up-Bay boat seems to be taking a trip back to the Ice Age. A Park Service naturalist is aboard to interpret the many facets of this most unusual National Monument, making the trip a learning experience. Everyone is encouraged to share what they see and it's relayed over the loudspeaker. Perhaps a black bear will amble over a talus slope. For sure there will be goats gamboling on 5,000-foot Mt. Wright. The *Explorer* quietly approaches nesting sites in the Marble Islands. Wherever food is plentiful—fish, plankton, shrimp—stirred up in shallows by the tide, there'll be flocks of sea birds: puffins, scoters, oystercatchers, cormorants, phalaropes, kittiwakes, guillemots, murrelets, and assorted gulls. More than 200 species have been sighted, plus shorebirds, including the ptarmigan (the state bird) and the majestic bald eagle.

And you'll learn about ice, which is usually near at hand. It's scooped up, pure and crystal clear, as needed for the bar. Bartenders swear it lasts longer than the mundane ice cube. Their authority is the ranger who explains how snowflakes fall high in the mountains, granulize, and become highly compressed on their hundred-year trip to salt water—thus works nature's slow-motion, automatic ice machine.

The longer the time spent in the monument, the better. It's possible to combine tours and perhaps include a night at the glaciers in the west arm via the *Explorer,* the day cruise on the *Thunder Bay* to Muir Inlet in the east arm, and optional flightseeing and fishing packages available from the lodge.

Personnel of Glacier Bay Lodge and the adjacent Park Service Headquarters work together to see that monument visitors get the most out of their stay. Enlightening films and talks are scheduled in the lodge in the evening. Naturalists escort daily walks on nearby rainforest trails and along the living water line. One trek that is never the same twice is through the fleeting world of sea creatures and plants revealed for a short time at low tide before being claimed again by the sea.

Another mini-cruiser worthy of mention, the *M.V. Fairweather,* daily traverses the upper reaches of the Inside Passage between Juneau and Skagway.

Fjord-like Lynn Canal

Capt. George Vancouver, famous British explorer (and name dropper), discovered this waterway in 1794. Assuming it connected with other seas, he called it Lynn Canal, after King's Lynn, his home in England. Actually, this fjord stretches north of Juneau and after sixty scenic miles deadends at Skagway.

Almost 200 years later, a Seattle-based travel company, Westours, in a sense rediscovered Lynn Canal. They felt that this area, bordered by snowy mountains, glaciers, steep timbered slopes, and supporting a wealth of sea and bird life, should be seen in broad daylight. And so they altered their cruise pattern along the Inside Passage and added a specially-built day cruiser for the best viewing of Lynn Canal's choice assets.

Their big, world-class cruise ships, Holland America's *S.S. Statendam* and the *Cunard Princess* sail north from Vancouver, B.C., and turn around at Juneau. From there passengers switch to the *Fairweather,* which links the longer sea leg with tour destinations throughout the heart of Alaska. Though smaller, the smooth, fast *Fairweather* has maximum creature comforts. They include a narrator and four attentive hostesses, besides the captain and crew, seats that recline, and cocktails for sale. A feast for the eyes is right outside the extra-large picture windows and is augmented by complimentary beverages and a hearty snack, served up with tidbits of local lore.

Informality is the keynote during the 5½-hour cruise. You'll learn about nature and how to identify whales, porpoises, seals, and seabirds. In season fishing boats will be netting salmon, King to sockeye. And you'll have your turn to see the view from the bridge, to scan the radar, to study the charts, to peek at the log, and to pick out some landmarks.

Passing what looks like an army post, with early 1900-style military buildings surrounding a large parade ground, you'll see that it is actually a town, Port Chilkoot, and also a National Historical Site. After World War II, the town's founders bought the substantial but little-used Fort William H. Seward as army surplus, and moved in. Right next door is Haines, traditional in appearance and started by

Presbyterian missionaries in 1881. These adjacent towns are now incorporated.

A trail led from this area to the Klondike gold fields before the better-known Chilkoot Trail to the north. Enterprising Jack Dalton staked it out, based on a well-used Indian route to the interior. Then he got *his* gold by charging a substantial toll to use the trail.

Most Westours comprehensive Alaska itineraries include the *Fairweather,* traveling either north or south. Northbound, after overnighting in Juneau, you are taken by motorcoach to the Yankee Cove Landing. It's several pleasant miles from the city, past green islands, quiet bays, and titillating glimpses of Juneau's most famous asset, the Mendenhall Glacier. Southbound, after overnighting at Skagway, passengers step on board at the gold-rush town's famous harbor. The "Klondike Passage" is an optional tour, Juneau to Whitehorse, or reverse. The circa $200 price includes a hotel room in Skagway and Juneau, or in Whitehorse, all transportation, transfers and baggage handling. Also popular is a fly/cruise tour starting from either end of the Fairweather run. Ground transportation is provided as needed to connect with the cruise and the scenic flight. This tour allows you to see contrasting but equally beautiful versions of Lynn Canal.

Gateways or Exits?

After Juneau, whether you consider the two most northern ports on the Inside Passage to be introductions to southeast Alaska, or exits from the mountain and sea-locked Panhandle, depends on whether you are coming or going. From both Haines and Skagway, overland routes lead from sea level and over mountain passes to connect with the Alaska Highway.

The 159-mile Haines Highway joins the Alaska Highway at Mile 1016. From Skagway, the White Pass & Yukon Railroad takes cars and passengers to Whitehorse, capital of Canada's Yukon Territory, within about 280 miles of the Alaska border. Here paving begins and continues through interior Alaska to Fairbanks, official end of the Alaska Highway at Mile 1523.

Klondike Highway 2 takes off from the ferry dock at Skagway and cuts through 60 unpaved miles to Carcross. It connects with Yukon roads leading to a junction with the Alaska Highway about 14 miles from Whitehorse. Motorcoaches, cars and RV's can traverse the sixty rugged but scenic miles of the new American and Canadian road, but everyone is advised to check conditions and regulations ahead before striking out.

From here on, a copy of one of the excellent detailed road travel guides (see *Additional Reading*) is invaluable for sightseeing and determining what creature comforts (or lack of them) lie ahead. They also point out interesting variations and loop roads for inquisitive travelers with plenty of time to explore and recreate.

Haines

A missionary, S. Hall Young, and a famous naturalist, John Muir, picked the site for this town meant to bring Christianity and education to the native Indians. The location is a beautiful one, on a heavily wooded peninsula with magnificent views up the Inside Passage and of the Coastal Mountain Range. Its Lynn Canal neighbors are Skagway, 15 miles to the north, and Juneau, about 75 miles to the south.

Since its religious beginnings in 1881, some sporadic happenings have influenced Haines. By 1897, it was a gateway and supply route to the Klondike in the Yukon via the Jack Dalton Trail, and it boomed in 1898 when gold was discovered nearby in Porcupine (now deserted). In 1903, an army post was started at Portage Cove, just south of town, and by 1905, Fort William H. Seward had a full garrison with two companies of soldiers. By 1918 there were four companies, and Alaskans were drafted from there for World War I. In 1923, they changed the name to Chilkoot Barracks, and for nearly 20 years this was the only Army post in Alaska. World War II of course put all of Alaska on the map, and units from Chilkoot Barracks were the nucleus for military installations in bigger cities and places such as Cold Bay and Dutch Harbor out toward the Aleutian Islands.

After the war, the deactivated Chilkoot Barracks were sold to a group of veterans "lock, stock, and barrel," you might say. They renamed their purchase Port Chilkoot and considered developing the vast recreational possibilities of the beautiful area which so far had concentrated on such basic industries as fishing, fish processing, mining, and lumbering. The adjacent communities merged in 1970 as the City of Haines, combined population about 2,000, all gearing up for the big city centennial celebration during 1981.

Together, they now emphasize the hunting and fishing, and camping at Chilkoot Lake, Portage Cove, and Mosquito Lake (don't let the name deter you—it's beautiful there). They are all within easy driving distance and offer unusual birdwatching. Though eagles stay in the Chilkat Valley all year, they concentrate at about Mile 19 on the Haines Highway in the fall. Their white heads a standout against blue sky and foliage, hundreds cover the river flats and perch in the trees during November and December.

"Haines Is for Hikers" is the lead for a folder describing the local trail systems. One system south of town on the Chilkat Peninsula takes in areas being developed as a large state park. Trails lead to Battery Point and Mt. Riley. The more strenuous one, the Mt. Ripinski Trail System, was named for a teacher in the Presbyterian boarding school, who settled in Haines in 1896. It's a day-long hike to the trail register on the higher northwest peak, but the view from the 3,610-foot summit is a photographer's delight on clear days: the contrasting communities; Lynn Canal bordered by its snowy mountains; waterfalls and alpine meadows.

In fact there is a great deal you can photograph in the area without such effort. You can drive toward the picturesque cannery at Letnikof Cove and take photos of the Davidson Glacier and the Rainbow, a hanging glacier that glistens in the sunshine and drops chunks of ice during rainy weather. And the walking tour of historic Fort William H. Seward is mostly a level one. A map and folder describing the buildings facing the parade ground gently guides visitors from one of the first buildings, the Cable Office, which is now an art shop, past officers' quarters, the former hospital, post exchange, barracks, and many more.

Totem Village, on the parade ground, includes a replica of a pioneer trapper's cabin and cache, a reproduction of a tribal house, an Indian drying and tanning rack for pelts, and a small collection of large totems. A totem pole 132½ feet tall, heralded as the world's largest, was carved here and dedicated to "all the Indians of Southeastern Alaska." Exhibited in Japan's Expo '70 at the Alaska Pavilion, this mighty totem is now in the village of Kake, Alaska. Though not part of the original post, Totem Village belongs here as part of the heritage of the Chilkat Indians, represented in other buildings of this living museum, still under renovation and reconstruction.

The Chilkat Indians

The Chilkat Indians, a branch of the Tlingits, were notoriously war-like a hundred years ago. Their strategic position helped them to guard mountain passes and waterways against most invaders who might have challenged them for the game-abundant forests and fish-filled fjords, lakes and streams. They managed to keep most visitors at a distance, the better to enjoy their way of living, in which work alternated with periods of leisure when they had time for artistic pursuits, especially woodcarving, weaving, and dancing.

Since then, with the inevitable encroachment of people, ships, planes, and roads, much has changed—for better or worse, depending on your viewpoint.

Today some Chilkats still beat drums, flash spears, war dance, and perpetuate some of the old ways. They do it to help preserve some of the best of their culture, and for visitors. For a number of years now, friendly Chilkats have been reviving their arts and crafts under the direction of Carl Heinmiller, a white man from Ohio and an expert woodcarver. He started projects like totem pole carving, mask- and costume-making, and lively Indian dancing as antidotes for the lack of activities for young people—both Indian and white—in Port Chilkoot, then newly incorporated and isolated. An Eagle Scout himself, one of his first efforts was to organize a Boy Scout troop.

He figured Indian dancing was a logical study project for the area, as a starter. But Carl came up against a blank wall and a generation gap when he went for advice to the elders of the close-by old Indian village of Klukwan. They had to be convinced that the young people and Carl were seriously interested before they would pass on traditional dances and mask designs which were inherited and private clan property.

Through museum research Carl carved masks the Indians couldn't distinguish from their own, and he helped the young people study and prepare intricate dance costumes, until finally the key leaders were convinced. Once the youngsters started learning the chants and peppy tribal dances, there was no doubt of their enthusiasm. Girls were asked to join the activities, and the project grew into Alaska Youth, Inc., which has received some help from the government through grants and appropriations.

Carl's rewards from the Indians was a gratifying honor. The Eagle (Scout) became a Raven in the clan, with a high and worthy Indian name. Since then the dancers have won honors in inter-tribal competitions, and have been ambassadors to cities in other parts of the world. In some places they left a souvenir at city hall—a carved totem pole.

The Chilkat Dancers are not the only result of Carl's help and concern for native Alaskans. Alaska Youth evolved into Alaska

Indian Arts, Inc. (A.I.A.), now directed by Carl's son Lee, while Carl assists and also serves as town magistrate. A.I.A., besides rekindling the natives' interest in their heritage, also provides employment for fishermen in the off-season, and for the handicapped. Handicapped himself since World War II, Carl understands the problems.

Though funding has been sporadic and the number of workers fluctuates accordingly, visitors always find the school intriguing. Inside the former fort hospital, now the Alaska Indian Arts Skill Center, people will be carving Alaska soapstone, jade, ivory, and wood, or perhaps etching silver, buffing copper, carving and painting wooden plaques, or making costumes. Outside, Tlingits may be carving a totem pole or other large item.

The fort gymnasium has been nicely remodeled as a little theater and is much used for community programs and plays. The Chilkat Dancers moved their performances there when the audiences outgrew the tribal house they authentically had reconstructed on the parade ground.

The Canadian Connection Via the Haines Highway

Haines is Mile 0 on the Haines Highway, a 159-mile road connecting the Marine Highway with the Alaska Highway at Haines Junction, Yukon Territory. Some people who take their cars on the ferry choose to disembark here and take this route to reach Anchorage or Fairbanks. Part of the Haines Highway follows the Dalton Trail, laid out and cleared by the indefatigable and high-handed Jack Dalton, who charged Klondike-bound travelers $150 per trip for using the trail.

The Haines Highway, skirting the eastern foothills of the St. Elias Mountains, leads over 3,493-foot Chilkat Pass, past snow-bordered lakes reflecting rugged mountains. This is the domain of snowpeaks, glaciers, glacial streams, and clear-water recreation lakes. Many travelers feel that the scenery along the Chilkat River estuary, which the highway parallels for 16 miles, is comparable to the Himalayas.

If you start early enough in the morning from either end of this highway there is time to sightsee and still reach the other end—seaward it's Haines; mountainward, the Alaska Highway—without being hampered by the lack of paving or the fact that the border closes up tight at night. If you have the time, it's well worth planning to stop over at one of the not-too-numerous resorts.

At Mile 21 a side road makes a 2-mile loop to the Chilkat village of

Klukwan, one of the oldest Indian settlements of the region and for
centuries before the white man a center of Tlingit culture. The
American bald eagle, no stranger in southeast Alaska, arrives in the
Klukwan area by the thousands in the autumn to feed on the late
summer salmon run.

At Mile 27, Mosquito Lake state campground is located 2½ miles
off the right side of the highway. The 33 Mile Roadhouse advertises
the last gas for 92 miles; better tank up. At Mile 35, the abandoned
Porcupine Mine and the ghost town of Porcupine can be seen across
the Klehini River from the road. The asphalt road of Alaska gives
way to the gravel of British Columbia at Mile 41. Depending on your
direction of travel, you must stop at either U.S. or Canada Customs,
almost next door to each other. No facilities nor accommodations
here, and they close up at night. Check current hours before starting
off on this highway, and local times. Alaska and B.C. are on Daylight
Saving Time; the Yukon Territory stays with Pacific Standard year-
round. Twenty-three miles onward, the road, after winding headily up
a mountain, crosses 3,493-foot Chilkat Pass. At Mile 91 the road
crosses into Yukon Territory. Two miles on are gas, a store, and a
café. At Mile 97, just before the bridge, a trail leads leftward to
Million Dollar Camp and waterfall, a fine picnic area. At Mile 106, a
tight, twisty, rough road leads 2½ miles to the abandoned Dalton
Post, established in 1892. At Mile 115, follow a sign that will send
you off the road half a mile to Klukshu Indian village, a small
settlement on the river of the same name. The village is on the old
Dalton Trail. Good photographic possibilities of the villages: fish
traps on the river banks, meat caches, log cabins, terrain of the
Dalton Trail. At Mile 125, Lake Dezedeash Resort and Lodge, at the
southern end of Dezedeash Lake, has rooms, horseback riding,
fishing, restaurant, cocktail lounge, store, gas, garage, and complete
hookups for trailers and campers open year round, a gateway to
Kluane National Park. Rooms, restaurant, cocktail lounge. At Mile
137 a side road on the left leads to Kathleen Lake Territorial
Campground, with 30 campsites, kitchen, and boat launch. This lake
has many grayling and rainbow trout and the rare kokanee, a
landlocked salmon. Be sure to have the right license—or all three—
for fishing in British Columbia, the Yukon Territory, and Alaska.
Half a mile up the highway is Lake Kathleen Lodge, with rooms,
restaurant, laundromat, and complete garage service. Haines
Junction, less than 17 miles on, has tourist accommodations—rooms,
store, garage. The junction lies 98 miles west of Whitehorse on the
Alaska Highway route from Dawson Creek.

Skagway

Skagway, 17 miles north of Haines, is the last port of call on the Inside Passage. It was the end of a gold rusher's sea leg of his journey, and the jumping-off place for the arduous overland trek to reach Canada's rich Klondike gold fields. Technically, it's the same for visitors today, but they accomplish the feat in a fraction of the time, and with none of the discomforts.

Skagway is an important link of the developing Klondike Gold Rush National Historical Park. It follows the historic path of the turn-of-the-century gold seekers, beginning in Seattle's Pioneer Square, the departure point. In Skagway, a sizeable downtown section of business buildings and homes—all listed in the National Register of Historic Places—is being restored. Two other segments of the Historical Park commemorate the Chilkoot Trail and the White Pass Trail. The project is International, as Canada develops portions from the summits of Chilkoot Pass and White Pass (International Boundary) all the way to Skagway's Canadian counterpart, Dawson City, of Klondike fame.

Skagway had only a single cabin, still standing, when the Yukon Gold Rush began. At first the argonauts swarmed to Dyea, nine miles west, but when it was found that a dock could be built at Skagway, this town became the great gateway to the Klondike. Skagway mushroomed overnight into as rich and wild a mixture of people as Alaska ever knew. Three months after the first boat landed, in July 1897, Skagway numbered perhaps 20,000 persons, with well-laid-out streets, hotels, stores, saloons, gambling houses, and dance halls. By the spring of 1898, according to a Northwest Mounted Police report, "Skagway was little better than a hell on earth."

The exciting environs of Skagway, topped by 7,000-foot-high mountains, is matched by the flavor of the boardwalks, false-front buildings, and old stores along the dirt streets that extend from the dock. In all Alaska, there is no town to match the pioneer flavor of Skagway. "Progress," in terms of modernization, is resisted in favor of tourist appeal. However, the accommodations are not only interesting and comfortable but also most attractive, such as the lately built, modern Westours Klondike, and Alaska's oldest, the modernized Golden North Hotel. The friendly residents will keep you busy with their list of things to see and do for as long as you stay.

In this town of about 800 people, time is kept standing still. To hear the locals talk, it was only yesterday that "Soapy" Smith,

Alaska's most notorious outlaw, and Frank Reid, representing the forces of law and order, met in mortal confrontation.

Volumes have been written about the heyday of this lively ghost town. You'll likely see them well-displayed in souvenir shops, among them Mike Miller's "Soapy," Howard Clifford's "Skagway Story," and Archie Satterfield's "Chilkoot Pass."

The gist of the Smith-Reid encounter was that bad guy Smith and vigilante good guy Reid met down at the dock and shot it out on a pleasant July evening in 1898. Smith died instantly; Reid passed away 12 days later.

The town built a huge monument at Reid's grave, and with a simple inscription summed up what he meant to the honest citizens: "He gave his life for the honor of Skagway." The original gravestone of Soapy Smith was whittled away by souvenir hunters, and now only a simple plank marks his burial place. The graves of both men are close together, in the town cemetery.

Local residents are full of enthusiasm. When cruise ships are in, they stage "The Soapy Smith Show" and "Skaguay (sic) in the Days of '98," with cancan girls, and preceded by play money gambling.

You can drive—or take a taxi—to Dyea, where a tent city of 10,000 sprang up overnight. Here the Klondike-bound began the long, agonizing trek to a lake, where they built boats to continue onward. The fearsome Chilkoot Trail, starting from near sea level, climbed a perilous slope to 3,739-foot Chilkoot Pass. They say that if a climber had to step out of line, he could freeze to death before someone would stop long enough to let him get back in. The last half mile was so steep that some enterprising souls built a "stairway" to the top, cutting 1,500 steps—and charged those who used the stairway a heavy toll. In 1898 an avalanche at Sheep Creek swept more than 60 men to their death. Many lie in Slide Cemetery, near the Dyea townsite.

For more than 60 years the Chilkoot Trail lay silent and in time became overgrown. Then the state began to clear and restore the trail, starting from the beach at Dyea to the Canadian border. The hike is not an easy one, but from the heights there are impressive panoramas. Many mementos of the early Chilkoot Trail still lie around, so the hike is a walk through history. Each year hikers make the trip to Lake Lindeman or Lake Bennett, where they can continue to Whitehorse or return to Skagway by train. Make arrangements for train tickets ahead, either direction. Guides are available in Skagway for those who want to follow the Chilkoot Pass Trail from Dyea to Dawson. The Klondike Gold Rush Park Visitor Center in the AB Hall on Broadway has maps and brochures. Or write to the Superintendent,

Klondike Gold Rush National Historical Park, Box 517, Skagway, AK 98840.

By Rail and Highway to the Yukon

In 1898 a narrow-gauge railroad was started along the White Pass Trail to Whitehorse. Two years later it was completed. The train ride is, for some persons at least, the high mark of an Alaskan visit. Its historic interest lies not only in following the old foot trail, which is clearly seen at points, but in the pause at Carcross, once a sternwheeler stop and now also a way point on the new Skagway-Whitehorse highway.

Motorcoaches and cars drive the summer-only highway link between seaport Skagway and the Interior Alaska Highway. The route follows the Skagway River across from the W.P. & Y.R. tracks. Then it climbs to 3,290 feet elevation, heads past Tutshi Lake, and follows along Windy Arm to Carcross. Here are the first locomotive in the Yukon, an early stage coach and freighter and, at the lake shore, the last of the sternwheelers to ply these waters. From Carcross came the men who made the first Klondike discovery.

The train route via White Pass and Lake Bennett serpentines up and down and around mountains, past vistas of mighty snow masses that seem to grow taller as the train withdraws, Lynn Canal, waterfalls, fields of wildflowers, gorges, lakes, and glimmering meadows.

Both routes are an experience. . . . but will this new do-it-yourself highway cut back the number of rail passengers, maybe make the W.P. & Y.R. as a tourist excursion economically unfeasible eventually? Only time can answer that. Meanwhile railroad buffs continue to opt for the informality of the W.P. & Y.R. and the chance to photograph the train maneuvering hairpin curves as its engine disappears into tunnels in rocky mountainsides. They hope the little old parlor car with its quaint upholstered seats, water cooler, and pot-bellied stove, will be retained for atmosphere, along with the modern cars with movable chairs and comfortable footrests lining the long picture windows. Passenger excursions continue to the summit and back, and also through trips either way for tour groups or individuals. Will the W.P. & Y.R. still serve that gandy dancer-sized lunch at the Lake Bennett station—tables laden, including big wedges of pie, and all included in the through fare? For information to help plan itineraries and to make reservations, write: White Pass & Yukon Route, P.O. Box 2147, Seattle, WA 98111.

From Whitehorse, the Alaska Highway's Mile 0 at Dawson Creek, B.C., lies over 900 miles south and east through Yukon Territory and British Columbia provinces. Those who have driven the whole distance will probably have "Alaska or Bust" written in dust on their vehicles, distinguishing them from those who chose the alternate water route, bypassing Dawson Creek.

In any event there are still almost 300 miles to the Alaska border (and paving) and 300 more to Fairbanks.

PRACTICAL INFORMATION FOR SOUTHEAST ALASKA

This section will point out some of what there is to see and do in this part of Alaska, and provide information about shopping opportunities, where to stay, and where to eat.

The beauty of the trees, islands, and mountains will be obvious, and so will the rain. If it precipitates a bit too much doing your visit, don't complain to a "native." They brag about the rain in Ketchikan and measure it on a gauge that says at the top, "Busted in 1949—202:55 inches!" They even drink to it at a waterfront bar, The Rainbird. So ignore it if it rains, and concentrate on all the pleasures at hand.

This potpourri is only a sample of what you'll discover in the main ports-of-call reached by ferries, cruise ships, and planes. As they say in Wrangell, "Help is as close as the nearest person." And every community has a center where you can talk with someone and pick up literature that will keep you traveling in the right directions.

ACCESS ROUTES TO THE SOUTHEAST PANHANDLE

BY AIR. From Seattle, *Alaska Airlines* and *Wien Air Alaska* fly direct to Ketchikan and Juneau. Alaska Airlines serves Ketchikan, Wrangell, Petersburg, Juneau, Sitka, and Yakutat. Local lines provide air-taxi service to smaller communities, deliver freight, and offer flightseeing trips and charters into remote areas.

BY OVERLAND HIGHWAY. You can drive to the Southeast, but the only access highways taking off from the Alaska Highway are the 110-mile Klondike Hwy. 2 and the 159-mile Haines Highway leading to the two northernmost ports in the Panhandle: Skagway and Haines. There is scheduled bus service, and motorcoach tours also travel these routes.

BY WATER. Year-round, ferries of the Southeast System of the *Alaska Marine Highway* connect Seattle and/or Prince Rupert with Panhandle ports. Smaller ferries make the rounds to smaller villages on the islands. In summer, there are many cruise ship sailings: *Holland America, March Shipping, Princess, Paquet, Royal Viking,* and *Sitmar* are the main lines. (Also see *Practical Information* for "The Rest of Alaska.")

 WEATHER FORECAST AND WHAT TO WEAR. The climate is comparable to the rest of the Pacific Northwest, but wetter. Full raingear that is light and easy to pack is a must. Include something to keep your feet dry on city streets or while exploring and hiking farther afield. Lightweight sweaters, pants suits, and slacks are comfortable for spring and summer. In autumn, the days may still be mild, but warmer slack outfits and perhaps a convertible-type topcoat will feel good for cooler evenings. In winter, add some wool, an overcoat or parka, heavier shoes or boots, head and hand covering, and you'll be up to anything going on out-of-doors.

Although clothing is casual aboard the cruise ships, as a rule there are also opportunities to dress up. Women may want to take an evening dress and men a jacket and tie. Just ask ahead about how formal or informal it may be aboard the particular ship you choose. Then you'll also be prepared for any special nights out in Juneau, Fairbanks, or Anchorage.

 GETTING TO KETCHIKAN, GETTING AROUND, GETTING INFORMATION *Ketchikan Visitors Bureau* is handily located next to the attractive new waterfront park downtown, right by City Pier, where the big ships dock. The ferries dock at their own pier to the north of the main business district. *Alaska Airlines* and *Wien Air Alaska* jets land at Ketchikan International Airport on Gravina Island across from Revillagigedo Island, and every half-hour passengers take a 10-minute shuttle ride to the Airport Ferry terminal, not far from the State Ferry terminal. There is regular bus service to town; and there is *Alaska Cab,* that also offers sightseeing charters. *Ketchikan Sightseeing/Northern Bus Co.* will be waiting to take those who have bought tickets for the one-hour, 12-mile sightseeing tour possible during the time the ferry is docked. For longer-staying visitors they'll be ready with the 2½-hour, 30-mile tour of Ketchikan and environs. Or, as they say in Ketchikan, all that's needed is "a pair of sneakers and an hour or two" to cover the high points of a walking tour at your own pace. It begins at the Visitors Center, and from there well-placed signs put up by the Chamber of Commerce lead you onward.

Getting to Wrangell, and Around, and Information. Tourism and services are very informal in smaller, waterfront-dominated Wrangell. Scheduled ferries dock near "downtown" just a block from the largest hotel, the Stikine Inn. When cruise ships, such as the *Vera Cruz* and the *Princess Patricia,* put into port, they tie up at the new City Dock, only a short walk away from the Inn.

The town appreciates the regularly scheduled ferries, and everyone loves having the cruise ships call. In fact, they greet them with music and dance—the dancers, ranging from young tots to the young-in-heart, may turn out for a lively cancan, in costume. They may be joined by some local Stikine (sti-keen') Indians, also of all ages, who dance in costume in the tribal house on special occasions. The band may be from the high school, or be a local family combo, with the youngest on mama's lap dodging her hot trombone.

If you arrive at the airport, taxis are available. And inquire about courtesy service to and from the hotels.

The *Wrangell Visitors Bureau* is at the high school on Church Street. They are open long hours seven days a week in summer, and when state ferries and cruise ships are in port. There are usually tours put together for the tour ships, and otherwise the Visitors Bureau is very accommodating and tries to arrange a guided tour if requested, often led by an enthusiastic student. Personnel at the Museum, on Second Street next to the library behind the post office, also dispense information, but the hours are shorter.

Getting to Petersburg, and Around, and Information. Petersburg, a little smaller than Wrangell, is just as informal. The high point, tourist-wise, is during May when they celebrate the good fishing and being Norwegian, but independent. They turn out to greet visitors arriving to help them celebrate, and some of the greeters may be a bold band of "Viking pirates." There's a taxi service, and buses can be arranged for getting around the area.

During the summer, visitors can find out what they want to know at the Petersburg Museum, First and F streets, open 1 to 4:30 P.M. daily. Otherwise, write to the *Petersburg Chamber of Commerce,* Box 649, Petersburg, AK 99833. If your name is Norwegian, you'll have it made.

Getting to Juneau, and Around, and Information. Juneau is a little over two hours by air from Seattle and about an hour and a half from Anchorage. The Municipal Airport is about nine miles from the City Docks downtown, where the ferries and cruise ships tie up. Air passengers can take a bus to town for about $4. A *Haida Cab* will cost not a whole lot more per person if you can find others to share it. Cars are for rent at the airport and also in town. When the legislature is in session, and it has been known to run into the tourist season in June, reserve ahead to be sure to get the car. The same is true for lodging.

Except for the downtown area, the capital is spread out enough so that those without their own transportation will want to sign up for a local two-and-a-half-hour tour, offered daily by *American Sightseeing* and *Gray Line* with offices in the Baranof Hotel, or *Alaska Sightseeing Co.* through Juneau Travel Service on Marine Way.

Otherwise, all around downtown Juneau is a favorite walking area. The *Chamber of Commerce* at Second and Franklin, catty-corner to the Baranof Hotel, has walking-tour maps. Most businesses have them on hand, too. Follow the map from the waterfront on up as high as you want to climb. Once you head away from Gastinau Channel, the route is increasingly up via narrow streets and wooden stairways, past homes clinging to town-confining Mt. Juneau and Mt. Roberts.

There is also an Information Kiosk on the waterfront. Manned by volunteers in summer, the booth is in the Marine Park by the seaplane docks and the Merchants Wharf shopping mall.

In 1980, the capital celebrated its centennial with special events all year. Some of the projects are permanent attractions. Look for the replica of an early log cabin church at Third and Main, a quaint contrast to the State Court Building, all metal and glass.

Getting to Sitka, and Around, and Information. Situated on the outside of the Inside Passage route, the former Russian capital of the Great Land is two hours by *Alaska Airlines* jet from Seattle. The ferries in summer make it to Sitka four times a week northbound and three times a week southbound. (Juneau is served twenty times a week.) Ferries dock seven miles from town. Sitka is a popular cruise ship port, with several ships together making close to a hundred stops during summer. Unlike at most other ports, ships anchor out in the harbor, and passengers are then taken ship to shore and back on launches that run frequently.

Buses can transport you to downtown hotels from the ferry dock and airport, and there are *Island Taxis* and *Hertz* cars for rent. Obliging *Sitka Tours* buses are waiting at the ferry to take people on a Ferry Stopover tour for well under $10 (you pay any admission charge along the way), returning to the gangplank in time for the sailing. The longer tours, $15, leave from hotels. They include admissions, but not transfers. Those who have bought tours aboard ship walk from the launch dock to the tour buses waiting nearby.

The *Sitka Visitors Center* headquarters is conveniently located in the beautifully designed Centennial Building. A big Tlingit Indian war canoe is mounted on the front of it. Inside you'll find a museum, auditorium, art gallery, Convention and Visitor Center offices, and lots of friendly people with advice on what to see and how to do it. The staff is enthusiastic, from students to "Double O's" ("Older Ones"). Many of the latter are retired Alaskans living in the Pioneer Home, the big building dominating the downtown square and marked by a flourishing hedge of Sitka roses. On the lawn, a two-ton bronze statue of a grizzled prospector honors all "sourdoughs." Some of the Double O's are history buffs who lived through much of Alaska's lively early-20th century history.

Getting to Haines and Skagway, and Around, and Information. There is no direct big-jet service to either town, but *LAB Flying Service* and *Southeast Skyways* fly regularly to Haines and Skagway from Juneau. Both towns are served by the ferries, and both can be reached by highway with motorcoach service. (See the *Exploring Southeast* and *Practical Information* sections.)

During Haines's Centennial years, 1979–1981, is a good time to visit. Take in the Haines Centennial Revue featuring the melodrama "Lust for Dust," and vaudeville put together by the active Lynn Canal Community Players. Dalton Trail Days fall over the Fourth of July to celebrate the rough-and-tumble days of Jack Dalton and his pack train route to the Klondike. The Southeast Alaska State Fair is a three-day festival held in August. Haines was once famous for its giant strawberries, and even had a Strawberry Festival as part of the Fourth celebration. A few people still cultivate them, and some of the mammoth strawberries still show up at the Fair.

As you enter Haines, the Visitors Center, marked by impressive Welcome Totem Poles, is at Mile One of the Haines Highway. They have maps and brochures, and suggestions for sightseeing and entertainment, camping, hiking, and other recreation. There is also an information desk at the Halsingland Hotel on the quadrangle of Port Chilkoot's Fort William Seward. They'll have information on local tours, times, and prices, and on subjects from bald eagle sightings to Indian dancing, performed frequently in summer.

Skagway is the northernmost Southeast port, the end of the line and turnaround point for most of the cruise ships and ferries, just as it was for the gold rushers. (One exception is Westours; the *Holland America* ships turn around at Juneau, and the *Fairweather* shuttles to Skagway.) Ships tie up only a short walk from downtown, near where Skagway's famous gunfight was held. Cruise ship passengers are primed for excursions up the highway or to the summit of White Pass by rail, or they may be on a tour continuing to the interior and north. Transportation will be waiting to take them and their baggage to hotels and/or exploring. Otherwise, there is taxi service year-round. Inquire at the *Alaska Liquor Store* about car rentals.

Skagway's Chamber of Commerce Visitor Information Center is next to the post office, on Sixth and Broadway. They'll know about town sightseeing, escorted or on your own, about campgrounds at Prospector Park and Liarsville, and how to get to the Gold Rush Cemetery, Reid Falls, flower gardens, Skyline Trail to the top of AB Mountain, and to Upper and Lower Dewey Lakes for fishing. Hotels housing tour groups dispense tour and entertainment information, and tickets, at desks in their lobbies.

SOUTHEASTERN SPECIALTIES

THE INDIANS. Ketchikan's *Totem Heritage Center* provides a good introduction to the history of the old totem poles here. And a leading Tlingit Indian wood carver may be at work on an authentically designed reproduction of one. *Totem Bight State Historical Site,* eleven miles from the city on the North Tongass Highway, contains excellent totems and a tribal house. *Saxman Totem Park,* three miles south of the city (behind Saxman Indian Village, named for an early-day teacher), has over twenty totems, among them a reproduction of the Lincoln totem. Watch for evidence of both the Tlingit and Haida art about town, especially in shops where typically Alaskan items are displayed.

In Wrangell there's much that's Indian, with a touch of the Russian still lingering. There are totems standing in town, and some well-kept ones on *Chief Shake's Island,* reached by a footbridge in the inner harbor. Tribal dances may be presented for tour groups inside the restored Bear Tribal house, where some of the chief's wealth is displayed along with other treasures.

Some exemplary totems are tucked away in unusual places. If you aren't watching for it you might miss the weathered mortuary pole with a kind-faced man hugging his knees. It is standing guard over by the oil docks. And note the Indian carvings on a house nearby.

At low tide mysterious carvings by long-ago Indians show up on rocks on the beach. One site is near the ferry dock. Another is reached by a boardwalk beach trail branching off from the airport road. Experts say these petroglyphs may have been chipped into the rocks as long ago as 8,000 years.

Haines–Port Chilkoot: Indian lore, arts, crafts, and dancing are perpetuated on the historic ground of turn-of-the-century *Fort William Seward*. Visitors can walk around the Totem Village on the parade grounds and see an authentic tribal house, trapper's cabin and cache, pelt-stretching rack, totems, and other replicas of early Indian and frontier living. Artists and craftspeople work in the Alaska Indian Arts Skill Center in one of the vintage buildings. Some may be working outside if the project is large enough, like a house pole or totem, or perhaps a dugout canoe. June through September the Chilkat Dancers perform several evenings a week in another of the renovated army buildings, now the Chilkat Center of the Arts. They wear colorful, authentic costumes and accessories crafted in the Alaska Indian Arts program.

Sitka: The Indian vies with the Russian background here, but holds its own at the *Sitka National Historical Park*, where the emphasis is Tlingit, past to present. Totem poles outside and inside the Visitors Center, excellent audio-visual programs, and the people—including some Natives who may be at work in the craft shops—help to interpret this side of Sitka's rich cultural heritage.

Ports like Petersburg may have an Indian side, but what you'll see there is mostly Norwegian. Juneau remembers its golden days, but the presence there is government. However, visit the *State Museum*, and if Chief Walter Williams happens to be on guide duty you'll get a rundown on all he knows (considerable!) about his heritage, plus his interpretation of some of his favorite dances. Skagway, namesake ancestral home of the Tlingit Indian tribe that once guarded the mountain passes, is much more wrapped up in its gold-rush past. Stop in at *Native Carvings* on the main street and you may find Richard Dick, an Alaska Tlingit Indian, working in wood and stone and willing to pass on some native lore.

Scattered around the islands are many reminders, in smaller Indian villages like Kake, Hydaburg, Angoon, Hoonah, Klawock and others, reached by plane or boat. On the way, bush pilots like Paul Breed of *SEA Airlines*, based in Ketchikan, are inclined to circle and try to point out some remains in deserted village sites, perhaps a totem or part of a tribal house, if they think you are interested.

 FISHING. To catch them around Ketchikan, consult *Ketchikan Marine Charters; Alaska Salmon Charters;* fish off the city docks; drive fifteen miles to fish out of Clover Pass Resort; fly forty-five miles to fish at Yes Bay; or fly about the same distance to fish and soak at Bell Island Hot springs. (The *Frontier Saloon* is the stage for the melodrama "Fish Pirate's Daughter"—and for Alaska slide shows, free popcorn, displays of Gold Rush antiques, sawdust floor, dancing, and live music.) The million-dollar, out-of-door *Deer Mountain Hatchery* adjacent to the Totem Heritage Center is self-guiding, and there'll be someone on hand to interpret, too. A branch of the state *Fish and Game Department* looks after this city-owned birthplace and nursery for King and coho salmon. It's free, open year-round, and you can learn all you want to know about salmon, including their unusual sex life.

Klawock (Kl-wahk'), an Indian community a short flight or a ferry ride from Ketchikan, has a notable collection of totems on a hill in town, but they also major in fish. Alaska's first salmon cannery was built in Klawock in 1878 by the Northern Pacific Trading and Packing Company. From this beginning Alaska's multi-million-dollar industry evolved.

At Petersburg, study the sculpture considered to be one of the Pacific Northwest's finest pieces of bronze art. It's outside the museum, and it honors all fish, including the halibut, Petersburg's mainstay. Inside the museum they boast the record-holding King salmon, 126½ pounds.

All Southeast communities, regardless of their other interests, all go in for sport and/or commercial fishing in varying extents. And they all hold fishing derbies in which visitors are invited to participate. Fishing regulations can be learned in local Fish and Game Department offices. Sporting and fishing gear stores, usually next to or on the waterfront, have current contest rules, licenses for sale, and lots of advice (free).

Throughout the Southeast, visitors will meet fish on the menu, and in some places be exposed to a favorite institution, the salmon bake, usually a good buy. Wrangell offers one that usually coincides with a cruise ship being in port. It's part of the sightseeing tour that ends up at the Roadhouse Salmon Bake, a few miles out of town. At Juneau, the Gold Creek Outdoor Salmon Bake at Last Chance Basin, where millions in gold has been mined, has long been popular with visitors and residents.

In their Sightseeing Alaska program, *Westours* offers a salmon bake and an air tour, all for under $100. They combine flightseeing with that old Indian custom, the salmon bake, in a setting among glaciers and wilderness at Taku Glacier Lodge. Tour groups fly in *Southeast Airways* float planes via the Juneau Ice Field, massive source of many mighty glaciers, including the Taku. They land at the dock of Taku Lodge, situated in a mossy rain forest. The dining room overlooks the aptly-named Hole in the Wall Glacier. Coming and going, the skillful and obliging pilots identify landmarks and glaciers and watch for wildlife on the move. In the long light summer evenings, sharp eyes may spot black bears bent on berrying, and sheep and goats on mountain ledges.

Sitka is inclined to put on a masterly salmon bake in the all-purpose Centennial Building, when requested by cruise ships or on other special occasions. Just ask if one is scheduled.

At Skagway, try the *Salmon and Sourdough Shed,* open evenings 5:30 to 9:00 seven days a week in summer, for dinners featuring barbecued salmon. It's in the Inn Annex right across from the Klondike Inn, under cover; they also serve lunch and breakfast.

HISTORY AND CLUES TO LOCAL BACKGROUND

In the Southeast (as well as in other parts of Alaska), when you look for the historical you find it involves museums, historic sites and buildings, shopping, sightseeing, and entertainment.

Passengers are briefed aboard cruise ships on what there is to see and do at each port, and they'll sell tours to expedite your doing it. Otherwise, inquire at Visitor Information Centers about the following attractions, and they'll also tell you about many more.

SOME MUSEUMS AND HISTORICAL PLACES. Ketchikan's *Tongass Historical Society Museum* is in the Centennial Building, built in 1967, the 100th anniversary of the purchase of Alaska from Russia. The museum shares the building with the public library. Seasonal displays feature the arts and crafts. Permanent exhibits in the museum include pioneer relics, minerals, Indian items and artifacts. Outside, Ketchikan Creek tumbles in rapids fought each season by salmon on their way upstream to spawn. Across the way is the town's famous (or infamous) Creek Street, with *Dolly's House.* Part of Ketchikan's history, it is also a museum, but quite a contrast to its staid neighbor, the Tongass Museum. It has just recently been opened to the public. Facing a boardwalk supported by pilings, this restored house of prostitution retains the furnishings and decor picked by Dolly herself. Of course the $1.50 admission is now just for looking.

The Wrangell *Historical Society Museum* across from the federal building has petroglyph carvings in its Indian section, and many local historical items. On the north end of town, a private collection of artifacts and nineteenth- and twentieth-century memorabilia is displayed in *Bigelow's Museum and Gift Shop.* Stop in for a refresher at the *Marine Bar,* near Shakes Island. It's on the site of Fort Dionysius, established when the Russians settled there in 1834, to keep the Hudson Bay Company from fur trading up the Stikine River.

Besides Juneau's big, well-planned, comprehensive *State Museum,* there are other jewels about town. The *House of Wickersham* is the house-museum of early-day Judge Wickersham. The tiny onion-domed *Russian Orthodox Church* is typical of religious structures of the nineteenth century. Some other buildings now considered historical are the *Governor's Mansion,* completed in 1913; *Behrends Department Store,* established in 1887; the *Bergmann Hotel;* and, would you believe, the *Alaska Steam Laundry.* (Also see *Exploring Juneau.*)

The not-to-be-missed *Sheldon Museum* in Haines is on hallowed ground. Its new home is downtown near the waterfront, on a corner donated for that purpose by the United Presbyterian Church. From here the surveys were made for the original mission dedicated to the Chilkat people, now the town of Haines. There is a display of the extensive collection of the museum's founder, pioneer citizen Steve Sheldon (1885 to 1960), and many other priceless community treasures. Much has been in storage awaiting the new museum. At adjacent Port Chilkoot is *Fort William Henry Seward,* established as a U.S. Army post in 1904 when the first contingent of soldiers arrived. The barracks, officers' homes, and other military buildings now serve as hotel, community buildings, informal school buildings of *Alaska Indian Arts, Inc.,* and private homes.

Skagway: As is often the case, it is the badman who lives on in legend. *Soapy Smith's Parlor and Museum,* on First Avenue, near the site of a famous gun battle, is privately owned. Sometimes it's open so visitors can see inside the quaint little building. The *Trail of '98 Museum* is open every day, including Sunday, 8 A.M. to 8 P.M. in summer so that visitors have every opportunity to see a fascinating collection owned and operated by the citizens of Skagway. The museum is on the second floor of the first granite building in Alaska. It was scheduled to be a college in 1900, but it became a federal courthouse instead. The city of Skagway bought it in 1956. City offices are on the first floor. Above, for $1 (children 50¢), you can browse as long as you wish over old court records preserved under glass, including Frank Reid's will and papers disposing of Soapy's estate. Besides Native artifacts, memorabilia of pioneers, stampeders and the Arctic Brotherhood, there are unusual miscellaneous items. How about a blanket made from the skin of duck necks and fortified by pepper bags sewn behind the skins for moth protection? The gambling paraphernalia from the old Board of Trade Saloon is on display, and on the grounds is a vintage White Pass & Yukon Route steam locomotive. As part of the *Gold Rush Historical Park,* there are many buildings in downtown Skagway, now under restoration, that qualify as museum pieces.

Sitka's varied background is well represented in the *Sheldon Jackson Museum* and on the campus of Sheldon Jackson College, now over a hundred years old. The museum has exhibits covering Indian, Russian, and American periods. Take a walking tour of the campus and you'll see such historic buildings as Pittsburgh House, on the site of the first indoor bathtub in Sitka! The original school, started by Presbyterian missionaries in 1878, was developed on the present site in 1882 by Dr. Sheldon Jackson, evolving over the years into high school and then college programs. Within walking distance around town are the *St. Michael's Russian Orthodox Cathedral* and its religious treasures and the *Sitka National Historical Park,* site of the Battle of Alaska, during which Russians destroyed Indian fortifications and secured the region for the Czar. *Castle Hill,* overlooking the downtown area and harbor, was the site of Baranof's Castle and of the Alaska transfer ceremony on October 12, 1867. Here, too, on January 3, 1959, was raised the first forty-nine-star American flag, signifying Alaska statehood. The *Sitka National Cemetery* was the first such designated by the United States west of the Mississippi. It started as a military cemetery during the transfer days, and the oldest grave is dated December 1867. The *Russian Mission Orphanage* building dates from 1842. It is now being restored as a national historic landmark by the National Park Service.

ENTERTAINMENT AND BARS. The favorite watering holes in towns usually are well patronized by the residents, who are quick to point them out to visitors. The same is true for the current entertainment. In towns from Ketchikan to Sitka, they may direct you to the nearest Elk's club if you are an Elk, or may take you there. Some "in" places that you might want to sample include the *Fireside Supper Club* in Ketchikan; *Kito's Kave*, a den of many decibels, in Petersburg; and *Juneau's Red Dog Saloon*, probably the best-known bar in Alaska. There's sawdust on the floor, giant bear traps and snowshoes in the decor—all to give a gold rush feel. Also in Juneau is the more sophisticated *Latchstring*, at the Baranof Hotel. At the Baranof, the Gold Rush Minstrels put on a dinner show for under $20 including tip and tax, and you can try an Ice Worm Cocktail for under $3.

Juneau entertainment leans heavily on the gold rush background. The Last Chance Players perform melodrama in the *Mining Museum and Opera House* near the now defunct Alaska-Juneau Gold Mine, a short walk from the Gold Creek Salmon Bake. "Pure gold" is described by six people who knew it well in the *Perseverance Theater* on Third Street in Douglas, 8:15 P.M. nightly, June 1 to September 15. There's an admission charge for each. Both the *Prospector* and *Yancy Derringer* are notably good bars. They allow for "attitude adjustment" certain hours before dinner by serving cheaper drinks.

In Sitka, the locals head for the excellent lounge and entertainment at the uptown *Shee Atika Lodge*, the *Canoe Room* at the Potlatch House, and the disco in the waterfront Sheffield House. Everyone applauds the Traditional Russian Folk Dances performed in summer by the New Archangel Dancers on the stage of the Centennial Building. In gold-rush gateway Skagway there's no lack of 1898 atmosphere. *Moe's Frontier Bar* is typical and popular. You can count on seeing "In the Days of '98" and "Soapy Smith" shows throughout the summer. (For some more leads, refer to the *Hotel* and *Restaurant* categories at the end of this section.)

 SHOPPING. Everywhere you sightsee and explore you'll be tempted by the myriad shops and art galleries. They'll be selling traditional and modern creations made from Alaskan materials. The source of supply may be a small "cottage industry" or a cooperative venture of several local artists and craftsmen. Some items and materials may be unique to an area.

In Wrangell you can buy a garnet from a Boy Scout. An unusual garnet ledge about five miles from town near the Stikine River flats was deeded to the Boy Scouts and children of Wrangell. Garnet fanciers have to deal through them. You are bound to find an Alaskan souvenir, perhaps purchasing it from the artist who made it.

Ketchikan's mix of artists and craftsmen—silversmiths, potters, sculptors, photographers, etc.—supplies the *Morning Raven*, on Mission Street. Look for paintings in art galleries such as *The Gathering* and *Scanlon's* on Creek Street near Dolly's House. The *Northland Silk Screen Studio* specializes in Indian-design prints. *Nancy's Jewelers'* a great variety of gold nugget jewelry includes a 14-karat-gold Rainbird charm. Look for Native crafts at the *Alaska Treasure Cache, Trading Post,* and *Authentic Alaska Craft.* For fun, especially if you'd like to try on an antique for a few minutes, stop by *Gin*

Palace Polly's. They'll snap your photo in the style of the late 1800s for about $10.

As you have gathered from the exploring section, Haines and Port Chilkoot are oriented toward Indian crafts. *Helen's Shop* on the main street of Haines has been an outlet for fine craft work and a source of local information cheerfully dispensed for over 30 years. At Port Chilkoot, for almost as long, they have been turning out authentically designed totem poles, masks, silver etchings, soapstone carvings, and other handicrafts. What they don't use in the Chilkat Dance programs they'll sell through the Alaska Indian Arts Skill Center. Look for notable newcomers on the arts-and-crafts scene. J. VanHoesen paints Alaskana and displays it in his studio in a 1904 building, originally the telegraph office for Fort William H. Seward at Port Chilkoot. *The Sea Wolf* sculpture studio on the Parade Grounds has the work of Tresham Gregg, who grew up in a nearby officer's quarters made into a family residence. The *Palette and Wheel* across from Portage Cove Campground features painters and potters inspired by the magnificence of upper Lynn Canal scenery, including Gil Smith, whose paintings hang in the State Museum and Governor's Mansion, the Anchorage Fine Arts Museum, and at the University of Alaska.

In Juneau, there are excellent modern shopping centers and fine shops dealing in original and Alaska-made products. The *7-Arts Gift and Fur Shop* across from the Red Dog Saloon displays the hand insignia, which stands for authentic native handicrafts. The *ANA (Alaska Native Arts) Cache* is on Franklin; the *ANA Gallery,* at Merchants Wharf. *Nina's Originals* on Seward St. creates distinctive fur apparel, and the *Baranof Gift Shop* off the lobby of the hotel has collector's items, including rare Russian icons on display. The proprietress, Martha Edwards, has served as president of the Alaska Visitors Association, the first woman to be elected to that position. If you're a bookworm, don't miss browsing in the *Baranof Book Shop* a few doors farther on. The Merchants Wharf, on the waterfront, of course, was recycled from the dock and an old seaplane hangar. It's now an intriguing shopping mall with restaurants and stores including the *Mt. Juneau Trading Post,* with Indian arts and crafts, ivory, jade, and gold jewelry and Eskimo artwork.

Skagway has a most interesting assortment of stores lining its boardwalk-bordered main street. Upstairs, the *Porcupine Trading Co. & Sourdough Vendetta* is a health food store with a very complete bill of goods and a place to have a snack. The *Red Onion* now sells "curios, jewelry and objects d'art," but for a dollar they'll let you go around back and upstairs in this 1898 building that was a saloon and bawdy house. Visitors can see and take pictures of the interior of this restored gold rush brothel, including the two restored "cribs." Long-established shops such as *Kirmse's Curio Store* dealt with the Yukon stampeders. *Dedman's Photo* has Alaska books and color slides, including a gold rush collection. And stop in at *Native Carvings, Richter's Jewelry, Keller's Curios,* and *Irene's Gifts. Artists of Skagway* is a cooperative outlet for one-of-a-kind items created by several local artists. Along with a storeful of quality merchandise, *Corrington's* has an Eskimo museum and a large collection of ivory pieces for sale. Across the street *The Alaskan*

Scrimshander, William Joseph Sidmore, may be at work etching on ivory. He uses the same skills that were used by sailors during long periods at sea, and that are still used by Eskimos, the master ivory carvers in the Arctic. You could spend hours in Skagway browsing, buying, and talking with the friendly shopkeepers.

Sitka, as in its Russian past, has a reputation for having well-stocked stores. On Cathedral Circle you'll find everything from Alaska Wild Berry Products to T-Shirts. *Tops & Things* has T-Shirts with Alaskan motifs and phrases, created by Stella Conway, a charter member of the New Archangel Russian Dancers. The Russian Bell is a jewelry store also selling authentic Native handicrafts. Old Harbor Books has a wide selection of books, maps, and nautical charts. *Ceramitique* makes things of native Sitka clay. *Alexanders* on Harbor Drive has Alaskan paintings. Walk along Katlian Street behind the waterfront Sheffield House for picturesque shops in the "old town." They buy and sell old books and charts in *The Observatory* and *Books Books Books. Taranoff's Sitkakwan Shop,* like its name, reflects a Tlingit/Russian background with Alaskatique. Mrs. Taranoff designed the "Little Drook" (*friend* in Russian) button that city guests get when they sign in at the greeting desk in the Centennial Building. Wear it. Everyone is *extra* helpful when they know you are a visitor.

SOME SOUTHEAST TOURS. A name like Misty Fjords conjures up a kaleidoscope of mountains, deep inlets, forests, wildlife, and glaciers—one of nature's spectaculars. Now there are tours for visitors with more time who want to visit America's newest National Monument, a remote and wild area forty miles east of Ketchikan. Combination cruise and air tours that include a trip to Misty Fjords and a stay in Ketchikan are handled by the Leisure Corporation, 207 Main St., Ketchikan, AK 99901. One-day cruises to the National Monument leave on scheduled Saturdays in summer, drop off and pick up service in conjunction with the cruises for canoers and kayakers, and custom trips are offered by Outdoor Alaska, Box 7814, Ketchikan, AK 99901.

Ask about the Club Alaska Experience offered by Westours as one of their new Sightseeing Alaska optionals, out of Ketchikan. Some tours fly with SEA to Prince of Wales Island where the Fabry Family Guides take over at their base of operations in the modern Fireweed Inn at Klawock. During the three- to seven-day stays they help guests discover local evidence of deep Tlingit Indian traditions, and steer people toward wholesome outdoor pursuits in this back-country paradise. Visitors can go fishing, crabbing (and cook it on the beach), and "Craiging." Craig, about six miles away, is where the stores are, including three liquor stores and the bars.

Kayaking enthusiasts might be interested in the opportunities in older, larger Glacier Bay. Write Alaska Discovery Enterprises, Dept. NS, P.O. Box 337, Juneau, AK 99802 for information on trips by canoe and kayak in this and other wilderness areas.

Out of Sitka's Crescent Harbor near the Centennial Building, *Allen Marine Tours* sail every evening at 6:30. They touch on life that is scenic, wild, historical and even industrial, as the ships sail by the pulpmill waterfront. In Petersburg take a long-time favorite, a Blue Star dinner cruise, seven hours exploring the Leconte Glacier's icy fjord.

AIR TOURS OF NOTE IN THE SOUTHEAST.
Weather permitting, at some time during your stay try to take an air tour of the vicinity. Some are short enough to fit in between ship sailings or during ferry stopovers. You'll get an entirely different perspective of Alaska's grandeur. Small planes serve the Southeast well, and there are flying experiences awaiting you unlike any found in other places in the world.

Some favorites are flightseeing tours that include a lift off and splash down right in front of busy harbor at Ketchikan or Juneau. *S.E.A.* (formerly Flair Air & Webber Airlines, now merged under Southeast Alaska Airlines) is based on Ketchikan's waterfront. Their forty-minute flight with an experienced Alaska bush pilot covers the waterfront while he pinpoints totem parks, rain forests, and anything else interesting below before he heads through open spaces between the mountains for a look at the lakes behind Ketchikan. The ninety-minute flight takes in the Misty Fjords National Monument and all the beautiful wilderness in between, over lakes called Mirror, Punchbowl, Goat, Swan, and Grace, and recreation area trails leading to cliffs of granite rising two thousand feet above the fjords.

Juneau sits under the vast expanse of the Juneau Ice Field. On a clear day you can see ice almost forever on *L.A.B. Flying Service*'s scenic charter tours, sharing the cost with three, four, or six people, depending on the size of the plane. You'll want your camera as they fly over the ice fields and Glacier Bay National Monument. Previously mentioned *Southeast Skyways* offers year-round air taxi service and sightseeing on their "Wings of Adventure" out of Juneau. *Glacier Bay Airways* has an office in the Glacier Bay Lodge lobby (as well as at Gustavus Airport) to expedite glacier flightseeing, camper drop-offs, and group transfers in the area. For many years *Channel Flying* has been the charter and scheduled flying link to small southeastern towns, always with an eye for the scenic routes that delight the passengers. *Alaska Island Air,* flying out of Petersburg, has something besides air space in common with *Channel* and *Southeast Skyways.* All three airlines have kept a Grumman Goose in their operations. The sturdy, still-popular nine-passenger amphibian was the main air connection for many Southeast destinations in the early days of flying in Alaska. A.I.A.'s Goose looks very natty, painted in their colors and sporting their totem pole symbol.

You'll appreciate the planes and "Colossal Aeronautical Tours" of *Skagway Air Service.* They stick with the local theme in cleverly and brightly painted Cherokee Sixes, and the slogan "We Can-Can-Can!" Climbing the gold rush passes and tracing the Trail of '98 by air is about a forty-five-minute tour, costing about $20 per seat, three-seat minimum. It is a real thriller for the money. Stop in at their office at 4th and Broadway for a brochure and more information on prices and flights.

SOUTHEAST ALASKA

While in Sitka, you can fly with an Eagle—*Eagle Air,* by float plane or helicopter. They cater to cruise ship passengers, arranging pickups by bus to the airport from the Centennial Building, or perhaps at a landing spot near the dock where passengers come ashore. During the forty-five-minute helicopter flight you see a bird reserve where hundreds of eagles nest, look into the once-active volcano crater of Mt. Edgecumbe, a Sitka landmark, hover around the heights where mountain goats gather—and it's likely that whales or seals will surface in the water around the many islands. The helicopter may even land for a few minutes on the top of the volcano or on an isolated scenic beach.

There are many more possibilities for tours than those touched on here. Some are mentioned in the Exploring section and some under Tours in the *General Practical Information* section. The Visitor Information Centers, wherever you find them, will be ready with suggestions for what you can do in the time you have available.

WHERE TO STAY. The informal possibilities include campgrounds, wilderness cabins and lodges, and hostels. The Forest Service is in charge of the cabins; consult the office nearest the area in which you wish to stay. Some wilderness lodges in the Southeast are mentioned in Exploring; refer to that category in the General Practical Information section for some more possibilities. There are youth hostels sponsored by the Methodist Church in Ketchikan, by the Northern Lights Church in Juneau, and by the Presbyterian Church in Sitka.

Camping in and around Ketchikan is regulated by the Forest Service because about ninety-nine percent of the island belongs to the National Forest. They tell campers to watch for new property markers. Forest lands recently acquired by the regional Native corporation are off-bounds to campers. The camping season is May 25 to September 5 for campgrounds at *Settlers Cove* and out the Ward Lake Road. The space is free, but there may be a fourteen-day limit on your stay. There is a camper parking area near the *Westside Shopping Center.* One near the *Westside Service Station* has a dump station and free water. *Clover Park Resort,* twelve miles north of the ferry dock, rents six camp units with all the amenities, including showers, restaurant, and laundromat. The campgrounds at Wrangell and Petersburg are far out of town. *Pat Creek Public Campground* is eleven miles from the Wrangell ferry terminal on the Zimovia Highway. At Petersburg you'll drive twenty-one miles to camp at *Ohmer Creek.* Inquire locally to see if there may be some closer ones.

There'll be plenty of places to camp in the northern section of the Panhandle, and your best source for finding out where the local visitor information center is. You'll be directed to campgrounds, public and private, in Sitka, Juneau, Haines, and Skagway, within sight of mountains and glaciers, and bordering saltwater beaches and freshwater lakes and streams. Or you may be invited to pitch your tent or park your trailer in the yard of a new-found Alaskan friend. It happens.

HOTELS AND MOTELS. Lodging prices tend to be lower in the Southeast than in the big cosmopolitan areas, but they'll be higher than in the lower 48's northwestern states. Few if any hotels fill the bill for a super-deluxe or deluxe category, according to Fodor's requirements. Here we'll call it Alaska Deluxe, which means the best and most expensive available. Based on double occupancy, a *deluxe* room will probably cost over $60 per night. *Expensive* will probably be $45 up to $60; *Moderate*, $35 to $45; and *Inexpensive,* under $35. These rough estimates are subject to the whims of inflation.

KETCHIKAN

Alaska Village. *Deluxe.* Cape Fox Corp. (Native) hotel being built high on a hillside overlooking Creek Street and town, will be Ketchikan's finest and biggest, with an $8 million Convention Center. Scheduled for March 1982.

Clover Pass Resort. *Expensive.* Cabins and fishing. Located 15 mi. from town.

Marine View Plaza *Expensive.* Recently upgraded, with grizzly-sized beds in Alaska-sized rooms. Waterfront-view highrise in West End Shopping Center, near ferry dock. Restaurant, lounge, and convenient shopping nearby. A complete convention center. 2415 Hemlock.

Gilmore Hotel. *Moderate.* Downtown. Restaurant and lounge. Airport and ferry courtesy car. 326 Front St.

Ingersoll Hotel. *Moderate.* Established, downtown, three-story hotel, with front rooms overlooking the waterfront. Dining room and deli-restaurant; lounge. At Front & Mission Sts.

Hilltop Motel. *Moderate.* 46 units across from air and ferry terminals. Two levels, large rooms. 3434 Tongass Ave.

WRANGELL

Stikine Inn. *Moderate.* 16 rooms, with television, coffee shop, dining room, bar. Free phone. Gift shop.

Thunderbird Hotel. *Moderate to Inexpensive.* 36 rooms, all with bath. TV available. Hunting, fishing, sightseeing.

Roadhouse Lodge. *Moderate.* Four miles out the Zimovia Highway, but they'll send courtesy car. Salmon bakes, restaurant, dancing.

PETERSBURG

Tides Inn. *Expensive.* Modest-size motel, with 23 units. Free continental breakfast. Hunting and fishing information, charters. 1 mi. W. of ferry terminal, N. 1st & D Streets.

Beachcomber Inn. *Moderate.* Homey, once a cannery. Boats and float planes tie up at dock. Restaurant and bar. A local favorite; a few minutes drive from town.

Mitkof Hotel. *Moderate.* Downtown. Some rooms with bath, clean and comfortable.

King Salmon Motel. *Moderate.* Handy to ferry dock. Restaurant and bar.

JUNEAU

Baranof Hotel. *Expensive–Deluxe.* Seven-story downtown hotel offering many conveniences. Some suites. No pets. No off-street parking available. Restaurant, bar, combo, dancing. N. Franklin & 2nd Sts.

Juneau Sheffield House. *Deluxe.* Over 100 rooms. Downtown. Restaurant, lounge. 51 W. Egan Drive.

Prospector Hotel. *Expensive.* Modest-size hotel with full facilities. Restaurant, bar. Sightseeing tours available. 340 Whittier Ave.

Breakwater Inn. *Moderate.* Three-story motel with pleasant rooms, overlooking boat basin. Dining room, bar. Pets OK. 1711 Glacier Ave.

Driftwood Lodge Motel. *Moderate.* Two-story motel with comfortable rooms, some units with kitchen facilities, several two-bedroom apartments. Restaurant. 435 Willoughby.
  Inexpensive are the Bergmann, Alaskan, and Summit Hotels.

SITKA

Shee Atika Lodge. *Deluxe.* 107-room Native Corporation-built hotel across from the convention center. Features Alaska Indian Art Shop.

Sheffield House. *Deluxe.* 80 rooms, waterfront, dining room, lounge, disco and boat dock.

Potlatch House. *Moderate.* Several blocks from downtown, but there is a courtesy car. Mt. Edgecumbe and harbor view from dining room, cocktail lounge with entertainment. 709 Katlian St.

Sitka Hotel. *Moderate.* Downtown hotel with elevator and 24-hour phone service. 60 rooms, some with choice harbor and island views. Easy walking to historic sites from Tlingit Indian/Russian American/Alaska Territorial past. 118 Lincoln St.

HAINES-PORT CHILKOOT

Captain's Choice. *Deluxe* motel units overlooking Lynn Canal.

Eagle's Nest Motel. *Moderate.* Open year round; camper park full hookup May–Sept. Just outside Haines.

Thunderbird Motel. *Moderate.* Modern motel units in this small downtown facility, all with private baths. TV. P.O. Box 159. Haines, AK 99827.

Halsingland Hotel. *Inexpensive.* Located in Port Chilkoot, and affording a view of Lynn Canal and surrounding glacial-sided mountains, this moderate-size, family-style hotel is in vintage army quarters of old Fort William Seward, facing former parade grounds near Totem Village, where Chilkat Indian dancers perform. Area bus terminal. Dining room features Swedish family-style dinners. TV, camper park, laundromat.

Mountain View Motel. *Inexpensive.* At Port Chilkoot. Kitchen units.

Town House Motel. *Inexpensive.* Conveniently located next to post office, library, and playground in Haines, this modern motel offers free coffee in the lounge, color TV, public phone, barbershop in the premises. At Third & Main. If you want to stay awhile, ask about the Fort Seward Condos. These apartments rent completely furnished by week or month (3-day minimum).

SKAGWAY

Golden North Hotel. *Expensive.* A gold rush remainder. All 35 rooms different; furnished with charming antique touches. You can't miss it; its golden dome is a landmark. Restaurant. 3rd & Broadway.

The Klondike. *Expensive.* Next to the Historic District, this large, expanding Westours Hotel houses tour groups. Original section recreates theme of Gold Rush through colorful decorations. Restaurant and lounge.

Skagway Inn. *Moderate.* Small, no private baths. Aura of gold rush in this vintage building on unpaved boardwalk-lined main street.

Klondike Safaris Bunkhouse. For the thrifty. Bring your own sleeping bag and they'll furnish the bunk. $6 a night; shower and towel extra; laundromat nearby.

 WHERE TO EAT. Meals, especially if you take advantage of local specialties, are fairly reasonable in the homey restaurants of smaller Southeast towns. They may run *less* in cost than this overall budget estimate: $4 to $8 for breakfast or lunch, and $8 to $30 for dinner. The categories and ranges for a complete dinner are: *Deluxe,* $20–$30; *Expensive,* $15–$20; *Moderate,* $9–$14; and *Inexpensive,* about $8.

KETCHIKAN

Clover Pass Resort and Restaurant. *Expensive.* Seafood specialties, probably fresh caught in their "front yard," the ocean, served with view. Salad bar and cocktail bar. Dinners only, except for Sunday brunch; open summers. Mile 15 North Tongass Highway.

The Helm Restaurant and Lounge. *Expensive.* Fantastic view from top of the Marine View Hotel. Steaks, prime ribs, seafood. 2415 Hemlock (west end of Ketchikan).

The Heritage. *Moderate.* Off Ingersoll Hotel lobby. Alaska-sized steaks. Lounge and nightly entertainment.

Hilltop Restaurant. *Moderate.* Features daily specials, sandwiches, fountain. Across from ferry terminal.

Kay's Kitchen. *Moderate.* Home cooking, especially soup and pies; crab and Shrimp Louie. Lunches only. Clever decor and great location overlooking busy Bar Harbor boat traffic. 2813 Tongass Ave.

The Narrows Supper Club. *Moderate.* Seafood, steaks. Overlooks scenic Tongass Narrows.

The Fireside. *Moderate.* Popular supper club located in downtown Ketchikan. Variety of dishes, with fresh seafood a specialty. Lounge, music, and dancing.

Angela's Delicatessen. *Inexpensive.* Custom-made sandwiches produced cafeteria style, next to Ingersoll Hotel.

Dairy Queen Brazier. *Inexpensive.* The newest more-than-a-hamburger-and-ice-cream-stand; seats 90. Besides small and super "brazierburgers," sells fish 'n' chips, fish sandwiches, and foot-long hot dogs.

WRANGELL

Aunt Winnie's. *Moderate.* You can count on the fresh local seafood, especially the tiny shrimp, the best you'll ever eat. In the Stikine Inn.

The Roadhouse. *Moderate.* Out of town, but sends courtesy car.

The Better Way. *Moderate.* On Front St. Has herb tea and vegeburgers. The **Wharf,** also *Moderate,* says come as you are for home cooking and Alaska hospitality.

PETERSBURG

Viking Room. *Expensive.* View of Wrangell Narrows comes with fresh local seafood and steak dinners. Shipwreck Room for cocktails. At Beachcomber Inn, Mile 4, Mitkof Highway. Reservations needed.
  Moderate, downtown, all near Fisherman's Wharf: **The Anchor; Irene's; Sandy's;** and **Mar's Café** (Chinese food). Or the **Elk's Club,** if you're an Elk (or a friend of one).

JUNEAU

The Diggings. *Deluxe.* At the Prospector Hotel there is live entertainment nightly, dancing and cocktails. 340 Whittier Ave.

Breakwater Inn Restaurant. *Expensive.* All remodeled, except the view of the channel. Serves seafood specialties plus regular fare.

The Latchstring. *Deluxe.* Alaskan paintings by Eustace Paul Ziegler and Sydney Laurence help decorate this handsome restaurant in the Baranof Hotel. Well-prepared food makes this one of the most popular dining-out spots in the capital city. The Gold Rush Minstrels base their show on early Juneau life and people. Ice Worm Cocktails are the bar specialty. The latchstring is out nightly. 2nd and Franklin.

Timberline Room. *Deluxe.* At the Cape Fox Sheffield House.

Yancy Derringer's. *Expensive.* Highly recommended by the locals to those who like harbor entertainment (small boats, planes, cruiseships, sea lions) instead of the traditional. At the Merchants Wharf; beef and seafood specialties; try to reserve a window seat. Mon.–Fri. 4:30–6:30 is for "Attitude Adjustment" and the drinks are reduced.

Mike's Place. *Moderate.* A Juneau institution! Seafoods and steaks are specialties. Live music nightly for dancing. Located across the bridge in neighboring Douglas. If you don't have a ride they'll pick you up.

City Café. *Moderate.* Variety of food and quick service in this clean, convenient cafe across from downtown ferry terminal. Chinese and American dishes. Fresh seafood, steaks, and best hamburgers in town. Orders to go. 439 S. Franklin.

Summit Café. *Moderate.* Intimate: serves only 18 for dinner. Try the tempura prawns. 455 S. Franklin.

Glacier Restaurant and Lounge. *Moderate.* Usually has seafood on the menu. Overlooks Mendenhall Glacier. Located at airport.

Inexpensive. Local favorites: **Bullwinkle's Pizza** and **Sally's Kitchen.** For vegetarians, or anyone, there's the **Fiddlehead Restaurant & Bakery. Dave's Dinghy** at the Marine Park is noted for Shrimp Louis.

SITKA

Channel Club. *Expensive.* A local favorite for view, steaks and salad bar; 3½ miles out the Halibut Point Road.

The Shee Atika Lodge. *Deluxe.* Uptown, newest, large hotel built by the Native Corporation, and the **Sheffield House,** built on a former dock, overlooking the beautiful, historic waterfront and islands, both with excellent food, entertainment, bars.

Staton's Steak House. *Deluxe.* Popular with residents. Downtown overlooking Sitka Sound. Also bar.

Potlatch Motel Canoe Club. *Expensive.* Magnificent view of water, with mountains beyond. Specialty is fresh-caught seafood expertly prepared. Bar. 709 Katlian St. in handsome Potlatch Motel.

The Nugget Saloon. *Moderate.* Seafood and do-it-yourself steaks at the airport.

Moy's Café. *Moderate.* Chinese/American, open 24 hours; and **Revards,** both near Cathedral Circle.

HAINES-PORT CHILKOOT

10-Mile Steakhouse. *Expensive.* Dinners only.

33-Mile Roadhouse. *Inexpensive.* 7 A.M. to 10 P.M. daily.

The Lighthouse, *Expensive,* and **Captain's Choice,** *Moderate.* Both overlook the boat harbor.

The Bamboo Room, Sally's View Street Café, The Kitchen Restaurant in the Chilkat Bakery, and the **Sourdough Pizza** are *Inexpensive* to *Moderate*.

Hotel Halsingland. *Moderate.* Super Swedish and American meals. Fresh-caught salmon and other Alaskan seafood are menu favorites, along with wild-berry desserts. Magnificent scenery from hotel area. Family-style meals have scheduled hours. At Parade Ground in Port Chilkoot.

SKAGWAY

Chilkoot Dining Room. *Expensive.* Bar. In Klondike Hotel.

Golden North Restaurant. *Expensive.* Gourmet gold rush cuisine.

Cosimo's Place. *Moderate.* Family operation leaning toward Italian food. Good salad bar. No cocktails.

Northern Lights Café. *Moderate.* Long-time Broadway favorite.

Salmon and Sourdough Shed. *Moderate.* Features boneless King salmon served from 5:30 to 9 P.M. Across from the Klondike.

Sweet Tooth Saloon. *Moderate.* Featuring home-baked goods, homemade soups, sandwiches, in attractive old-fashioned ice-cream parlor decor.

ANCHORAGE

Alaska's Big Apple

If you have been intrigued by the variety in Alaska's skylines so far, wait until you see Alaska's "Big Apple." They've been busy adding towers to already tall buildings—the Anchorage Westward Hilton, the Captain Cook—and building new ones, such as the Sheraton. Facing mountains on three sides and with marine views as well, they are surrounded by scenery that is probably unsurpassable in quantity and quality. In addition, situated at the upper end of Cook Inlet, the city is in a hub position in relation to the rest of Alaska, as well as the world. The roads converge in Anchorage. The busy International Airport is a world air crossroads.

Starting as a tent camp in 1913, the 67-year-old city has gone farther in less time than almost any world city you might name. Modern, cosmopolitan Anchorage is the financial and business metropolis of the state, as well as the focal point for the creative arts and education. Besides a community college and a branch of the big University of Alaska, there is a new institution in town—a four-year private school being recycled from the former Alaska Methodist

79

ANCHORAGE

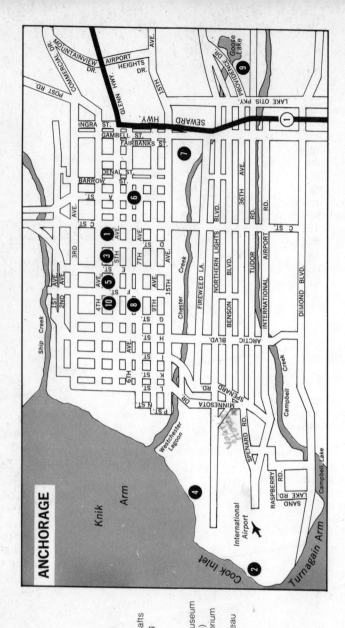

Points of Interest

1) Alaska Native Arts & Crafts
2) Captain Cook's Landing
3) City Hall
4) Earthquake Park
5) Heritage Library
6) Historical & Fine Arts Museum
7) Mulcahy Field (Baseball)
8) Sidney Lawrence Auditorium
9) University of Alaska
10) Visitors' Information Bureau

University, closed because of financial problems. Its goals are far-reaching, as defined by its new name, Alaska Pacific University. Its aim is to prepare pioneering spirits for the twenty-first century. Here, in developing, strategically located Anchorage, they hope to spur a meeting of the minds involving all Pacific Rim countries, affiliating with the colleges and universities of Japan, South Korea, Samoa, Hawaii, and especially China. It's an ambitious endeavor, with funding no small problem. If it works, a valuable cultural and economic link will be established between nations of the Third World and the United States.

By 1917, Anchorage was established as the busy construction base and headquarters for the nation's first (and still only) federally built and operated railroad. Then the Alaska Railroad extended from seaport terminal Seward to Nenana and on to Fairbanks, with branch lines to some mining areas with intriguing names like Chickaloon, Chatanika, and Moose. Still in use are the Fairbanks to Seward track and a spur across the narrow neck of the Kenai Peninsula south of Anchorage. It was built in 1942 from Portage, where Turnagain arm (off Cook Inlet) deadends, through the mountains to Whittier on Prince William Sound. It was needed in World War II for moving military necessities from tidewater to Anchorage and Fairbanks. This Whittier cut-off shortened by about fifty miles the distance between inland Fairbanks and access to an ocean port. It gave the railroad two important terminal ports, at Seward and at Whittier, connecting with oceangoing vessels.

In 1940, Anchorage was still only a small town of 3,500, but World War II triggered the action, and the keynote has been growth. New industries and energy-resource discoveries, particularly oil-related ones, have managed to keep the city and its environs booming. Studies made ten years ago predicted there would be 225,000 people living in Anchorage by 1980. Those statistics are pretty much on target. The 1978 census showed a population of more than 202,000, and they now forecast another 50,000 or so residents will be added by 1985.

Annually, over three million people pass through Anchorage International Airport, on domestic and foreign flights and cargo operations to and from major world cities. Over the pole, London is only nine hours away. Eastern United States, the national capital, and New York are 7½-hour flights. Seattle is 3 hours away; Los Angeles, 5; Honolulu, on the same time as Anchorage, is 5½ hours south. Japanese visitors, of which there are many, fly from Tokyo to Anchorage in 7½ hours.

Because it's big, there is more to see in Anchorage than within any other city in the state. Moreover, the active Alaska Visitors Association headquartered there and the enthusiastic Anchorage Convention and Visitors Bureau are determined to make the city a destination for all seasons and all people. Some brochures now are printed in Japanese and German to accommodate some of their best customers. They are developing a language bank, and they claim that when needed they can call on people to help out in Arabic, Afghanistan, Native Alaskan, Finnish, Chinese, Dutch, French, Hebrew, Hungarian, Italian, Korean, Malayan, Norwegian, Polish, Portuguese, Spanish, Russian, Swedish, Turkish, Vietnamese—in addition to Japanese and German. There are also special aids for the deaf and blind, as well as other handicapped persons.

Anchorage is young among world cities, and perhaps some of its folks are a little self-conscious about not having an image they can really pinpoint and call their own. It's not a gold rush gateway, ex-Russian capital, salmon capital, oil capital, etc.—titles that other, smaller Alaskan towns can claim. But they can't compete with Anchorage's lively, cosmopolitan bustle, only minutes away from vast frontier wilderness. This helps make it the state's leading convention center, attracting national and international organizations.

PRACTICAL INFORMATION FOR ANCHORAGE

 WEATHER AND WHAT TO WEAR. In the southcentral and Gulf of Alaska regions, winter relinquishes its hold to capricious spring late in April, so prepare for changeable weather and dress in layers you can add or peel off as needed. Overshoes, hat, gloves, and an all-purpose coat will come in handy. During summer the temperature average is in the middle 60s. Be prepared with a sweater for cooler evenings, though they are long and light. During this area's spectacularly colorful fall—golden trees, blue skies—light wool shirts, slacks and pants suits are ideal. Though temperatures are rarely extreme in winter, they can range the Fahrenheit scale from the 30s to 15° below zero. Bring appropriate dress for whatever outdoor activities attract you as participant or spectator—perhaps skiing, snowmobiling, or skating.

The Interior offers surprises, particularly those hot summer days in Fairbanks when the temperature sometimes tops 90° F. Light-weight clothes feel best, but if you are heading for wilderness areas such as Mt. McKinley National Park, take a coat or jacket. Spring weather is changeable and cool, as is autumn, when everyone wants to be out enjoying nature's fall color and wildlife display. Bring warm layers of clothing you can adapt as needed. Winter is cold. On top of the warm layers, add a winter coat or down jacket, warm gloves, winter boots, cap, even earmuffs. It won't hurt to have long johns underneath all of that!

TOURIST INFORMATION. Call the Hot Line, 276-3200. A recording gives the events of the day, the time and the place, and number to call for more information or for reservations, if needed. There might be a rock-climbing demonstration or a film on mountain rescue, a musical at the Fine Arts Museum, a trip through the Candy Kitchen; something special in the way of nightlife, an ethnic exhibit where you can sample the food, or whatever spectator and participant sports are on. Many are the same as in the Lower 48, except that in Anchorage there is curling, more ice skating, and probably more ice hockey in winter. In summer, the *Glacier Pilots,* a semi-professional baseball team, play at Mulcahy Field in the evenings. The main headquarters for the state-wide, plus chapters out-of-state of the *Alaska Visitors Association* and the active *Anchorage Convention & Visitors Bureau* are at Plaza 201, East 3rd Ave., Anchorage, AK 99501. Better yet, stop in at the ACVB's attractive log cabin at Fourth and F. Along with almost everything else you might want to know about Anchorage, they collect menus. Looking through them and comparing prices helps a traveler stay within a budget.

GETTING AROUND. Downtown is neatly laid out with numbered avenues north and south and lettered streets east and west. There is much of interest in a reasonably compact area, and good walking-tour maps are available in many places. An inexpensive alternate to walking (or driving your own vehicle) is the People Mover, the local bus system. The central station is at 6th and G. downtown. Pick up a schedule or call 272-4411. The bus network covers residential and business districts with shopping malls where there are some major retail stores—*Penney's, Lamonts, Montgomery Ward, Nordstrom's, Sears Roebuck & Co.*—and many specialty shops. The People Mover is for exploring farther afield, too, like perhaps at the *Alaska Zoo,* which is about five miles south on the Seward Highway from Anchorage, then left on the O'Malley Road for about two miles. The zoo is non-profit, city-owned, and leased to the operators who have programs for 8 or 9,000 school children and almost one hundred thousand visitors a season, late spring through fall. Some forty species of wildlife inhabit the spacious grounds. Visitors follow the paths to the "stars" of the zoo. Native Alaskans, polar bear Binky and her cubs reside in their new grotto and pool. Perhaps a distant relative of the mastodons whose frozen remains are still being found in Arctic tundra, long-time resident Annabelle the elephant lives in a new $150,000 house. Though the zoo charges admission, it also depends on donations, so bring along any leftover meat or fish (no bones, please) when you come. There are cans to put it in, and donation jars for any spare cash.

Anchorage also has a commuter bike program, and last summer about 1,500 persons checked out the free bicycles. There are a number of bicycle paths in and around the city. "Earth Cycles" expects to have 20 bikes this summer. Identification and a $5.00 deposit are required.

MUSEUMS, LIBRARIES, AND HISTORICAL PLACES. Both Elmendorf Air Force Base and Fort Richardson have free *wildlife museums;* ask at their gates. Anchorage International Airport includes many stuffed animals in its decor on Concourse C. The *Historical and Fine Arts Museum* has permanent and changing displays of Indian and Eskimo art and artifacts, and there is often a cultural event scheduled in the auditorium.

The *Heritage Library* in the National Bank of Alaska Building at Northern Lights and C Streets has old publications, maps, and artifacts. The *Z. J. Loussac Public Library,* 427 F St., has a comprehensive section on the North. Among the historic buildings and places to see and photograph: the *Wendler Building* is the oldest one in Anchorage, at 4th and 1 Sts.; *Kimball Building* at 500 W. 5th was bought at the original townsite auction and keeps its early store-front look; *Pioneer School House,* the first one, at 3rd and Eagle. The site of the original 1915 Anchorage tent city is at Ship Creek on the Whitney Road. Anchorage's first airstrip is now *Delaney Park;* on 9th Avenue, it still looks like a landing field. Probably the most unusual site and tourist attraction was created by nature. The 135-acre *Earthquake Park,* at the west end of Northern Lights Blvd., is a true testimonial to the devastating 1964 shake-up. From Earthquake Park there are grand views of 20,320-foot Mt. McKinley, 17,400-foot Mt. Foraker, the Talkeetna Mountains to the northeast, and the Chugach Mountains to the east.

NATURE ATTRACTIONS. Besides the aforementioned Alaska Zoo, there is bird watching at Ship Creek, Potter's March, and Lakes Hood and Spenard. In summer, allied with the Anchorage Audubon Society, *Westours* has Nature Tours leaving at 7:30 P.M. from the Anchorage Hilton. During the next 2 to 2½ hours, they make stops at the Potter Marsh and Glen Alps area. Another unique Anchorage activity is Bore Tide Viewing, along the Anchorage–Seward Highway, when the water rushes into Turnagain Arm. For the best time, they say to check the low-tide schedule in the Anchorage newspaper. To see it at Milepost 32.6 from Anchorage, add 2 hours and 20 minutes. For another good spot about 4 miles farther, add 2 hours and 45 minutes to the low-tide time. Other places recommended for tide viewing are Earthquake Park, at the end of the Northern Lights Blvd.; Bootlegger Cove, at the end of W. 5th Avenue; Resolution Park, at the corner of 3rd and L Streets, where the statue of Captain Cook looks across at Mt. Susitna's famous "Sleeping Lady" profile; and Bird Creek, on Turnagain Arm.

FOR SPECIAL INTERESTS. In a city that has a whole festival dedicated to it—the Fur Rendezvous—there are bound to be places where visitors can see it, feel it, and buy it. The *Anchorage Fur Factory,* 120 E. 5th Avenue, is owned and operated by a large Mexican family. Tours are free. At *David Green Furriers,* 130 W. 4th Avenue, Perry and Jerry, both master furriers and sons of founding father David (now deceased), will show small groups the premises, including the storage room where the best fur coats of Anchorage residents are kept until needed in winter. The tour is spiced with tales from long-time experience in the fur trading and processing business. Both companies have craftsmen at work in the back rooms, and both appreciate advance notice for tours.

Ask the sales clerk at *Alaska Native Arts and Crafts,* 425 D Street, about watching Native craftsmen at work there. At the *Oomingmak Musk Ox Producers,* there aren't any of the creatures on hand, just items made of the wool by members of the co-op; some may be there knitting.

If you are interested in gold panning, try the *Alaska Prospectors,* 4409 Spenard Road. They operate Saturday afternoons from 1-6 P.M. in summer. The Ericksons have a *gold mine* you can visit. It's near Girdwood, about a mile from Mt. Alyeska, on the Anchorage Seward Highway.

CULTURAL EVENTS. Some of the organizations enriching community life are the *Alaska Artist Guild; Anchorage Arts Council;* the *Civic Opera Association;* the *Concert Association; Anchorage Film Society; Alaska Repertory Theatre; Anchorage Symphony Orchestra; Theatre Guild;* and the *University of Alaska,* Anchorage, Performing Arts Center. And there are art shows, flower shows, square and folk dances, festivals, events and always something on the drawing board. Like 1984. While talking with new-found friends in the Bar and Grill at Simon & Seaforts in Anchorage, we learned that Alaskans were bidding for the next World's Fair. They had plans for a bang-up Alaska-style Expo '84. Though the state has since lost out to New Orleans, undaunted, Alaskans are rallying with plans for their own exposition in 1984, based on the 25th anniversary of statehood. The theme of the Exposition will be people and Alaskana. This will involve Russian Americans. British-Scandinavian-Spanish furseekers and explorers, gold rush argonauts, the military, homesteaders, in fact, all the roots.

TOUR INFORMATION. The *Anchorage Convention & Visitors Bureau* (ACVB) has lists of flightseeing services in the area, both by small plane and helicopter. *Alaska Sightseeing,* 327 F Street, and *Grayline/ Westours,* 527 W. 3rd. offer tours of the city and environs. *Alaska Tour Center,* 838 W. 4th, includes all major tour destinations, many off the beaten path, and they handle the top sportfishing packages in the state. They can advise on their Best of Alaska Tours. For additional listings see *Practical Information* sections at the end of the Exploring details.

ANCHORAGE HOTELS

Categories are as stated in previous chapter under "Hotels and Motels."

Anchorage International Inn. *Deluxe.* Big, down to its king and queen size beds. Restaurant, bar, convention facilities. By airport; courtesy car service.

Anchorage Sheraton. *Deluxe.* The newest, on Calista Square at 6th & Denali, near downtown. Elegant décor, including jade stairway in foyer. Rooftop restaurant/lounge, ballroom, and healthclub with whirlpool and saunas.

Anchorage Westward Hilton Hotel. *Deluxe* (Bristol Bay Native Corp.). 502 rooms downtown double tower. Coffee shop, dining rooms, bars. 3rd & E St.

Captain Cook Hotel. *Deluxe.* Large, well-decorated rooms in huge hotel. Three towers of view rooms. Some suites. Parking lot. Coffee shop, dining room, cocktail lounges with entertainment. 4th and I St.

Golden Lion Hotel. *Deluxe.* Cocktails, dinner, 83 queen-size rooms. Free parking. 36th & New Seward Highway.

Holiday Motor Inn. *Deluxe.* Large motor inn. three levels. Attractive rooms. Indoor pool. Dining room, cocktail lounge with entertainment nightly, except Sun. 239 W. 4th Ave.

Sheffield House. *Deluxe,* recently remodeled, 2 new restaurants and 3-level Penthouse Lounge, highest in Anchorage, with view, 720 W. 5th, downtown.

Anchorage TraveLodge. *Expensive.* Pleasant, three-story motor inn with coffee shop, dining room, bar. 3rd & Barrow.

Barratt Best Western Inn. *Expensive.* 100 rooms, a few with kitchenettes. Restaurant, bar, and courtesy car to and from airport, 3 minutes away. 4616 Spenard Rd.

Inlet Towers. *Expensive.* 135 hotel-apartments, kitchenettes; beauty shop, sauna rooms, laundromat. Near downtown at 1200 L St.

Northern Lights Inn. *Expensive.* 130 rooms. Restaurant, lounges (live music), beauty and barbor shops. Free parking. 598 W. Northern Lights Blvd.

Red Ram Motor Lodge. *Expensive.* Two-story, medium-size motel with two main dining rooms, cocktail lounge. At 5th & Gambell St.

Traveler's Inn. *Expensive.* Two-story motel, with comfortably furnished rooms, coffee shop, dining room, bar. 720 Gambell St.

Hillside Motel & Camper Park. *Moderate.* 26 rooms, some with kitchenettes. All hookups, even phone, hot showers, laundry. 2150 Gambell St.

The Inlet Inns. *Moderate.* Were older hotels; rooms with bath and some kitchenettes. Seasonal rates. Limo service. Largest Inn is 119-room **Downtown,** 539 H St. Waterbeds at **Merrill Field,** 224 E. 5th, and at 15th and Gambell. Other Inlet Inns at 4th and Sitka, and at 5th and Karluk.

Johnson Motel & Camper Park. *Moderate.* Small motel with hookups, showers, near Mt. View Shopping Center. Many conveniences within walking distance. 3542 Mt. View Dr.

Mush Inn Motel. *Moderate.* Large motel near Merrill Field. Free transportation to and from airport. Restaurant & bar nearby. Covered parking; security guards. Family rooms, kitchenettes. Heated water beds! 333 Concrete.

Voyager Hotel. *Moderate.* Rooms with kitchenettes, restaurant, sandwich shop, bar. Highly recommended for location and comfort. 501 K St.

ANCHORAGE RESTAURANTS

Price ranges are as stated in previous chapter under "Where to Eat."

Crow's Nest. *Deluxe.* Sweeping view of historic Cook Inlet from this fine restaurant atop 9-story Captain Cook Hotel. Seafood and steak. Whale's Tail room, on ground floor of same hotel, is also recommended. At 4th & I Sts.

Elevation 92. *Deluxe.* Seafood. 92 feet above sea level; with superb inlet view. Dinner and lunch weekdays; dinner only weekends. 3rd & K Bldg.

House of Lords. *Deluxe.* Ground-floor restaurant in Sheffield House. 720 W. 5th. Elegant food and service. Try the just right Filet of Halibut Olympia with a special fluffy sauce. Fitting climax to a spectacular meal is Café Diablo, prepared with style at your table.

Josephine's. *Deluxe.* The new Sheraton's elegant roof-top restaurant.

Top of the World Restaurant. *Deluxe.* Award-winning restaurant. Located in the Westward Hilton Hotel, this is a most popular spot for fine dining. Wide selection on menu. Cocktail lounge. Reasonable coffee shop also available. Top of the world restaurant and lounge open afternoon and evenings. 3rd & E Sts.

Stuckagain Heights. *Deluxe.* Somewhere nearby in the Chugach Mountains, overlooking the city, but so exclusive they don't tell you how to get there until you make reservations. Phone 333-8314.

Clinkerdagger, Biggerstaff and Petts. *Expensive.* Very popular; reserve! Old English-Tudor atmosphere, and a wide selection of anything you want. In the Calais Building on C St.

Club 25. *Expensive.* In the Wendler Bldg., oldest structure in town. Quality seafood/steak. Small; reservations a must. 410 I St.

Club Paris. *Expensive.* 417 W. 5th Ave.

Garden of Eatin'. *Expensive.* Fine steaks and seafood are served in this Quonset hut that was first a homestead. Open 6–10 except Sunday and Monday (and all winter, when it is closed). Reservations required. 2502 McRae Rd.

Monkey Wharf. *Expensive.* Quick lunch, longer dinners with conversation piece being monkeyshines (real ones) behind an enclosed bar. 529 C St.

Simon & Seaforts. *Expensive.* A saloon and grill dedicated to capturing the spirit (and spirits) of the turn-of-the-century Grand saloon. Congeniality with good food at 420 L St.

The Upper 1. *Expensive.* Located at Anchorage's International Airport. Local favorite is "Sunday Smorgasbord Supreme" from noon daily. Varied menu. Cloudhoppers Lounge.

The Cauldron. *Moderate.* Good-for-you things leaning toward, but not entirely meatless. Homey, with live folk or classical music nightly. 328 G St. Also takeout lunch menu.

Downtown Deli. *Moderate.* Local food landmark between the Captain Cook and the Anchorage Westward Hilton. Many notables have endorsed their tasty specialties and unique made-to-order dinners. 525 W. 4th St.

One Guy from Italy. *Moderate. The* place for Italian food (closed Tuesdays). At least 43 different specialties, 25 kinds of pizza. They're open to suggestions . . . those written in Italian are given priority. In the "Z" Plaza at 3024 Minnesota Drive.

Oriental Gardens. *Moderate.* Japanese and Asian specialties are lobster, tempura, seafood. In relaxing surroundings 7 miles out of town on Old Seward Highway.

Peggy's Airport Café. *Moderate.* One of Anchorage's long-time popular dining eating spots. Visitors are urged to try sourdough hotcakes and Peggy's homemade pies. At 1675 E. 5th St. Opp. Merrill Field.

Rabbit Creek Inn. *Moderate.* Attractive dining room with fireplace. Charcoal-broiled steaks and seafood served in Hearth Room. Roast prime rib specialty. Soft lounge entertainment on weekends.

Rice Bowl. *Moderate.* Good Chinese-American cuisine. Charcoal-broiled steaks and Chinese dishes. Orders to go. 232 W. 5th St.

Rubinis. *Moderate.* Myriad Italian specialties. 721 Muldoon Rd.

The Balcony. *Inexpensive.* Claims to be able to fill you up for under $5 or $6. In the University Center.

Thirteen Coins. *Inexpensive.* Amazing menu variety and daily specials. Across from the Hilton.

There are 2 dinner shows in Anchorage in the summer (both about $21): *The Alaska Story.* Multi-media look at past, present and future of "The Great Land." Presented after dinner in the Aft Deck banquet room of the Hotel Captain Cook. *The Alaska Show and Sourdough Buffet.* Anchorage Westward Hilton. Entertainer Larry Beck recites the most famous poems of Robert W. Service and presents other nostalgic reminders of pioneer and goldrush days.

SOUTH CENTRAL & INTERIOR ALASKA

Where the Roads Go

The bulk of Alaska, with plural personalities and multiple faces, is contained in the huge, pan-shaped peninsula that extends eight hundred miles north and three time zones west of the Southeast Panhandle. This diversity is reflected in the character of the people, in the characteristics of the land, and in the economy. Thus, within the Interior, visitors may encounter Native Athabascan Indians, and in the Gulf of Alaska–Cook Inlet south-central areas there'll be descendants of Eskimo offshoots and of Russian settlers. City populations blend people from all over the United States and the world. The mix is concentrated in the two largest cities, Anchorage, at the gateway to the Interior, and Fairbanks, within it.

There is great variety in a terrain that has been shaped by major rivers and geologic upheavals. It's a land still being formed, sometimes violently, by earthquake and by volcanic eruption. Glaciated mountains contrast with flat valleys that were sculptured by now retreated glaciers. The climate, mild to severe, influences the activities of the residents (and visitors). The economy depends on the use of a wealth of natural resources including such notorious ones as oil and gold, as well as other minerals. Coal may be on the verge of redevelopment as a source of energy in some areas. Agriculture has a good start in the rich valleys of the Tanana and Matanuska rivers.

Many routes lead to South-Central and Interior destinations, where the highway network lends itself to circuit travel. This is the best way for visitors to see the most without duplication, whether they are on their own or with a tour.

Anchorage and Fairbanks are pivot points. International airports link them with the world. Highways connect them, through Canada, with the rest of the continental states, and with each other. Keeping up with all the circle travel possibilities is like getting involved in a lively square dance. Besides those in Alaska, there are circle routes to get there, as we shall see as we continue to follow the "Grand Circle" tour mentioned in the introduction.

On to Whitehorse

The newly built Skagway–Carcross Highway completes the newest circle back to the Alaska Highway and on to the capital of the Yukon Territory, Whitehorse. From there a bigger swing takes in gilded, gold rush ghost Dawson City before returning to the highway at Tetlin Junction, still over 200 miles from Fairbanks.

Whitehorse

Yukon Territory is vast, wild, exhilarating. It contains almost 208,000 square miles and perhaps 20,000 persons, more than half of whom live in and near Whitehorse. Whitehorse, the seat of government of Yukon Territory, has a population of over 15,000 and, by incorporating a king-size surrounding area in 1971, has become the largest city in Canada in area—168 square miles. No other town has over 1,000 persons. In all the far-flung territory there are probably 12 communities with a population of more than 100—including Old Crow, an Indian settlement far north on the Porcupine River and remote from any road.

Whitehorse, the territorial capital, is a clean, friendly city, with fine accommodations. They range from hotels to campgrounds and include a youth hostel near the jet airport. Some exceptional restaurants and burgeoning shopping centers are contained in this big bend of the Yukon River.

Meriting visits in and around Whitehorse are: Miles Canyon, through which the dam-tamed Yukon flows; MacBride Museum, on whose grounds are the Sam McGee Cabin, built in 1899; the Hydro Dam and Fish Ladder; the spirit houses in the Indian cemeteries; some log "sky-scrapers" and the Anglican Old Log Church, built in 1900, and now a church museum; the mural in the foyer of the Whitehorse City Hall; the special northern art displays in the Yukon Regional Library; and the sternwheeler S.S. *Klondike,* now a National Historic Site. Three-hour boat excursions include the M/V *Schwatka* cruise up the Yukon and through Miles Canyon, and downriver to Lake Laberge.

Whitehorse is headquarters for some diverse attractions. One is the Royal Canadian Mounted Police, renowned for keeping law and order in the Yukon since 1894. Others are the Yukon Sourdough Rendezvous, featuring dogteam races at the end of February and the "Frantic Follies," a local-talent vaudeville show, using the theme of the Gold Rush era, staged from mid-June through August.

The Visitors Information at 3rd and Steele has lists of attractions, and Atlas Travel in the Travelodge Mall sells all kinds of tours.

Dawson City, Yukon Territory, Canada

Gold rush buffs are bound to want to continue to the end of the Trail of '98 at Dawson, gateway to the Klondike gold fields. Planes and buses go there, but driving the almost 500 mile Klondike Loop Highway adds only about a hundred miles more than taking the direct Alaska Highway route that passes the beautiful Kluane Lake area.

The highway is dirt, but well kept up in summer, and campgrounds, stores for groceries and gas, and accommodations are open for business at well-spaced intervals. Following lake shores, through forests and over gentle mountains and high scenic plateaus keeps the scenery interesting, highlighted by old settlements from Indian to mining.

Down to fewer than 900 people, about 30,000 below what it had in 1899, Dawson City clings tenaciously to its fabulous past. Streets remain as they were at the turn of the century, and visitors find glamour in the silent, shuttered ramshackle stores and houses and the miles of flower-bordered boardwalks. But some pioneer buildings are still open and operative or under restoration as historic shrines by Parks Canada, including the Flora Dora Hotel, post office, Canadian Imperial Bank of Commerce, where Yukon bard Robert W. Service worked from 1907 to 1909, and the old administration building. Also intact is Service's two-room log cabin where his "ghost" recites his poems daily during the summer months. Near the Service cabin is Jack London's cabin. The "Gold Room," above the Bank of Commerce, has an exhibit of early-day equipment for weighing, measuring, and melting gold. The S.S. *Keno*, "the historic sternwheeler that pioneered the Yukon," is now a historic museum, but the "Yukon Lou" paddles past an Indian fish wheel and sternwheeler "graveyard" to ghost town Moosehide during a 2-hour tour. Side trips lead to dredges, still seen on the creeks, to legendary mines, and to "Poverty Bar," where you can pan for gold on Bonanza Creek. Dawson Hardware Museum is a Gold Rush era museum; it has old bottles for sale. The Klondike Mine's railway locomotives rest in Minto Park, and an outdoor Mining Museum at Front and Queen Sts. hoards more mining memorabilia.

The federally restored Palace Grand Theater stages "The Gaslight Follies," nightly at 8, during the summer season. Afterward, everyone heads for Diamond Tooth Gertie's in the Arctic Brotherhood Hall. The Klondike Visitors Association runs the operation: floor show with can-can girls and *real* 1900 gaming tables, under special government blessing. It's the only legal gambling hall of its kind in Canada (annual membership $2). On or near August 17, all of Dawson and visiting gold buffs take a long holiday to celebrate Discovery Day, when a gold strike was made on Bonanza Creek. Festivities include a raft race on the Klondike River. Reserve ahead to be sure of a place to sleep.

Back of Dawson, from the crest of a mountain called Midnight Dome, men still look down on valleys not much changed since a muskeg settlement was the focus of the world's imagination. On June 21 you can see the midnight sun barely dip down behind the 6,000-foot Ogilvie Mountain range in the north before it rises again.

Crossing big rivers, such as the Pelly and the Stewart, on the Klondike Loop, was more exciting before bridges replaced small ferries. But there is still a ferry across the Yukon at Dawson that carries people and cars free, when the river is ice free, generally May to October. There are public campgrounds on both sides and a trailer park in Dawson.

From Dawson City, Yukon 3 is locally known as the 60-Mile Road. In the early 1900s it was a wagon road for freighting to the gold mines. The border is 67 miles from Dawson and you can't cross without going through customs. They have their hours: 9 A.M. to 9

P.M.; 8 to 8, Alaska Time. Allow enough time to avoid an overnight delay. There are no places to stay on the Canadian side. Moreover, it is 71 miles from Dawson City to the first facilities of any kind, including gas. You'll probably breathe a sigh of relief when you make it to Corbett's Boundary House, four miles beyond the border. Camping and trailer spaces, cabins, café, gas and oil, tubes and tires, and minor auto repairs. From Corbett's it is little more than 100 miles to Tetlin Junction, on the Alaska Highway at Milepost 1,301.

North via Kluane Lake

Leaving Whitehorse and the Yukon River, the Alaska Highway moves on to Haines Junction at Mile 1,016. Here, the great pike meets the Haines Highway connecting the Interior and Inside Passage seaport Haines.

Beyond Haines Junction the country is open, with thin woods, except to the west, which is full of the St. Elias Range. Seen on a clear day is a score of pristine, soaring peaks, seemingly impenetrable. Three of the peaks are more than 16,000 feet high with the loftiest, Mt. Logan, 19,850 feet, surpassed only by Mt. McKinley, the highest mountain on the continent.

Canada's Kluane National Park is still in the planning stages, but it's bound to be a winner wildlife-wise and scenically. Until there is road access to the Park, highway travelers will have to settle for skirting 35-mile-long Kluane Lake, the Yukon's largest. Lodges and motels, some oldtimers, some new (but all modernized), and campgrounds and picnic spots are well-spaced along this beautiful lake. Spring through fall the lake trout fishing is big—some over 50 pounds. Boats and guides are for hire at several fish-oriented camps and lodges. Watch for Dall sheep in the hills at Mile 1,060. Kluane Historical Society, at Mile 1,093, has a small but excellent museum of local artifacts. Burwash Lodge, on the shore of Kluane Lake, has been operating since 1904.

Beaver Creek, not too long ago, consisted only of some Indian huts off the road and a lodge. Now there are motels, a trailer park, service stations, cafés, cocktail lounges, some open 24 hours, and some year-round. The post office functions on Tuesdays and Fridays; Canada Customs and Immigration office here is open 24 hours. The Alaska-Yukon Territory border is 21 miles onward. Remember to set your watch back one hour to Alaska time, and to check in at the Port Alcan U.S. Customs & Immigration Station. It is open 24 hours a day, year round, and everyone entering Alaska must stop.

The northern end of the Klondike Loop (Taylor Highway) from

Dawson joins the Alaska Highway at Tetlin Junction, Alaska, at Mile 1,301. The Forty-Mile Roadhouse, named for the river that was the setting for gold strikes in 1886, has log cabins, café, 24-hour wrecker, general car repairs, souvenirs—all open 24 hours.

If you are interested in museum-towns, take the Taylor Highway from Jack Wade Junction (his deteriorating dredge is still there), to Eagle, a tiny village of almost 200. There are gold diggings to ponder along the 163 miles, and when you get there you'll find a general store, gas, meals, and lodging, including the pioneer Eagle Roadhouse.

A post office was established here in 1898, when Eagle had 750 persons more than its present population of 50. In 1901 Eagle became the first incorporated city in interior Alaska. For many years it was the main port of entry from Canada, via the Yukon River. A telegraph line from Valdez to Eagle was completed in 1903. Eagle was the seat of the first court in the interior, established by legendary judge James Wickersham. The courthouse is one of Eagle's several museums. The Amundsen Cabin is another. Some remains of Ft. Egbert, established in 1889 and abandoned in 1901, have been restored, and original buildings preserved. Visitors can walk around the parade ground surrounded by officers' quarters and utility buildings, and see the old Mule Barn with brass nameplates for each mule. The active and eager Eagle Historical Society conducts free tours, through the museum and around town daily in summer.

At Mile 1,314 is Tok (pronounced *Toke*), one of the most important junction settlements in Alaska. Anchorage is 328 miles west; Valdez is 260 miles west, then south on the Richardson Highway. Fairbanks is 206 miles north of Tok. The state maintains an information center here that includes displays and pictures and literature from all over Alaska, ferry schedules, and free coffee. In recent years Tok has grown enormously, so that today it has up-to-date accommodations, cafés, campgrounds, service stations, a clinic, a garage, gift shops, general stores, churches, a four-year high school, and an Alaska State Troopers Post. There are also laundromats, a movie theater, a bank, a post office, guide service, and charter flights.

The settlement here is a good place to spend a night, just to get acclimated to Alaska, and to peruse Tok's hospitality helps.

Alaska's Alaska Highway

The rest of our Grand Circle Tour continues along gold-dusted trails that have evolved into fine highways, and pauses in cities with a golden past, from Fairbanks to Valdez. More riches of nature are sampled en route, at McKinley Park, and while crossing Prince William Sound.

Heading north from Tok Junction and continuing counter-clockwise, the Grand Circle touches on many of the treasures of Alaska's interior and southcentral regions.

Beyond Tok, the Alaska highway slants northeast to skirt the Alaska Range, whose 500-mile arc straddles southcentral Alaska in a tremendous display of raw power and height. The grandest peak is 20,320-foot Mt. McKinley.

Delta Junction, at Mile 1,422, is technically the end of the Alaska Highway, with an impressive marker saying so. Here the World War II-built Alaska Highway merges with the historic Richardson originating from gold rush port Valdez, now serving oil tankers. Together they continue to Fairbanks, commonly considered the end and goal of Alaska Highway travelers.

There's a glowing welcome at the log-cabin information center run by the Delta Chamber of Commerce, open 9 to 6 during the summer: a hearty handshake, free coffee, and, to show off, a certificate for reaching their end of the Alaska Highway.

Delta Junction is the home of Ft. Greely, a U.S. Army arctic testing and training center. This, and establishing a permanent pipeline maintenance station here, has bolstered the economy and population, now 800 in town, 3,900 in the area. Farming is coming to the fore throughout the rich Tanana River valley. Fishing lakes with pike, trout and whitefish, and many game birds and animals attract visitors, but the biggest novelty is buffalo-watching. (And eating, if you are in Delta the first Sunday in August for the Chamber of Commerce Buffalo Barbecue.) Twenty-three animals were let loose on the Big Delta game reserve in 1928, and now the bison number more than 500. They gather in numbers at a saltlick across the Delta River, easily seen from the Richardson Highway about 4 miles from the Junction. They are sometimes seen along the highway and have no qualms about nonchalantly sauntering across the road. There are good tourist accommodations at Delta, and there is a public campground a mile up the highway.

At Mile 1,451 on the Richardson (Alaska) Highway stands Richardson Roadhouse, a pioneer hostelry on the old trail between Valdez and Fairbanks. Here is one of the few authentic old caches visible from the road. (An Alaskan cache is a mounted, covered miniature cabin in which supplies and furs are stored. It is elevated to prevent bears and other animals from getting at the contents.)

End of the Road in Fairbanks

You've made it, officially, when you drive through Fairbanks to the bank of the Chena River, First and Cushman. The good news, a mileage marker, stands next to the sod-roofed, log cabin Visitors Center. Stop in between 8:30 and 5 weekdays, and someone will be ready to tell you all about the abundant number of hotel rooms, campground space, and wide range of restaurants. Between pipelines is a good time to visit; the city has much to offer, but at a less frantic pace.

Fairbanks has come a long way since 1901, when it got its start on the basis of a rumor and a boat trader's need to make a cache and "hole in" for the winter. The place he picked was here on the bank of the Chena, and the rumor concerned gold possibilities nearby. In 1902, the rumor was verified by Felix Pedro who found gold on his namesake creek. 1903 and 1904 were stampede years. Judge Wickersham moved his District Court from Eagle to the booming new gold town. The Judge had named it Fairbanks for his Senator friend from Indiana, who later became Vice President of the U.S.

Fairbanks today is Alaska's second largest community, with a city population of more than 27,000 and a trading area population (Greater Fairbanks) of more than 60,000. It is a military center, seat of the University of Alaska, a leading airway terminal, an important center of space communication from unmanned satellites, and its International airport also serves Arctic villages and oil fields of the North Slope.

Young (like most Alaska cities) and weathering boom and bust, Fairbanks has been growing and building rapidly. Though generally more costly, there's almost everything here that one might look for in the same sized city in the south 48 states, including tennis, swimming, and golf at the Fairbanks Golf & Country Club (public invited), the northernmost.

Looking around, the signs of the past are present, perpetuated in nostalgic bar decor, entertainment, small cabins overshadowed by tall buildings, and in curio shops and museums. In the environs, large dredges surrounded by piles of leftovers (tailings) are reminders of the glory days of gold mining and smelting. Mixing casually on the downtown streets are Eskimos, Indians, prospectors, big-game guides, homesteaders, famed scientists visiting the university, and hosts of government experts.

Summers are warm and bright. This is emphasized by the annual baseball game ushering in the summer. At midnight on June 21, a

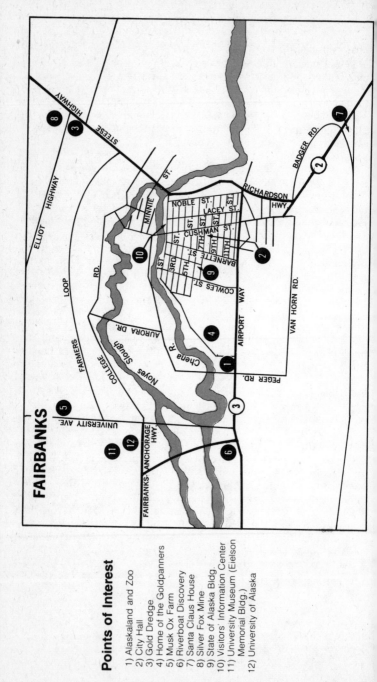

FAIRBANKS

Points of Interest

1) Alaskaland and Zoo
2) City Hall
3) Gold Dredge
4) Home of the Goldpanners
5) Musk Ox Farm
6) Riverboat Discovery
7) Santa Claus House
8) Silver Fox Mine
9) State of Alaska Bldg.
10) Visitors' Information Center
11) University Museum (Eielson Memorial Bldg.)
12) University of Alaska

baseball game is started—and played through to the finish without lights. People fish, hike, camp, climb, go boating, and rev up for the big Yukon "800" Riverboat Race.

It can also get cold in Fairbanks. The young people say that winter temperatures of 60 below zero are rare; more often the coldest is 40 below. But old-timers recall when for six weeks on end the thermometer never showed above 45 below, and went down to 60 below.

Life does not slow down in winter. Besides many fine cultural events, there are spectator and participant sports activities, indoor and outdoors: basketball, dog-sled racing, curling, ice hockey, skating, snowmobiling and skiing (two easily-accessible ski slopes are in the Fairbanks area).

Fairbanks is in the heart of the interior. It is the northern terminus of the Alaska Railroad, which extends south to seaport Seward on the Gulf of Alaska. Ft. Wainwright, a cold-weather test field, is next door to town. Eielson Air Force Base is 23 miles away.

The University of Alaska, founded in 1917, spreads out over 2,300 acres. Students from almost every state and many foreign countries attend. It is farther north than any other institution of higher learning in the world. There are more than thirty modern buildings on the main campus, in Fairbanks, and branches in Alaska's four time zones. Besides the senior campuses at Juneau and Fairbanks, there are twelve community colleges and ten extension centers throughout the rest of the state. Some 28,000 residents in smaller communities and villages sign up for the assorted courses offered in their area, and almost 12,000 are enrolled at Fairbanks. That's a high percent of learners among the total population.

The university is strong in research, communications and environmental studies, striving toward developing new industries in agriculture and aquaculture, not only for Alaska, but for the world. Besides the traditional curriculum, students can study fine arts such as music and drama, with much community encouragement whenever and wherever they perform, sometimes far afield in a small Native village. More unusual subjects deal with Native heritage and languages—Yupik, Eskimo, and Inupiaq. The university's location lends itself to geophysical studies of phenomena such as the aurora borealis. And the far north offers unique recreation—dog sledding, ski touring, marathons—when people want a break from their books.

City tours include the attractive campus, with its surprising arrays of bright flowers in summer. The driver points out the student union building, or Constitution Hall, where Alaska's constitutional convention was held in 1955. They allow time in the expanded and updated university museum. On display in a beautiful new building are thousands of items covering arts and crafts, wildlife, botany, anthropology, paleontology and mineralogy. The aim is to interpret and put into proper perspective Alaska's natural and cultural history.

Alaskaland was created in 1967 as the Alaska State Centennial Park, to commemorate a hundred years of American ownership. The city now maintains and operates this large free outdoor museum of Alaskana. It is open all summer and has an information center at the main entrance. Its 44 acres provide visitors with a "mini tour" of the 49th state. Alaskaland has a Gold Rush town, constructed primarily from buildings that once stood in Fairbanks' downtown area, with period items in the Hensley House; the first church built in Fairbanks; a Pioneers' Museum; a Robert W. Service Museum; old cabins that house gift shops and artisans; the sternwheeler *Nenana,* in its prime the queen of the Tanana-Yukon fleet; the Crooked Creek and Whiskey Island narrow-gauge railroad, which carries visitors around the 44-acre park; Native Village, with examples of dwellings from all parts of Alaska; Alaskaland Zoo, with moose, bears, and caribou; the Mining Valley section, built from cabins on creeks around Fairbanks.

Some other suggestions: bird watch out College Road in a former dairy (Creamer's) pasture; visit the university's experimental farm; paddle into the past on the stern-wheeler "Discovery"; hoist a couple to the past in the Malemute Saloon at Cripple Creek Resort, once a mining camp.

Highways Out of Fairbanks

Although the Alaska Highway ends in Fairbanks, a look at the map shows roads continuing beyond: to the east, to the west, and north to the Arctic Ocean at Prudhoe Bay.

Surprisingly, on the brink of the Arctic, some roads lead to hot springs. These were appreciated especially by miners wintering over and waiting for spring thaws in order to begin sluicing again. Watching wild life, rockhounding, berry-picking in season, and camping are popular along the road, open year round, that ends 60 miles east of Fairbanks at Chena Hot Springs.

The Steese Highway (summer only) partly follows prospectors' trails. It passes through once popular mining country, with appropriate mementoes showing up from remnants of ghost towns and mining sites to residue left by dredging operations—sometimes the dredge itself, rusting and idle. Eagle Summit is the highpoint where, weather permitting between June 20 and 22, there is an unobstructed view of the midnight sun. Many varieties of wildflowers add color to the wilderness vista, and caribou migrate through in fall. Most of the creeks, even the forks, have unusual names, given by miners staking claims. "Tough Luck" and "Lost" creeks could tell a story, perhaps. Mammoth Creek is named for the gigantic fossil remains of animals roaming in Alaska before the glaciers came. A branch of the road veers off to Circle Hot Springs before the Yukon River stops the Steese at the town of Circle.

Fort Yukon

Speaking of circles, Circle City is a take-off point for a very important one—the Arctic Circle. The invisible arc that marks the end of the Frigid Zone is at latitude 66° 33 minutes north. From Circle City, *Air North* flies about 55 miles northwest to Fort Yukon, above the Arctic Circle. Each passenger receives an "Official Arctic Circle Certificate." Most tourists, however, fly direct to Fort Yukon from Fairbanks (daily scheduled flights).

The 2,081-mile Yukon River, cutting an arc to reach the Bering Sea, makes its northernmost bend above the Arctic Circle. Here, where the great stream expands to a width of three miles, stands this Athabascan Indian village of about 500, or perhaps fewer. Today, even though its population has dwindled in the past two decades, it is the largest Indian village on the Yukon. Although it is above the Arctic Circle—and the post office does a thriving tourist business for that reason—summers are mild, sometimes quite warm. The mercury has climbed close to 100 degrees here—some people say it has actually hit 100—but winter temperatures have gone down to 78 below zero. Summer sunshine of 24 hours daily occasions 10-foot sunflowers and giant strawberries. In winter there are several days when the sun never gets above the horizon.

Athabascan women engage in handicrafts, such as elaborate beadwork. A prized example is an intricately beaded white moosehide altar cover, displayed in a log church, one of many historic buildings dating from nineteenth century Hudson Bay Company trading days. Fur trapping and fishing, in which fish wheels are used to catch salmon, are main occupations. The town has a lot of malamutes, which pull tourist wheel-equipped sleds in summer and in winter are used, despite snowmobiles, to pull residents' runner sleds. Many of the Indians still live in log cabins.

The Elliott Highway and the "Haul Road"

The Elliott Highway is gravel, well maintained but tricky when wet and while pulling a trailer. It shares traffic with the North Slope Haul Road to just beyond the small village of Livengood, a mining town founded about 1915. Then the Elliott heads southwest. At Mile 110, a side road leads 12 miles to the relocated Indian settlement, Minto. Manley Hot Springs, almost 50 miles farther on, was a booming trade town for the mining area in the early 1900s. Now the Manley Roadhouse, old-fashioned hospitality with family-style meals, and the Trading Post—cabins, store, gas, and small museum—survive at Mile 157, the end of the highway. The hot springs, with temperatures as high as 136 degrees Fahrenheit, are on a hillside just below the entrance to town.

Those intrigued by the novelty of driving as far north as possible, and in seeing and following the route of the pipeline, are allowed to share the Haul Road—for a way. Turnaround point is Mile 56, after crossing the Yukon River Bridge. Between pipelines (oil and gas) is a good time to do it, with supply traffic lessened.

The pipeline passes under the highway, and parallels it on high ridges. There are sweeping views as it snakes over hills and disappears into hollows. Approaching the Yukon River, a 5-mile rough gravel road leads to a campground with a boat launching area on the river bank. The Bureau of Land Management maintains the site, 7-day limit.

The North Slope Haul Road has been turned over to the State of Alaska, but whether eventually the rest of the 360 miles through the spectacular Brooks Mountain Range to Prudhoe Bay will be open to the public has not been decided at this writing. Conservationist arguments against: cost of maintenance, difficulty of guarding the pipeline, patrolling such a wilderness road, potential damage to the delicate ecology and to the isolated villages, brought on by increased recreational use—all these factors keep the Haul Road's future in doubt. It still awaits a proper official name, but a good guess is that its "popular" one will be hard to change.

South to Anchorage by Rail and Road

The government-owned Alaska Railroad operates between Fairbanks and Anchorage, an 11-12 hour trip.

Along with more than 50 regular stops, the trains halt at any promising spot to let off or pick up fishermen, hikers, or homesteaders. Informative brochures provide a running account of what is to be seen, and the upper doors of the vestibules are open for the benefit of photographers. This helpfulness on the part of the railroad is reflected in the camaraderie of the passengers; by the time destinations are reached strangers are "old friends."

Fairbanks residents ride the railroad for one-day outings, particularly to Nenana, on the Tanana River, and to Mt. McKinley National Park. Nenana, a modernized Athabascan village of about 500, offers photographers fish wheels and an ancient cemetery. However, the village is best known for the Nenana Ice Classic. Thousands of Alaskans and Yukoners bet on the exact day, hour, and minute of the ice breakup on the river in the spring, with $100,000 or so in cash going to the lucky winners.

The all-paved George Parks Highway, with many tourist facilities, is the most direct road now connecting Fairbanks and Anchorage. The 370-mile route traverses rugged and beautiful terrain with a bonus. It passes right by the portal of Mount McKinley National Park, very convenient for rewarding stopovers. Before this highway was completed in 1971, the only access to the park (except for the railroad) was a long drive via the summer-only, gravel Denali Highway. The Denali veers west from the Richardson Highway at Paxson, south of Delta Junction, and 133 miles later joins the George Parks Highway near the park entrance.

Mt. McKinley National Park

The highlight of Alaska's interior, North America's loftiest peak, has been accustomed to the limelight over the years. It was revered by the Indians, admired by English and Russian explorers, and has been tackled by mountain climbers beginning with three sourdoughs. They missed the true summit in 1910, but another party made it in 1913. Many climbing parties have followed, some making the news because of success, many others because of disaster. In 1979, a successful ascent was made by dog team!

But the most important developments since the large area was reserved and set aside for nature lovers as Mount McKinley National Park in 1917 lie with proposed expansion and use of wilderness areas here and throughout the state. And there are some who would change the name of the mountain back to its original one. The Indians, who were in awe of the massive snowy peak, called it Denali, meaning "The High One," or "The Great One."

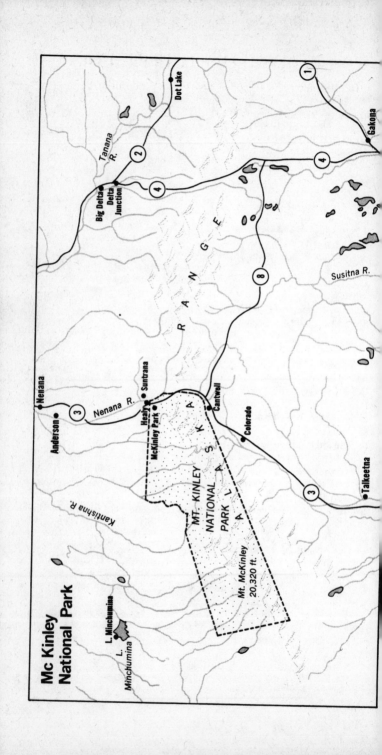

In December 1978, under the 1906 Antiquities Act, President Carter added about 6,094 square miles to Mt. McKinley's 3,030 square miles. Yellowstone was still our oldest but no longer our biggest National Park. Denali National Monument, which surrounds McKinley Park on three sides, was placed under the National Park Service. The purpose of the expansion was to include spectacular scenic areas such as Cathedral Spires, a group of several mile-high geological formations, and also to include all of the Mount McKinley massif which lay outside the former boundary. Another major goal was to preserve ecosystems, leaving undisturbed the calving and migrating territory of the caribou, the domain of the wolf and the grizzly bear, as well as the many lakes that are nesting areas for myriad waterfowl, including the endangered trumpeter swan.

No permanent regulations have been established yet for Denali National Monument. For a while, those able to hike into the back country from the end of the Park Road or from Alaska Highway #3 may use it. To fish, they'll need a license; otherwise the rules will be similar to those for the National Park. Future developments under discussion are a visitor center and hotel in adjacent Denali State Park.

Everyone agrees that nowhere in Alaska are wild animals better seen in their native habitat than here. More than 130 varieties of birds have been counted in the park; almost 40 species of mammals dwell here, including caribou, moose, bear (grizzly and black), Canada lynx, red fox, Dall sheep, porcupine, and beaver. In late June, caribou assemble on the tundra plains, and early in July the herds, sometimes numbering thousands, begin their annual migration northward to summer ranges.

The forests along the streams in the lower valleys consist of aspen, willow, birch, and black and white spruce. The tundra is a mosaic of alpine shrubs, fireweed, lichens and mosses, monkshood, and lupines. Wildflowers seem to pop up almost everywhere. Waterfowl splash in the ponds, shore birds wing furtively from roost to roost, song birds rend the air with gorgeous tones.

Some say the best time to see the park, for sheer beauty, is in late August. The trees and tundra flame scarlet and orange, russet and pink, yellow and gold. This incredible tapestry burns with rage for a few days or two weeks at most. Then, quickly, overnight, a frost sets in, and the fire is extinguished. A few weeks later the park hotel boards its windows and closes its doors, the tourists depart, and the long winter sets in. Not everyone leaves then, however. Rangers patrol the park using the sturdy dog teams and sleds that summer visitors saw during demonstrations at Park Headquarters. Winter enthusiasts bent on mountaineering or cross-country skiing can use dog power, too. Write to Denali Dog Tours, P.O. Box 1, McKinley Park, AK 99755, and they'll tell you about their tours and gear-hauling services.

The great attraction of the park is, of course, Mt. McKinley. Its main (south) summit is 20,320 feet high; its north summit, 19,470 feet in elevation. The closest approach to the mountain from the park road is 26 miles, but the space seems to enlarge rather than diminish it. Most summer visitors are not inspired to climb this grand peak and prefer admiring it whenever it reveals itself.

1979 was proclaimed Year of the Visitor in McKinley Park. To mark it the Park Service put out a Collector's Edition of *Denali Alpenglow,* summing up activities and services promoting the spirit of the National Park Service Organic Act of 1916: "To conserve the scenery and the natural historic objects and the wildlife therein and provide for the enjoyment of the same in such manner and by such means as will leave them unimpaired for the enjoyment of future generations."

An effective and energy-saving means of achieving this is the shuttle bus that transports sightseers and recreationers deep into the park. Controlled traffic—in fact very little traffic since private vehicle travel has been replaced by the wilderness shuttle—has increased the possibilities of animal sightings. Some animal counts made a few years ago, and since the system was started, show that visitors have been seeing moose and caribou on over 90% of the shuttle trips into the park. Grizzly bear haunt certain favorite areas, and they claim Dall sheep are practically guaranteed. An eight-hour tour, to Eielson Visitor Center, begins through spruce woods. At 2,500-foot elevation the road rises above the timber line. Eight miles from the hotel, one sees the first view of Mt. McKinley. The view from Stony Hill Overlook, 61 miles from the hotel, is dramatic. Though much of the time the mountain may be shrouded by fog or clouds, the chance of seeing all or part of it at any time—even by moonlight—is well worth the gamble.

At Eielson Visitor Center there is a head-on view of Muldrow Glacier, largest northward-flowing glacier in Alaska, which stretches between the twin peaks of the mountain the Indians considered high enough to be the home of the sun. From Eielson, 65 miles into the park, the McKinley Park Road continues another 20 miles past Wonder Lake, North Face Lodge, and a short distance farther, high on the ridge above, the mountain's namesake, wilderness Camp Denali.

Be advised that in line with their policy of conservation and protection, park authorities warn that anything is subject to change, if they determine it's necessary.

Be sure to stop at the Riley Creek Visitor Center near the entrance, when you first arrive at the park. It's open in summer from early morning until late evening, and they'll have the latest information on shuttle buses, rules and regulations, campsite availability, hiking trails, and other worthwhile park activities: campfire talks, nature walks, wildlife tours, and sled dog demonstrations. (Also see *National Parks and Monuments* and *Wilderness Resorts* under *Practical Information*.) Denali Flying Service, headquartered in the railroad station, offers reasonable and exciting flightseeing tours for close-up views and photography of rugged McKinley's glaciers and cirques. Outside the Park, from McKinley Village, raft trips take off down the Nenana River. Alaska Raft Adventures' 12-mile float ($25) through moose, sheep, and other wildlife country suits most everyone. You should probably be fairly hardy. It's required you be at least 12 years of age for the 4-hour "Healy Express" ($35) through Nenana Canyon and its exciting white water. For the range of adventures—all day, an evening, overnight, or a few hours—and specific information write: Box 66 McKinley Park, AK 99755.

After McKinley Park, the Alaska Railroad and the George Parks Highway (#3) parallel each other much of the distance. They pass through towns of Willow, Wasilla, and Palmer, skirting the Matanuska Valley as they continue to Anchorage.

Westward to Anchorage

Those who have taken Alaska Highway #2 or Richardson Highway #4 will turn onto the Glenn Highway #1 that leads southwest to Anchorage. The turnoff point for the Alaska Highway is Tok Junction, where the 125-mile Tok Cutoff joins the Richardson at Gakona Junction. From Tok there'll be adequately spaced and well-equipped commercial campgrounds and roadside attractions, such as the Mentasta Athabascan Gift Shop & Store Co-op, Inc., with native arts and crafts, plus birch-bark items, mukluks, and beaded work. There is also a campground with fireplaces, laundromat, and groceries. The Indians live six miles away, but nearby they have built a model of an Indian village to show how it was in the old days.

At Mile 65 a side road leads 46 miles to the old Nabesna Gold Mine, no longer operative, but interesting to see. There are many spectacular views en route, the fishing is good in lakes and streams, but the road may be only fair. Twenty-eight miles up the road to Nabesna is Sportsmen's Paradise, a lodge open June to Nov. Sandwiches, gas, fishing, boating.

Onward to the Junction and the meeting of the Gakona and Copper rivers, the scene includes panoramas of the Copper River Valley and the Wrangell Mountains, including 16,237-foot Mt. Sanford and 12,010-foot Mt. Drum. The Richardson and Glenn highways merge here and continue together for the next 14 miles.

Two miles below Gakona Junction is Gulkana, founded in 1903 as a U.S. Arm Signal Corps telegraph station. Twelve miles farther, at Mile 139, is the South Junction of the Glenn and Richardson highways. This was the only junction before the Glenn Highway was extended to Tok. Here the highways separate near the town of Glennallen, named for two army officers who were active in mapping the Copper River region. The Richardson continues south to Valdez. The Glenn Highway heads almost due west to Palmer, then follows along the Knik Arm of Cook Inlet to Anchorage.

Beyond the junction the highway enters a vast plateau. Back of it are legendary fishing streams that can be reached only by pontoon-equipped plane; from the highway it is possible to see small herds of caribou and an occasional grizzly or black bear. Dall sheep may also come into view. If you tramp into the bush, you may see muskrat and beaver.

The 187-mile road from Glennallen to Anchorage passes streams, forests, wildflower fields and homesteads, lakes, particularly Tolsona, mountain views, such as 17,400-foot Mt. Foraker, and glaciers, including Tazlina and the Matanuska, one of the oldest and largest in Alaska. Its state public campground is at Mile 101 and trails lead along the bluff overlook, a great vantage point for taking photographs. At Glacier Park Resort, Mile 102, you can rent a motel room, or hook up your trailer, and then walk on the mighty Matanuska.

Fifty-four miles from Glacier Park is Palmer, the hub of the Matanuska Valley. It was here that farmers and mechanics from the Middle West arrived in the spring of 1936 to become Alaska farmers. Very few of the original colonists are still around. But the rich soil of the Matanuska Valley has been productive, and Palmer today is the state's leading farming center, the only one (so far) that is based almost entirely on agriculture. The Matanuska is renowned for its giants—cabbages up to 60 pounds, turnips more than seven pounds, and Alaska-sized potatoes. They are exhibited at the Alaska State Fair, held annually; 11 days before, and ending on, Labor Day. Matanuska Valley museums at Palmer and Wasilla have early farm tools utilized by first Matanuska Valley colonists as well as arts and crafts of the area. Knik, 14 miles southwest of Wasilla boasts the Sled Dog Mushers Hall of Fame. Although the Glenn Highway slices through the valley, at the base of the Chugach Mountains, the panorama is best seen by a short drive from Palmer to Wasilla. *If* the state capital is moved from Juneau, between here and nearby Willow is the chosen site.

Palmer has excellent tourist facilities as well as a city camping park, which can accommodate 40 trailers and 50 campers.

From Glennallen to Palmer there are so many places to camp, obtain automobile services and products, find cafés and lodgings that it seems unnecessary to detail them. From Palmer to Anchorage there is even a greater density of tourist facilities. In the 48 miles between Palmer and Anchorage there is something, it seems, just about every mile. About 15 miles out of Palmer, en route to Anchorage, is the University of Alaska Matanuska Farm, better known in these parts simply as the "Experimental Farm." Corn has been raised here with good results, perhaps indicating a new crop for the valley. A model dairy herd, almost pampered by the agronomists, is for public viewing as well as experimentation. On a summer day the farm is never free of tourists; considering how little publicity it seeks, it gets a lot of visitors. Photographers will be interested in the "Family Gardens," where colorful vegetables and flowers form a vivid foreground for the white-clad Chugach Mountains.

Outside Anchorage

When travelers opt to start with Anchorage, flying there direct, the largest, most sophisticated city is their introduction to Alaska. Following our Grand Circle, though, Anchorage is the exit point for deciding the route home.

From here, some travelers may fly all the way to their take-off point. Some will connect with an Inside Passage cruise, or the ferries, for the trip back. Others, especially if they by-passed Mile 0 going, may return the length of the Alaska Highway. They'll head from Anchorage to meet it, then south to complete the arc, via Dawson Creek, B.C.

Whether a gateway or a getaway, Anchorage will be the starting point for trips farther afield: by plane, highway and/or South central ferries; on their own, or on a tour.

(For details on Anchorage itself, see the separate chapter on that city, earlier in this book.)

Exploring in Circles Outside of Anchorage

There are smaller circle trips (all reversible) out of the big city that can be done overnight or within a few days, depending on where you might want to linger and relax. Take the Glenn Highway through the Matanuska Valley to the South Junction beyond Glennallen. Circle to the left and you can follow the Richardson Highway almost 200 miles for a jaunt via Fairbanks. Or circle off sooner at Paxson, about a third of the way along, where the summer-only Denali Highway stretches 135 dirt miles to Cantwell and a junction with Highway #3, about 26 miles from the entrance to McKinley Park.

Circle to the right and you'll travel the state's oldest highway, the Richardson, to Valdez. From there the circle swings across Prince William Sound, through mountains, and back to the Anchorage Seward Highway, where you have two choices. "Circle to the left" and explore the wild, big, and beautiful Kenai Peninsula and neighboring Kodiak Island, all connected by the Southwest Marine Highway System of ferries; "circle to the right" to complete the circuit at Anchorage.

On to "Swiss Alaska" via the Richardson Highway

After South Junction, the scenery gets even better. The highway rises to glacier-draped mountain heights before it drops down to the sea-level delights of Valdez in its alplike setting. Car travelers and motorcoach tours stop to look and photograph impressive views from 2,771-foot Thompson Pass. They drive up to the icy tongue of the Worthington Glacier that almost licks the highway. Some walk the short path to where they can set foot on the mighty river of ice. The route passes through green, waterfall-laced valleys and claustrophobically narrow Keystone Canyon before reaching oilport Valdez.

The road to Valdez parallels an army telegraph line built in 1900 and a trail used by feverish argonauts to reach the Yukon River and the Klondike gold diggings. Now it also parallels the southern portion of the 800-mile pipeline which starts at Prudhoe Bay and ends at

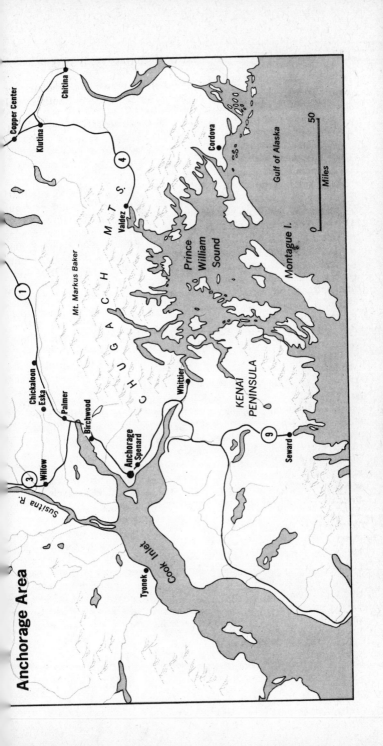

Anchorage Area

Valdez. You'll see the pipeline, from time to time, snaking over the hills, hugging mountains and fording streams and rivers. Accommodations along the way are not only diverse, but interesting. One of the fanciest is The Ahtna, at the Richardson and Glenn Highways Junction, built with local funds from the "People of the Copper River." In contrast, is the long-established Copper Center Lodge and Trading Post, still in use, modernized, serving excellent meals, and with cocktail lounge and curio shop. The lodge started as a roadhouse during the Yukon Gold Rush and was the first hostelry in the Copper River Valley, in 1896. Before 1900 there were hundreds of log cabins in and near Copper Valley, built by argonauts who arrived exhausted after crossing the treacherous Valdez Glacier. Many of the men perished from scurvy and frostbite, and a large number returned to Valdez, where they took boat passage back to the States. Only a few indomitable souls remained in the valley, enough to start a post office in 1901. Scarcely one of the log cabins or descendants of the early miner-settlers remains today, but Copper Valley has the "feel" of being rich in tradition.

The informal possibilities for eating, sleeping, and recreating are often spectacular in this vast wilderness area. State waysides and campgrounds are situated to make the best of the rugged, spread-out mountains, the Wrangell Range, and then the Chugach Mountains.

Willow Lake, five miles farther, mirrors the lofty peaks of the Wrangell Mountains. Two miles on there is a picnic wayside, affording superb views of the 100-mile-long, 60-mile-wide Wrangell Range. At this point, if you are an imaginative soul, you might think of the Wrangell Range as holding fast in its glacier wildness a mysterious and untamed Shangri-la. Get off the road a dozen miles or so and you may confront grizzly bears, black bears, moose, mountain goats, Dall sheep, beavers, muskrats, ptarmigan, and spruce grouse. If you get lost in season, you can stay alive on fat blueberries and lowbush cranberries; in summer the streams are thick with salmon.

There's good fishing, including tasty grayling, at Squirrel Creek Campground.

Near here is a side road leading to Chitina, 33 miles off, on the Edgerton Highway. There is some colorful, rugged scenery along this road, with grand views of the Copper River Valley and of very interesting geologic formations. The first 19 miles are paved and after that the road is gravel. About 24 miles from the junction there is a state public campground at the foot of Liberty Falls. Chitina, a former mining town, is now a supply base for the farms and tiny hamlets of the area. Chitina Cache Store has groceries, hardware, and supplies for anglers; fine salmon fishing in summer and many lakes with grayling. Chitina Saloon has cold drinks and live music on Saturday and Sunday nights. If you want to hear some backcountry music in a real down-to-earth atmosphere, this is the place. Less than a mile from Chitina is a small Indian village, with an old log church. In the three miles to O'Brien Creek there are several spots for do-it-yourself camping. An ancient railroad trestle at the creek will excite photographers.

Along the way there'll be lodges located at fishing rivers: Tonsina Lodge, Tiekel River Lodge, Tsaina Lodge—all generous with information. Besides stores for supplies and gas, there are gift shops with intriguing names: The Grizzly, The Aurora, and Serendipity.

Above timberline favorites are the campground right at the Worthington Glacier, and Blueberry Lake Wayside, near Thompson Pass. Thompson Pass forms an eastern anchor of the Chugach Range, with Anchorage at the western end. The area is a wonderland of alpine wildflowers—so don't be in a hurry to leave. The structures you see below, as you start to descend the pass, are the remains of an old mining camp and roadhouse. There are, in the next 11 miles, especially in narrow Keystone Canyon, a number of historical markers, waterfalls and waysides. The highway spans the terminal moraine and milky glacial streams of the Valdez Glacier and a mile later enters the site of Old Valdez, which was so damaged by the Good Friday earthquake of 1964 that the town was relocated several miles to the west of the former townsite. At the entrance to the new town you can park at a turnout and, if you come in August and early September, stroll across the road to see pink and silver salmon spawning.

"Valdez Please"

Valdez, pronounced to rhyme with *please* (the natives instruct visitors by saying "Valdez please"), has a population of about 7,000 people. It is near the head of a fjord and is one of Alaska's most thrilling locations. To more than a few people, Valdez is the "Switzerland of Alaska." Everywhere you look up you seem to be surrounded by alp-like snowy peaks. The town is a key gateway to camping grounds in the Chugach National Forest. There are enough photographic possibilities—in the mountains, fjords, woods, lakes—to fill a book. Valdez Museum has many artifacts of the Gold Rush and early seafaring days.

Some main attractions are the excellent fishing, cruises to Columbia Glacier, and the tanker ships at the terminal, loading and leaving with oil for refineries to the south. The ice-free year round port is busy, and especially so in the summer. Make reservations ahead, if not camping, or on a tour.

From Valdez you can take a state ferry to Cordova, Whittier, or Seward.

Cordova, named by Spanish explorer Fidalgo, flourished as the rail port for the Kennecott Copper Mines until they shut down in 1938. Now the town lives off the sea, packing and processing a large percent of diversified seafood in its modern canneries. Petroleum explorations in the area have raised high hopes for development of oil-related industries. The 1964 Good Friday earthquake lifted the area about seven feet, changing its face and harbor, but not the super surrounding scenery. Eyak Lake, Cordova, is held fast by mountains never entirely free of snow, and it is a popular winter sports area. Summer recreation includes swimming in the town pool and camping and hiking in the surrounding Chugach National Forest. However, the Chugach National Forest is more than trees. A highlight of this circle trip out of Anchorage is exploring the Chugach's watery domain with its sea birds and marine mammals.

Crossing Prince William Sound

The state ferry M/V *Bartlett*, small cruise ships, private and charter boats cross between Whittier and Valdez. The *Glacier Queen I* and *Glacier Queen II*, new in 1980 and bigger, major in Columbia Glacier Cruises: Box 34, Anchorage AK 99510. The ships cover the sea leg of popular circle tours out of Anchorage mentioned in the earlier section, "Exploring in Circles Outside of Anchorage." The route is part of the Alaska Marine Highway System which cuts through the Chugach National Forest here, past the land administered by the Forest Service under the U.S. Department of Agriculture. Because it abuts the Sound, all the wildlife therein, finny or furry, is the responsibility of appropriate departments. The ferry crossing takes about seven hours and allows a leisurely inspection of sea life and one of the largest of Alaska's tidewater glaciers, the Columbia. Ships approach the face, pause awhile, and toot their whistles, usually triggering an ice fall. About half the Columbia's face is visible from the deck of a ship entering the bay. Visitors see 2½ miles of sheer cliff rising 160 to 260 feet above sea level. They say ice may extend down as deep as 2,300 feet in some places.

As glaciers go, this is an active one, flowing seaward about 6 feet a day, faster in summer than in winter, and often calving icebergs from its face. The beautiful deep blue color, most intense on cloudy days where a chunk has just broken off, is caused by reflection and refraction from the highly compressed ice crystals. Like prisms, they break sunlight into all the colors, but reflect back mostly a gorgeous "glacier blue."

Various forms of food—microscopic animal and plant life and plankton flourishing among the debris carried by the glacier—attracts larger feeders to the glacier's face. The naturalist aboard the ferry who interprets the prolific sea life here and throughout the crossing, is often an enthusiastic young college student majoring in forest and wildlife subjects.

Everyone watches for whales, of course. The kind most likely to show in comparatively shallow Prince William Sound are the black-and-white, dorsal-finned killer whales, which are actually the largest of the dolphin family. The small (up to 30 feet) Minke Whale is often seen. The Humpback Whale (up to 50 feet) is seen occasionally, as is the Gray Whale, especially during late spring.

You can practically count on seeing porpoises. The Dall Porpoise is playful, and small schools often follow alongside ships and play in the bow waves. The shy Harbor Porpoise avoids ships, but watch for them where tidal currents meet or in tide rips. Harbor seals abound, especially around the Columbia Glacier. Ships sneak up on seals sunning on ice cakes so that passengers can try for photos. If you see a small mammal floating on its back, flippers up, possibly carrying a little one on its chest, it is probably a sea otter, once hunted almost to extinction. Protected by the Fur Seal Treaty of 1911, it has recovered and is now about 30,000 in number, mostly in this area.

The Sound is definitely for the birds. Marbled Murrelets are the ones you'll see the most of, followed by Black-legged Kittiwakes, Tufted Puffins, and Glaucous-winged Gulls, according to the minimum estimate by the Bureau of Sport Fisheries. Other colorful ones are black Oystercatches, Murres, and the spectacular chestnut-colored, blue-and-white-plumed Harlequin Duck.

The environment is so engrossing that it seems no time at all before the ferry docks at Whittier.

Approaching Anchorage from the South

With its two almost-skyscrapers, seaport Whittier looks as if it should be a booming community. This was a busy seaport base during World War II, and those gaunt, mostly empty buildings against the mountains once held a self-contained military community of Army men and their families. They housed offices, clinic, people, stores, recreational facilities—a whole city. Now there is a small boat harbor by the docks, and Whittier is the vacation home of some thirty or forty people from Anchorage. They claim it is an excellent base for fishing and other outdoor recreation.

Most visitors in transit spend only long enough to board the train, which also carries vehicles. The trip from Whittier to Portage takes about half an hour, and you won't see a great deal. The first tunnel is 2½ miles long, and the second is one mile. Between them you get an idea of the size of the mountain barrier and glimpses of the Portage Glacier. Those with their own transportation drive onto the railroad flatcars; those on tour hop aboard the waiting motorcoach and ride to where the train stops and lets vehicles off at Portage. Then they are driven north along fjord-like Turnagain Arm to Anchorage, completing the circle tour.

Exploring South of Anchorage

Car travelers and tours bent on exploring the large wilderness areas to the south reached by road and ferry head out the Anchorage–Seward Highway. The highway and the Alaska Railroad parallel Turnagain Arm as far as Portage, and it's beautiful all the way. Mt. Alyeska Ski Resort and the Portage Glacier, an hour's drive from Anchorage, are probably the most popular tourist attractions in the area. Along the side road to the Portage Glacier Recreation Area, there are easily seen salmon spawning areas. From the parking area, there are clear views across Portage Lake with floating blue-white icebergs to the glacier, 2½ miles distant. The Visitor Center here interprets the area and schedules nature walks. Besides campgrounds and picnic sites, there is a day lodge with dining room, bar and gift shop.

Ten miles beyond the Portage Glacier Recreation Area turnoff is Turnagain Pass, a popular winter recreation area for cross-country skiers and, in recent years, snowmobilers. Twelve miles farther there is a meeting with a road coming in from (or leading out to) Hope, 16½ miles off. A pioneer mining settlement on the Upper Cook Inlet, Hope is still alive, with about 90 year-round residents. It is a summer retreat for some Anchorage people. Porcupine Forest · Service Campground is about two miles past Hope.

Nineteen miles past the meeting with the Hope Road, Alaska 1 forks. The left fork, which continues to Seward, becomes Alaska 9. The right fork is designated as Alaska 1. Thirty-eight miles beyond the forks the highway from Anchorage, now Alaska 9, reaches its end at Seward.

Seward

An important port nestled at the foot of the Chugach Mountains, Seward was badly damaged by the big earthquake, but it has been rebuilt. The population of Greater Seward is under 3000. It is the southernmost terminus of the Alaska Railroad and home port for the state ferry M/V *Tustumena*. On the opposite side of the Kenai Peninsula from the city of Kenai, Seward is a favorite vacation area for sports fishermen from Anchorage, who come to Resurrection Bay to try for salmon and sea bass. Founded in 1903 as a sea (and later railroad) terminal and supply center for the Alaska Railroad, Seward is today considered to be one of the best-equipped and most favorably sited cargo ports and fishing harbors in the North American West. Fisherman may have their catches canned, smoked, or frozen by firms in the city.

Seward is very conscious of the 1964 earthquake. A slide show, "Seward is Burning," shown at 2 P.M. in the library illustrates the damage done by the Good Friday tremor. The presentation, in summer, is held in the basement of the City Hall. Photographs of the big quake are on display at the State and City Office Building. A museum in the building's basement holds artifacts of the white pioneers as well as Aleut-made baskets. Paintings by prominent Alaskan artists, together with Russian icons, are exhibited at the Seward Community Library. A painting done in 1925 of the Resurrection, with an Alaska background and motif, hangs in the 1906-built St. Peter's Episcopal Church. For local information, visit the Information Cache, in the old railroad car "Seward," at 3rd & Jefferson. The city has two municipal campgrounds, open May through Oct. 15. Thousands come to Seward on July 4 to see the annual Mt. Marathon Race, to the top of 3,022-foot Mt. Marathon and back. Started in 1909 as a wager between two sourdoughs, the race begins and ends in downtown Seward. The 1974 record is 44 minutes and 11 seconds. Hikers go at a slower pace up a well-marked trail for the view of Resurrection Bay. The Silver Salmon Derby starts the second Saturday in August and runs 8½ days of round-the-clock fishing for more than $40,000 in cash and merchandise prizes. Charter planes fly to Harding Ice Cap, one of the world's largest icefields. The excursion boat Seagull explores Resurrection Bay and comes close to a Steller sea lion colony. Hospitable and eager, Seward boasts that it provides "the best and largest camper, trailer, and boat parking facilities in Alaska."

From Seward you can take a state ferry to Kodiak, Port Lions, Seldovia, Homer, Valdez, and Cordova. For rates regarding schedules, berths, and tariffs for vehicles, write Division of Marine Transportation, Pouch R, Juneau, AK 99811.

Continuing to Explore the Kenai Peninsula

To reach the north side of the Kenai Peninsula, return 38 miles to the forks and turn left, onto Alaska 1, the Sterling Highway. This area has boomed with oil and natural gas exploration and development, and it is popular for recreation and for fishing and hunting. Fishermen line the Russian River during salmon and trout runs. The Kenai-Russian River campground next to the Sportsman's Lodge is starting point for Alaska Campout Adventures floating the Kenai River to Skilak Lake.

Eight miles beyond Sterling lies Soldotna, one of Alaska's newer cities. Little more than a mile from Soldotna is a junction with the Kenai Spur Road. Eleven miles down this road is Kenai, the largest city on the Kenai Peninsula. Its urban population is some 6,000, and its greater city population (meaning the environs added to the city) is about 17,000.

Kenai

One of the oldest permanent settlements in Alaska, Kenai, on Cook Inlet, was founded by the Russians in 1791. The oldest of the Russian Orthodox churches—Russian Orthodox Church of the Assumption of the Virgin Mary—was built in 1896 and its replica built before 1900 is still in use. But basically Kenai is a very modern community. Discovery of oil and natural gas in the late 1950s turned Kenai from a sleepy village into a swift-paced community. From a scenic outlook in "Old Kenai" you can see, from late spring until autumn, thick herds of beluga whales scouring for food fish. Visitors are made welcome at the Kenai Packers salmon cannery during salmon packing season. The 80-acre municipal park accommodates small pickups and campers.

Everyone in the Greater Kenai Chamber of Commerce is keen on travel to the town of Kenai and the rest of the big peninsula. You'll know it as soon as you step inside their headquarters and information center in "Moosemeat John's" cabin off the Kenai Spur road in mid-Kenai—or if you write to Box 497, Kenai AK 99611. They'll ply you with maps, literature, and advice, all most useful. They also have rental tour tapes on hand for walking or driving around Old Kenai, and a Black Gold driving tour of the Industrial part.

Beyond Kenai the road continues for 27 miles, to Captain Cook State Recreation Area. They are working toward 250 campsites, varying from wooded to beach areas, the delight of rockhounds and beachcombers. Between Kenai and the recreation area, on the shore of Upper Cook Inlet, there are some thrilling overlooks of Cook Inlet including panoramas of two volcanic peaks, 10,116-foot Mt. Iliamna and 10,197-foot Mt. Redoubt.

The highway passes through moose country, and you'll likely see some in the Kenai National Moose Range. In 1941, this big area was set aside to protect the stamping grounds of moose that grow to giant size on the Kenai. The Kalifonsky Beach Road runs two miles to Kasilof, founded by the Russians in 1786. The Indian fishing village that followed is gone now, and the population scattered, but an early log schoolhouse by the road displays artifacts.

Russian traders founded Ninilchik on fur farming and fish in 1820. Among the area population of 450 are several of their descendants, many Russian-speaking. Antique log homes, fishing shacks and a Russian church high on the hill are reminders of the town's Russian-American beginnings. Ninilchik State Campground lacks water, but the beach has clams and fishing is good.

The Anchor River attracts silver, king salmon, rainbow and steelhead fishermen. The Anchor Point road ends at the beach where a marker informs that this is the most westernly point accessible by continuous road system on the North American continent. During the peak fishing times, the campgrounds will be overflowing, especially at the river mouth. The well-situated Anchor River Inn features the latest fishing information among its many services.

Homer's at the end of the road

The Sterling Highway gives up at the tip of an almost 5-mile-long finger of land extending into fjordlike Kachemak Bay, the Homer Spit. In summer, much of the town of Homer's activity is based on the salt chuck surrounding Homer Spit, where there is a small boat harbor, ferry and big ship docks, bars, hotel, campground, and beaches. Fishermen cast for trout and salmon from the shore. Campers beachcomb, and "live off the land" by digging clams or catching fresh crab for supper. Delectable seafood is sold in the dock shops and served in the restaurants.

Bird and sea life flourishes among Kachemak Bay's islands, fjords, glaciers, and even volcanoes. St. Augustine on its island 70 miles away across Cook Inlet sometimes entertains with an impromptu "sound and light" show. Bay excursions leave from the dock, and the Skipper zeros in on seabird nesting islands, lifts shrimp and crab pots (traps), picks up and lets off campers at Kachemak State Park, across the Bay, and stops at Halibut Cove, once a thriving fishing town, and now home of several artists.

In the latter 18th century, about the time of the American Revolution, Russian explorers and trappers were paying calls near Homer, even before Captain Cook sailed by. Homer was founded in the spring of 1896, and given the first name of the head man of the first industry there, gold mining. Next came coal mining, followed by the growth of fishing—all kinds—and its satellite industries; farming, including a short-lived fox farming try; and homesteading. Exploratory offshore oil well drilling near Homer in Lower Cook Inlet may turn up an oily future. At present, tourism is a mainstay.

Homer's residents are unusually artistic, probably inspired by the matchless scenic surroundings. Their works are displayed in several galleries and studios, and visitors are welcome. Drop by the Homer Artists Gallery and the 8 x 10 Art Studio, landscaped with native plants and flowers, in town. About 12 miles from town is the secluded studio of a long-time respected resident artist, Norman Lowell.

The Alaska Wild Berry products has a taster's stand in summer, and their kitchens and gift shop, preparing and selling unique berry and sea food packages, are open year-round. The Pratt Museum is sponsored by the Homer Society of Natural History. Besides pioneer, Russian and Indian, and sea otter displays, they've added a saltwater aquarium, holding sea life from Kachemak Bay.

Sightseeing excursions follow the Skyline Drive along the rim of the green and flowering bluffs rising behind Homer. They pass original homesteads, many now with modern (and luxurious) log buildings, and pause at views of the Grewingk Glacier, one of many spawned by the Harding Ice Fields just across the Bay.

For close-up views, air taxis and helicopters fly out of Homer.

Maritime Helicopters hover over volcanic Augustine Island, McNeil River noted for fishing (by people *and* bears), the Barren Islands and Lower Cook Inlet for spotting whales, seals and porpoises. Cook Inlet Aviation tours fly around the rookeries, islands and fjords of Kachemak Bay. If you are interested in small isolated towns across the bay from Homer, they arrange for sightseeing layovers in English Bay, Port Graham and Seldovia, none of them accessible by road.

Homer, a leisurely day's drive from Anchorage, is a popular weekend destination for Alaskans. Visitors from "outside" fly in from Anchorage for one day or overnight package tours, and there is bus and ferry service, between some points on the Kenai. Kenai Adventures specialize in personalized mini-van sightseeing tours. Itineraries are flexible; some include flying and ferry trips, with room for optional activities such as river rafting, fishing, camping, hiking—even gold panning. Write P.O. Box 2834, Anchorage, AK 99510 for the current program, or inquire in Anchorage at 5501 E. 38th, Court 4 (Rick Ross, owner).

Seldovia

Seldovia seems to retain the charm of an earlier Alaska, perhaps because of its isolation. No roads reach there, only small planes and boats, and state ferries of the Southwest Alaska Marine Highway System. The town's Russian flavoring shows in its onion-domed church and its name, derived from the Russian place name which translated "herring bay." Visiting fishermen use lots of that small fish for bait. With it they catch record salmon and halibut and king and Dungeness crab. They find the fishing good whether dropping lines in the deep water of Kachemak Bay, or casting into the surf for silver salmon while standing on the shore of Outside Beach, near town. But the serious fishing is commercial and large scale, beginning with netting them and continuing through the processing in the big Wakefield operation.

Crossing to Kodiak

From Homer, ferries serving the Gulf of Alaska head across a stretch of the Pacific Ocean to the town of Kodiak on Kodiak Island, the largest of a group bordering Shelikof Strait, which leads up to Cook Inlet. Across the Strait are the lofty volcanoes of the Alaska Peninsula.

The waters between the mainland and Kodiak Island are not always calm; indeed, they are at times as turbulent as any waters off the Alaska coast. In giant swells the *Tustumena* pitches, yaws, and rolls, and passengers who rush out on deck to look at the angry sea are stung by salt spray and buffeted by ruthless winds. Still, the scenery is itself worth the voyage. The spooky Barren Islands, the mystic-looking head of Marmot Cape, the broken hills of Afognak Island, and the sunsets, blazing as though the whole world were on fire, give the passage an odd, arresting beauty.

The only other way to get to Kodiak, unless you have your own boat or are signed up with one in the large fishing fleet working out of Kodiak Harbor, is to fly. *Wien Air Alaska* flies direct from Seattle to Kodiak, and from Anchorage. *Western Airlines* flies there from Seattle in summer; *Kodiak Western Alaska Airlines* serves Kodiak on a charter basis and serves remote areas by scheduled amphibian aircraft. By careful planning and timing you might be able to combine some tours and flights to see the Katmai, Kodiak, and Homer—three choice wilderness areas—before returning to the big city.

Kodiak is a great place for a short course in Russian-American history. It all began here, almost 200 years ago. On tour or on your own, you'll be well exposed to the island's scenic and historic landmarks, with the accent on Russian-American history.

The first Russian settlement, in 1784, was at Three Saints Bay, near present Kodiak, which dates from 1792. The town's heyday was at the turn of the 18th century, when it was headquarters for the rich fur trade, and governed by Alexander Baranof. (He later moved the capital of then Russian America to Sitka.)

The Kodiak colonists hewed and carved Russian-style wooden homes and built ships from plentiful Sitka spruce. They fired bricks and ground grain shipped from Russian settlements in California. Returning ships also carried back ice for bars and restaurants and bells for California missions and Russian Orthodox churches. The iron and brass bells were cast in Kodiak's busy large foundry.

Kodiak's Holy Resurrection Church parish was established in 1794 by Father Herman, one of the original missionary monks. He came from St. Petersburg (now Leningrad) via Siberia by small wooden ship in 1793. In 1970 he was canonized here, Alaska's—and North America's—first saint of the Russian Orthodox Church. Inside the church, thrice rebuilt after disasters, but always in the original style, there are valuable icons and some treasures of St. Herman, also called the "Fisherman's Saint." Among them are the cross and heavy chain he wore to show his love for God.

The one building left from 1793, said to be the oldest wooden structure on the West Coast of the United States, is now a museum. Portions of the original log walls, chinked with moss, show inside. On the lawn outside is a millstone used by the early Russians.

The Russian American era ended with the Purchase of Alaska by the United States in 1867. For the next 70 years Kodiak plugged along as a fishing town, visited by Baptist missionaries in 1886, and covered by volcanic ash in 1912, when a volcano 100 miles away blew its top. The town boomed when the World War II Naval Base was established at Fort Abercrombie, eight miles from town. The fort is now a National Historical Site with a campground. There are leftover bunkers here from when Kodiak was "home" for 25,000 troops and was heavily fortified.

Some scenic drives radiate out from town to many attractive, though mostly unimproved, campspots along bays and coves and a fossil beach. A road winds to the summit of 1400 Pillar Mountain, and a view of Kodiak, Shelikof Straits, the distant peninsula, and many more archipelagolike, lush, green islands.

From the size of the harbor and the number of boats, it's obvious that fishing is the main industry of this town of 5,000 people, 700 or so of whom are native Aleuts, mixed with Russians and Scandinavians. The fishing boats and hardy crews brave the stormy Gulf of Alaska and the moody Aleutian Islands.

Kodiak was the greatest loser in the 1964 earthquake, when seventy people died. The tidal waves that followed swept away the whole business district, tossing big fish boats from their moorings and far inland.

Now a rebuilt downtown with fine shopping mall and the boat harbor attract tourists and photographers. The waterfront, lined with marine suppliers and other fish-oriented businesses, plus the assorted fishboat traffic, keeps them snapping. For atmosphere, stop in and bend an elbow at the dock-side B & B Bar. It stands for Beer and Booze, and the place is a popular fisherman's hangout.

Besides fish and its Russian-American background, Kodiak claims two giants, one on land, the other in the sea. The Kodiak brown bear, weighing up to 1,200 pounds is the largest carnivore on earth and is a prized hunter's trophy. King crab may spread 4 feet or more, pincher to pincher. You can meet up with this sea monster in one of 15 seafood processing plants, or at lunch or dinner along with other seasonal Kodiak specialties: shrimp, halibut, salmon, and tasty local scallops.

If you want to pursue a Brownie, or other game animals for

trophies or photos, allow time to arrange for an expert guide. Bear harvesting and hunting areas are closely regulated for preservation. Otherwise, if you want to bear watch or take photos, charter planes fly to salmon streams where bears gather to fatten up on fish. Other flightseeing tours take tourists over Afognak and Raspberry Islands where elk graze, and around the Barren Islands, home of seals and sea lions.

Every August, Kodiak puts on Frank Brink's "Cry of the Wild Ram" at the Frank Brink Amphitheater at Monashka Bay. Out-of-doors, rain or shine, the historic drama about Baranof goes on, so dress for the occasion accordingly.

Celebrations come often in this lusty fishing town. Notable ones are the three-day early May King Crab Festival with crab races, St. Herman's Day, on August 9, the Jaycee Labor Day Rodeo, and September's facetious Great Buskin River Raft Race. Five beer (or juice) breaks are written into the rules.

PRACTICAL INFORMATION FOR SOUTH CENTRAL

AND INTERIOR ALASKA

Note: All Practical Information for these areas is contained in the Practical Information for the Rest of Alaska section, following the next chapter, "The Fringes of Alaska."

THE FRINGES OF ALASKA

Nome, the Arctic Circle, and More

Even though a "bush" airline advertises "Fly the Arctic before it's paved" and "See the Arctic Circle before it's a traffic circle," no public roads lead to the fringe areas in far northern and far western Alaska. To rub noses with Eskimos, you'll have to fly. But the end of the road does not signal the end of adventure. Planes head far north and west out of gateway cities. Some fly to the Bering Sea Pribilof Islands, headquarters for guided seal and birdwatching tours and superb nature photography. Some fly out the Alaska Peninsula to the Katmai National Monument. Here fishing and nature-watching are the main course with Baked Alaska for dessert. A highlight of the Monument is the eerie, seared, moonscape-like area called the Valley of Ten Thousand Smokes. Other package tours from Anchorage and Fairbanks make large flying circuits across that intangible Arctic Circle. These modern Arctic expeditions combine facets of gold rush, Eskimo and Russian heritage, and the North Slope oil fields.

Practically speaking, it's best to take a package tour. They come in sizes from a day to several, and they are priced accordingly.

Generally, the pre-paid and thus non-inflatable (for duration of your trip) package tour prices cover the many air miles round trip to the Arctic destination, airport transfers, hotel, and services of an in residence "expedition leader," perhaps a Native. A good tour guide can be a valuable catalyst as he interprets the unusual environment, scrupulously delivers all promised tour features, issues warm parkas for outdoor activities, if needed, and orientates his charges to the essential establishments: hotels, restaurants, shops, churches, and bars, if any. Some communities are dry, or vote liquor in or out depending on whether such revenue is currently needed.

Meals are not included, and the price may seem high. Eating can add $25 to $30 a day; more, if you research the local bars also. The source of supply is far away, and freighting is expensive, whether by air year round, or during the summer months when the Arctic seas are liquid and barges bring in some of the year's supplies. But eating can be an interesting experience. In the past, the brave could sample muktuk, whale skin with some blubber still attached, or even order a whale steak. With conservation concerns and hunting quotas, the Eskimos may not be able to spare any. However, the menu may feature other Arctic delicacies such as reindeer steak, salmon, or shee fish in season.

The main tour destinations, reached by jet, are Nome, Kotzebue, Barrow, and Deadhorse at Prudhoe Bay. Smaller Eskimo villages, such as Gambell, Point Hope, Shishmaref, Savoonga, Selawik, Kiana, and Noatak, may be visited via smaller bush planes. It's possible to stay overnight by making arrangements ahead. Usually through local airline offices, if no other package tours are offered.

Flying north, the change in terrain is obvious soon after leaving Fairbanks. There are views of the multi-billion dollar pipeline, and the meandering Yukon River, as the last snowy mountain barrier gives way to the flat vast treeless plain, gently sloping north to the Arctic Ocean.

If it's your first trip, the first sight of an Arctic community is rather grim. The tiny weathered buildings are almost lost in the expanse of tundra, the vegetation that covers the permanently frozen ground. The top few inches melt and vegetate in summer, supporting flowers, berries, and other low-growing plants. It's also the home and feeding grounds for nesting birds and small Arctic animals, lemmings, parka squirrels, foxes, and larger ones, caribou and reindeer. The polar bears will be off on icepacks lurking in the distance off shore; rarely near settlements.

Waves constantly wash the shore, and it appears that a big one might easily inundate the roadway and houses stretched along the beach. At Point Hope, on a small peninsula jutting into the Chukchi Sea not far from the U.S.S.R.-U.S. International Boundary, erosion compelled the Eskimos to move their centuries-old whaling town inland. The site is a favorite dig for archaeologists. They have found evidence of Eskimo culture and habitation going back some 4,000 years. The uprooting hasn't been easy. It is hoped visitors will continue to be welcome to attend the happy whaling festivals held after each successful season, and that some of the intriguing facets of old Point Hope will be saved.

For example, the graveyard, with its fence made of giant whalebones, is the town's landmark, and very photogenic. A sod, whalebone and driftwood home should also be preserved as an outdoor-indoor museum-piece. These time-mellowed dwellings are an amazing adaptation to the harsh environment. Even when lighted and heated only by seal oil lamps, they are surprisingly cozy and comfortable inside.

Kotzebue, Barrow, and Nome

Both Kotzebue and Barrow are above the Arctic Circle. Kotzebue, about 30 miles north of it, was established as a reindeer station and permanent trading post about 1897. The area was influenced by "outsiders" long before that, however, including Baron von Kotzebue exploring for Russia. He sailed into the sound off the Arctic Ocean in the first part of the 19th century. Some souvenirs his party left behind include blue Russian trading beads on display in the Ootukahkuktuvik ("place for having old things") museum and some Eskimos with Russian names.

Barrow's unique location has always attracted visitors, too: explorers, adventurers, and Arctic researchers. During World War II, its strategic position made it a key point in the Defense Early Warning System (DEW Line). The adaptable, durable Eskimos, naturally best fitted for Arctic survival, played important roles in all the activity. Barrow is now gearing up for more development activity at Pet 4, the nearby Naval Petroleum Reserve.

The Arctic has been changing, no doubt about it, and the natives welcome the addition of creature comforts: utilities, medical facilities, shopping malls, schools, and communication systems. Yet many are reluctant to forego the ways of the past. Tourism seems to be an industry that they can live with—even develop—with enthusiasm. Native corporations have been investing capital from land claims settlements in new modern hotels with all the comforts they think visitors want. And most of the residents are willing to share aspects of their fascinating way of life, past and present.

You'll visit with Eskimos in Nome, too, though Nome was a white man's town in the beginning. The King Island Eskimos who lived on a rocky island in the Bering Sea had been coming to the area for centuries to pick berries, and to fish in summer. After gold-rush Nome was established at the turn of the century, the King Islanders continued to make the 13-hour trip from the island. They paddled large oomiaks (skin boats) filled with families and supplies, prepared to camp under their oomiaks on the beach. In 1959, when the BIA school was closed, they moved to Nome permanently and settled in frame houses.

Many of these Eskimos still go back to hunt, and to check on their homes in the old ghost town clinging to the cliffs of King Island. Flightseeing trips often swing by for a look. The natives have continued their excellent ivory carving, and a dance group—tots to senior citizens—entertains with age-old story-telling dances and songs.

Gold rush memorabilia are all over Nome. Tour groups get a short course in gold rush history in the audio visual "Story of the Gold Rush," a blend of old pictures and narration. Then they strike out to see what's left. This includes gold fields still with giant dredges sitting in their private lakes and surrounded by piles of rocky tailings. Some are working now, because of profits made possible by the higher price of gold. Gold fever proves contagious when visitors practice panning at a small private operation on the tour agenda. What you pan you have to give back, but they'll give you a tiny free sample in a vial for a souvenir. If you get the hang of it, then try gold panning along Nome's famous beach, where anyone can pan and keep it, just like in the old days.

Nome's night life is notorious, naturally, because of its gaudy, lusty reputation in the past, and there are a number of bars willing to help prove it. However, the most sensational night show takes place above the Arctic Circle, starring the midnight sun.

For 36 days in summer, the sun doesn't drop below the horizon in Kotzebue. In Barrow it stays on stage for 82. Photographers snuggle down in their warm, colorful, borrowed parkas and shoot away. Sometimes all night. By fixing your camera in one spot (on a tripod is best) and shooting at 15-minute intervals, you can catch multiple exposures on the same film, as the sun arcs from east to west, without touching down in midsummer.

No two Arctic tours will be exactly alike, but you'll see the most of whichever place you choose to stop overnight. In all the towns, you'll be exposed to things Eskimo, from entertainment (dancing and games) to watching them go about their summer work of garnering food for winter. With almost 24 hours of light there is activity round-the-clock as they mend nets, fish, bring in seal and beluga, a small white whale, which they butcher on the beach.

In each town there are good shopping possibilities. You'll find typical and beautiful hand-crafted items in the stores, or perhaps make your purchase directly from the artist. After the dances, they spread out their wares.

Some towns boast of specialties. Kotzebue, for example, has *a* tree, referred to as the "Kotzebue National Forest." Several years ago, some tree-hungry fellows at the nearby Air Force Station brought in the lone spruce, planted it, nourished it, and coaxed it to grow.

Not to be outdone, Barrow brags about having the purest air in the world, give or take some whiffs agreeable to Eskimo noses but a bit ripe for cheechakos (newcomers). The adjacent Naval Arctic Research Laboratory backs up the claim. It's noted for Ice Island exploits, oil exploration and experiments in Arctic living. They say that dust and pollutants caused by vehicles, fires, etc., are soon whisked away by brisk Arctic breezes.

Prudhoe Bay

In each place there are unusual museums to browse through, with displays you aren't likely to see elsewhere. Deadhorse, the "town" for the Prudhoe Bay area, might well be preserved as a huge museum complex, for now and future generations. The costly, much-publicized Arctic oil and gas project is complex and varied. Overnight tours there explore activity on the tundra from oil pipes to sandpipers. Among the birds, wildflowers, summer-migrating caribou, and abundant ground squirrels, the guide will show you Prudhoe's forest, too, a stand of mature willow trees that grows only to seedling height on the edge of the Arctic Ocean.

The field tour surveys the scene: wells, stations, and oil company living complexes, small cities in themselves. The guide is prepared to explain things you may have read about, including the multi-million dollar research programs for preserving the ecology, and special tundra vehicles called Rolligons. Their great weight is distributed so that it scarcely makes a dint as it passes over the delicate terrain.

When to go? Most people visit in summer, but you can sample the Arctic in winter, too. Winter tours are based in Nome from February to the middle of May, with appropriate activities such as dog sledding and fishing through the ice. Early Arctic visitors, taking advantage of thrift season tour prices, may encounter the "break-up" of shore ice as the scene shifts from winter to a fleeting spring, then into summer.

We've barely touched on the magnificence and stark beauty of the Arctic, and the lifestyle of its fascinating, durable residents. Still with one mukluk in the past, they appear to be looking forward to a prosperous future. Go visit as soon as you can.

The Katmai

The Katmai National Monument is a wild, remote landscape on the Alaska Peninsula, bordering Shelikof Strait across from Kodiak Island.

Moose and almost 30 other species of animals, including foxes, lynx, and wolves, share the scene with bears fishing for salmon from stream banks, or standing in the water. Ducks are common; so are whistling swans, loons, grebes, gulls, and shore birds. Bald eagles can be seen perched on rocky pinnacles by the sea. Altogether, more than 40 species of songbirds alone can be seen during the short spring and summer season. Marine life abounds in the coastal area, with the Steller sea lion and hair seal often observed on rock outcroppings.

Compared with roads and facilities at Mt. McKinley National Park, it is quite primitive, but therein lies its charm.

Valley of Ten Thousand Smokes

Visitors have been coming to Alaska's Katmai area for over 4,000 years, except for a four-year lull. For centuries, the original Native, Eskimos and Aleuts, used to summer here, attracted by plentiful fish and game that they used for stocking up their winter larders.

On the morning of June 1, 1912, a green valley, more than 40 miles square, lazed below a mountain called Novarupta. Then the earth quaked, and for five days the violent tremors continued. On June 6, the quakes subsided, and the green valley breathed peacefully again. But a few hours later rivers of white-hot ash were pouring over the valley. A foot of ash fell on Kodiak, 100 miles away. Winds carried the ash to eastern Canada and Texas.

While Novarupta was belching forth pumice and scorching ash, another explosion took place six miles east. The peak of Mt. Katmai collapsed; where there had been a mountain top there was suddenly a chasm almost three miles long and two miles wide. Simply put, the molten andesite that held up Mt. Katmai had rushed through newly created fissures to Novarupta and been spewn out. Sixty hours after the first thunderous blast from Novarupta, the great eruptions were over. More than seven cubic miles of volcanic material had been ejected; the green valley lay 700 feet under ash. Though no one was killed, the Natives fled from Katmai, Savanoski, and other villages.

By 1916, things had cooled. A National Geographic Expedition, led by Dr. Robert F. Griggs, reached the valley. It seemed full of steaming fumaroles. What they reported inspired Congress to set it and the surrounding wilderness aside as a National Monument in 1918. At first sight, Dr. Griggs came up with an apt name, Valley of Ten Thousand Smokes.

The Natives never came back, but they have been replaced by sightseers, fishermen, hikers, and outdoor enthusiasts, who migrate here in summer, attracted by the fish and wildlife, and by the volcano-sculpted Valley of Ten Thousand Smokes (which have now cooled down to only a few, after 68 years). No roads lead to the Monument, at the base of the volcano-studded Alaska Peninsula, 290 miles southwest of Anchorage. Getting there is an all-Alaskan wilderness fly-in experience, and Wien Air Alaska includes it on their Southwestern triangle tours.

From Anchorage, Wien jets wing along Cook Inlet, rimmed by lofty snowy peaks of the Alaska Range. They land at King Salmon, near fish-famous Bristol Bay, where passengers transfer to a smaller plane, at home both on land and water, for the next hop. In twenty minutes, the amphibian plane splashes down in Naknek Lake, in front of the Monument Headquarters, next to Brooks River Lodge. A motorboat lassos the plane, tows it to shore, and then everyone walks a plank from plane hatch to the beach.

From Brooks Lodge, a daily tour bus with a naturalist aboard may still drive the 23 miles through the Monument to the Valley Overlook, where those who wish can hike the easy one-and-a-half-mile trail for a close-up look at the pumice-covered valley floor. The depth of the sand flow is evident where the rushing Ukak River has cut a deep channel, leaving a sheer cliff of pinkish layered residue, called volcanic "tuff." Cross sections are 200 to 300 feet high.

However, if this tour has been discontinued, people can—and do—

travel in the Monument and through the Valley in the style of the early-day visitors, on foot and with backpacks. There's a campground at Brooks River, and the Ranger Station dispenses regulations and advice. But there are easier ways, a flightseeing tour with Katmai Air Services, for example. From the air, early trade and hunting trails show up, and deserted Native villages. In season, roaming moose and brown bear are spotted. Jade-green lakes now fill some old volcano craters, and the sulphur smell of some "smokes," still sending up signals in the Valley, wafts into the plane.

Brooks River and Naknek Lake are hot spots for fly fishing. In fact, the trophy rainbow fishing is so fantastic, only artificial lures and single hooks are permitted. Fish-watching is another popular sport. A short walk up river to Brooks Falls, salmon are easily seen and photographed as they leap the eight-foot barrier in their compulsive, epic struggle to reach their native grounds during the spawning season.

Besides Brooks Lodge, Wien Air Alaska has other fly-in camps and lodges in their "Angler's Paradise." Outdoor-minded families can headquarter there and satisfy assorted interests. From Grosvenor Lake and Kulik Lodge on Nonvianuk Lake, the avid fishermen can fly off with a pilot/guide to fish for Arctic Char and Grayling, Northern Pike, and Rainbow Trout that reach trophy size, feeding on the abundant natural food in myriad lakes and streams. Nonfishers can take float trips, boat trips, hike, rockhound, plus observe and photograph birds and wildlife, hard-working beaver to bears, who are also avid fishermen. They say if the fisher appears extra big, shaggy, and has four legs, use caution and common sense, and allow plenty of elbow room. Usually there's no problem. Accommodations are mostly shared cabins, but with hot and cold water, private bathroom with shower, heat, and lights. Anywhere it's otherwise, they'll tell you what to expect.

Beyond the Katmai and the Alaska Peninsula lie the farthest reaches of Alaska. The treeless, semivolcanic Aleutian Island chain stretches more than a thousand miles and separates the North Pacific Ocean from the Bering Sea.

With the exception of U.S. Naval bases, the settlements are quite small, the largest being close to the several airports on "The Chain." The hardy Aleuts are expert at commercial fishing or work in canneries, and as guides for hunters and fishermen.

In the Bering Sea, some 200 miles northwest of Cold Bay are the Pribilof Islands, misty, fog-bound breeding grounds of fur seals, protected now from the rapacity of large-scale hunters by international treaty. At one time they were near extinction. In May the mating seals come home from far Pacific waters, and the islands see scenes of frenzied activity. When a thousand bulls scold at the top of their lungs or roar jealously, the sounds roll out several miles to sea.

Tours fly to St. Paul, largest of the Pribilofs, but for the most part, these outposts, almost in tomorrow in time and next door to Siberia in space, are visited (by air and sometimes by sea) by those who have business there, or by persistent, inveterate travelers addicted to way-out destinations.

This, then, is Alaska, a state catapulting out of the past. In two or three decades some say it will be far tamer, less awesome, more comfortable and some of it preserved only in storybooks. Meanwhile, the annual number of visitors just about balances the overall population, a little over 400,000. And the hospitable residents appear pleased to share with kindred souls wherever they meet them, in the cities and towns or in the "bush."

PRACTICAL INFORMATION FOR THE REST OF ALASKA

Note: Practical Information for southeastern Alaska follows the chapter on southeastern Alaska, earlier in this book, and there is also a separate chapter on Anchorage, with its own Practical Information section.

HOW TO GET THERE. *By air:* Scheduled airlines fly direct and from gateway cities in the Lower 48 states, Hawaii and Canada: Alaska Airlines, Northwest Orient Airlines, Western Airlines and Wien Air Alaska. The deregulation of air travel is causing changes in who flies where. In spite of higher fuel costs and other inflationary reasons, more competition encourages air-fare bargains. Watch newspaper ads and ask your travel agent about discounts, coupons, and other "supersavers." For up-to-date flight information, how to get to gateway cities, and fares, contact a travel agent or the nearest local airline office. Air France, British Airways, Japan Air Lines, Lufthansa, Korean Airlines, KLM Royal Dutch Airlines, Sabena Belgian World Airlines, SAS (Scandinavian Airlines System), and Northwest en route from Japan, touch down in Anchorage on their international flights, with stop-over privileges.

By highway: By car, camper, trailer, or motorcoach, the Alaska Highway is a real wilderness-road adventure. It stretches 1,529 miles from Dawson Creek, British Columbia, to Fairbanks, Alaska. The various access routes necessary in order to reach Mile 0 at Dawson Creek will easily add another thousand miles. Allow at least three weeks for a round trip. Some 900 miles through Yukon Territory are good, wide graded gravel—up to the Alaska border, where the paving starts.

The Alaska Highway is kept open the year-round, but the most popular driving season is from May through September. The alternate to driving the whole distance is to connect with the Southeastern Alaska Marine Highway System at ferry ports Prince Rupert, B.C. and at Haines and Skagway in Alaska.

By bus: Alaska Yukon Motorcoaches (TravAlaska Tours), Suite 555, 4th & Battery Bldg., Seattle, WA 98121. Scheduled weekly service between Seattle and Alaska via Prince Rupert and the Alaska Marine Highway System. In Canada, *Coachways System,* 125 5th Ave. S.W., Calgary, AB. Connects Edmonton, AB and Prince George, BC to Whitehorse, YT., then on to Fairbanks via *Alaska Coachways,* 208 Wendall St., Fairbanks, AK 99701. *Greyhound Canada* serves southern cities from Vancouver, BC to Prince George and Edmonton. Or take the motorcoach tour route: *Alaska Green Carpet Escorted Tours,* 345 N.E. 8th Ave., Portland, OR leave from Seattle and Vancouver, B.C. *Greyhound World Tours,* Greyhound Tower, Phoenix, AZ 85077 offer 21- and 22-day escorted expeditions from Vancouver, BC, Seattle, and also from some eastern cities. *Hyway Holidays* (Westours), 100 West Harrison Plaza, Seattle, WA 98119 go north to Alaska from Seattle via the Canadian Rockies and an Inside Passage cruise.

By water: Ferry: The ferries of the Southeast System of the *Alaska Marine Highway* broke the isolation of the Inside Passage towns in 1963. They connect Seattle and/or Prince Rupert with southeast Alaska ports. The main ones are Haines, Juneau, Ketchikan, Petersburg, Skagway, Sitka and Wrangell.

Largest of the ferry fleet is the *MV Columbia,* which carries 1,000 passengers, 184 vehicles, and has 96 staterooms. The *Malaspina, Matanuska,* and *Taku,* also named for big Alaskan glaciers, are not much smaller. They are luxury liners, with fine dining rooms, cafeteria, snack bars, and cocktail lounges. Reserve staterooms. Otherwise it is acceptable to sleep in a reclining deck chair between ferry ports, or roll out on deck in a sleeping bag. Public washrooms with showers are available.

Whether you travel on foot, or by car or camper, motor bike or bicycle, the Inside Passage is a popular and scenic alternate route to driving the whole distance on the Alaska Highway. Passenger and vehicle fares are rated on a through basis, with no charge for stopovers. Foot passengers simply get a stopover from the purser. Vehicle space has to be reserved ahead, when you buy your ticket. Cabin fare is port-to-port for one continuous trip. Meals are not included. The fare structure is complex, covering varisized vehicles between many points. The schedule is also involved, and departures sometimes depend on the right time and tide. Distances are figured in hours of running time, rather than miles. Seattle to Skagway is about a thousand miles, or about 60 hours, if all goes well. It's about 6 hours Ketchikan to Wrangell, the next port, and 3 to Petersburg, beyond. It takes only an hour from Haines to Skagway. Write to *Alaska Marine Highway,* Division of Marine Transportation, Pouch R, Juneau, AK 99811; phone (907) 465–3941 or 465–3940.

Contact the *B.C. Ferry Corp.,* 818 Broughton St., Victoria, B.C., Canada V8W 1E4 about Canadian ferries operating between Vancouver Island, and Prince Rupert, B.C., Canada.

By cruise ship: Cruise ships plying the Inside Passage come in large sizes and are of assorted nationalities, often reflected in the service and cuisine: French, Italian, British, Norwegian, Dutch. Cruise-ship travel appeals to those who like their magnificent vistas served in comfort and luxury without the hassle of packing and unpacking. In Alaska, shipboard fun and games have stiff competition. Almost round-the-clock daylight in summer and southeast Alaska's marine and mountain grandeur encourage healthful deck sightseeing and photography. There are "shore leaves" in the towns—all different, but with typical Alaskan flavor—for exploring and shopping. Over a dozen different cruise ships sail from Vancouver, B.C., Canada; Los Angeles; and San Francisco. Most of the regulars plus some newcomers will have many sailings along this traditional "invasion" route to Alaska, used by Indians, explorers, fur traders, gold seekers, adventurers, and now tourists. Often the cruise is the "sea leg" of a tour that covers other sections of Alaska by assorted transportation on land and by air.

Incidentally, today's Alaska cruises are another example of "history repeating itself." Cruises were advertised in the '90s, boasting the latest convenience—electric lights in the staterooms! Here are some main ships likely to be sailing to Alaska, in summer, and addresses you can write to for information: S.S. *Statendam, Cunard Princess*—Westours, Inc., 300 Elliott Ave., Seattle, WA 98119. S.S. *Rotterdam,* Holland America Cruises, Two Pennsylvania Plaza, New York, N.Y. 10001. *Island Princess, Sun Princess*—Princess Tours, Suite 1800, Fourth & Blanchard Bldg., Seattle, WA 98121. *Pacific Princess*—Princess Cruises, 2029 Century Park East, Los Angeles, CA 90067. *Fairsea*—Sitmar Cruises, 10100 Santa Monica Blvd., Los Angeles, CA 90067. *Royal Viking Star*—Royal Viking Lines, One Embarcadero Center, San Francisco, CA 94111. S.S. *Vera Cruz*—Strand Cruises, Ste. 611, 470 Granville St., Vancouver, BC V6C1V5, Canada. S.S. *Universe*—World Explorer Cruises, P.O. Box 2428, Laguna Hills, CA 92653. *Princess Patricia*—C.P. Rail Alaska Cruises, B.C. Coast Steamship Service, Pier B, Vancouver, B.C., V6C2R3, Canada. M.V. *Odessa*—March Shipping Passenger Service, One World Trade Center, Suite 5257, New York, NY 10048.

HOW TO GET AROUND. *By air:* Because of its vast size and modest highway system, Alaska has long relied heavily on air transportation. The state has the world's highest ratio of licensed pilots. There are more than 150 air-taxi and contract-carrier lines operating in the state, including these of the famed bush pilots, who offer dependable transportation to isolated points. More than a dozen carriers operate within the state, linking all the principal cities and towns by air.

By car: Highways cover about a fifth of the state in the southcentral to interior sections, from the Kenai Peninsula to Fairbanks and to the Yukon Territory. The Alaska, Richardson, Glenn, Seward-Anchorage, Sterling and

Haines highways are all paved, the latter except for the Canadian portion. Many of the feeder roads near Alaska's larger cities are also paved. Maintenance is difficult due to annual freezing and thawing and pavement may be rough in spots. Take it easy and allow more time for Alaskan miles.

Despite its generally good condition special precautions and preparations are needed for an Alaska Highway journey. A mile-by-mile guide such as *The Milepost* (see Recommended Reading) will answer most questions about the pleasures and perils. In the unpaved portion the roadbed can vary from mud to blinding dust. Delays are inevitable due to constant road maintenance efforts while crews repair and upgrade sections during the long light days of summer. Flying gravel is probably the worst problem. Some suggested protections are clear plastic headlight covers, a bug and gravel screen for radiators, and a rubber mat under gas tanks. Start out with vehicle, including tires, in top condition. Foremost among winter driving precautions is knowing how to drive under severe, possibly hazardous and unpredictable winter conditions.

For winter driving cars require antifreeze and proper-weight oil and grease. Heavy clothing and sleeping bags should be carried for use until help arrives in case of mechanical breakdown.

Car rental: Cars are available from most main firms—*Avis, Hertz, National*—almost anywhere. Reserve in advance during peak travel months July and August. Gas and oil are extra; license regulations are the same as everywhere else. It's possible to rent one place and drop off another by arranging ahead. Check for car rental offices at airports and in the local directories, or through local office in your area. R-V's: *Number One Motorhome Rentals of Alaska,* 322 Concrete, Anchorage. AK 99501 and others collaborate with airlines on fly/drive packages. *Alaska Tour and Marketing* has developed a Fly/Drive program among their "Best of Alaska" destinations. Assorted length itineraries include highlights such as McKinley Park, the new Skagway to Carcross Highway, and a flight to Glacier Bay with an up-Bay cruise. The price doesn't include meals, but does offer other good things: an ATMS Bonus Book for discounts or special services en route, a helpful planning kit with guides, maps, etc. Write for details and price ranges to *ATMS,* Suite 312, Park Place Bldg., Seattle, WA 98101, or inquire in Anchorage at the Alaska Tour Center, 838 W. 4th Ave.

By bus: *Alaska-Yukon Motorcoaches, Coachways Systems, Greyhound,* and tour companies give inter-Alaska service. Within Alaska scheduled service: *Mar-Air Bus Company,* Box 422, Haines, AK 99827. Connects with ferry, and runs between Haines-Haines Junction, Whitehorse, and Fairbanks. Also has local sightseeing tours in this very beautiful part of southeastern Alaska. In season, tours include Bald Eagles and their nesting grounds, and migrating salmon. *Transportation Services, Inc.,* 1040 East 1st Ave., Anchorage, AK 99501. They serve Anchorage to Seward, Homer, Valdez, and points between. Also main stops, including Mt. McKinley National Park, between Anchorage and Fairbanks. In winter they have daily round trips to ski area Mt. Alyeska, and year-round offer group charter service.

By rail: The narrow-gauge *White Pass & Yukon Route* offers 110 miles of spectacular scenery between Skagway, Alaska, and Whitehorse, Yukon Territory, a major city on the Alaska Highway. This interesting railroad follows the route of gold prospectors on their Trail of '98. The cost of the trip includes a luncheon at Lake Bennett, British Columbia, where the train changes crews. Passengers may travel either from Skagway to Whitehorse, or the other way around. It is hoped that the new highway access will not effect any great changes in this route, and that sightseeing excursions to the summit and back, and also the "package plan" for travelers who want to ship their car or camper truck from Skagway to Whitehorse (or vice versa) over this historic route, instead of driving the summer-only dirt highway, will be continued. For current prices, schedules and other details in advance, write White Pass & Yukon Route, P.O. Box 2147, Seattle, WA 98111.

The Alaska Railroad, operated by the Federal Railroad Administration of the U.S. Department of Transportation, provides passenger and freight service between Anchorage and Fairbanks. Daily, May to Sept. For winter schedule and more information write The Alaska Railroad, Pouch 7–2111, Anchorage, AK 99510.

For a small charge added to the through fare, passengers may stop over in Mount McKinley National Park while en route to Anchorage or Fairbanks. A spur running between Portage (near Anchorage) and seaport Whittier carries passengers and vehicles. Food and beverage service is available in the dining car.

By ferry: Besides the 4 large ferries serving southeast Alaska, there are three smaller ones that connect with smaller ports with intriguing names: Metlakatla, Hollis, Hoonah, Angoon, and Pelican. The *LeConte, Chilkat,* and new *Aurora* ferries have no staterooms, but do have cafeterias and snack and liquor bars.

The Southcentral System of the State Ferries does not connect with the Southeast System. Two ferries connect ports on Cook Inlet and Prince William Sound. The *Bartlett,* named for a revered Alaskan senator, covers Prince William Sound from Valdez to Cordova and Whittier, where passengers and cars are portaged by rail through a mountain tunnel to connect with the Anchorage-Seward and Sterling highways leading down to Kenai Peninsula, or along Cook Inlet to Anchorage. The *Tustumena,* another glacier namesake, links Gulf of Alaska and Kenai Peninsula towns: Seward, Homer, Seldovia, and island towns Port Lions and Kodiak.

Other means of transportation: In the right season, visitors can take short turns aboard dog sleds, though there are few around, now that they've been displaced by snowmobiles, which are also popular with tourists. Also, rafting, canoeing, riding, hiking and pack trips are offered in summer.

 TOURIST INFORMATION SERVICES. "AVA" and "DOT" are excellent information sources, and also travel agents in and out of Alaska. The *Alaska Visitors Association,* P.O. Box 2220, Anchorage, AK 99510

operates a clearing house of its membership's information pieces, which they'll dispense in answer to specific area and activity requests. Write the *Alaska Division of Tourism,* Pouch E, Juneau, AK 99811. Ask for their official travel book *Discover the Worlds of Alaska.* Almost every community in Alaska has a tourist contact center. The Chamber of Commerce in the towns you wish to visit will supply information regarding hotel, motel, and lodge accommodations. DOT has ben branching out: The Alaska State Asian office is at 1-40, 4-Chome, Toranomon, Minato-Ku, Tokyo 105, Japan. European Office: Vesterborgade 16, DK-1620 Copenhagen V, Denmark. For Austria, Germany & Switzerland it's *Tourplan Marketing,* Marcusallee 49, D-2800 Bremen, West Germany. In Anchorage stop by Anchorage International Airport *Visitor Information Center,* Baggage Claim Area, Main Terminal, and the *Tourist Information Log Cabin* at 4th & F. In Fairbanks, at the Chamber of Commerce *Log Cabin* on the bank of the Chena River Slough by the Alaska Highway sign, First & Cushman. Alaska Highway travelers may stop for information and free coffee at the Tok Chamber of Commerce hospitality center, Mile 1314, open 8 A.M. until midnight in summer, every day.

For information on touring and ferry service, contact the *Alaska Marine Highway System,* Div. of Marine Transportation, Pouch R, Juneau, AK 99811. Phone (907) 465-3941. Ferry and general information also at the State Center, Pier 48, Seattle, Washington 98104. Phone (206) 623-1970.

For information on hunting and fishing regulations, write the *Dept. of Fish & Game,* Subport, Juneau, AK 99811.

The Superintendent, *Katmai National Monument,* Box 7, King Salmon, AK, 99613, or National Park Service, 334 W. Fifth Ave., Anchorage, AK 99501, supplies information on private touring of the monument, including kayaking, canoeing, and backpacking.

For information on Chugach and Tongass National Forests, and reserving a $5 Forest Service Cabin, write to the Regional Forester of each, at Federal Office Building, Box 1628, Juneau, AK 99801.

For camping and recreational opportunities on Alaska's National Resource Lands and reservations for three public-use cabins (all in the Fairbanks area) contact the State Director, Alaska State Office, *Bureau of Land Management,* 555 Cordova St., Anchorage, AK 99501.

Some other aspects a visitor might want to know something about include oil and gas: *Alaska State Division of Oil & Gas,* 3001 Porcupine Drive, Anchorage, AK 99504. Mining: *Alaska State Division of Geological Survey* (same address as above); and *Mines Information Office,* Pouch M, Juneau, AK 99811. Agricultural information is dispensed by the *Cooperative Extension Service,* University of Alaska, Fairbanks, AK 99701, and the *Alaska State Division of Agriculture,* Box 800, Palmer, AK 99645. To learn about the business climate and job possibilities consult the *Alaska Department of Commerce & Economic Development,* Division of Economic Enterprise, Pouch E.E., Juneau, AK 99811; the *Alaska State Chamber of Commerce,* 208 NBA Bldg., Juneau, AK 99801; and if you are really serious about job opportunities, check with the *Alaska State Employment Service,* Box 3-7000, Juneau, AK 99811.

Department of Tourism & Information, Box 2703, Whitehorse, Yukon Territory, Canada.

SEASONAL EVENTS. Alaskans are prone to celebrations year-round, and for almost any reason, iceworms to whales. Visitors are always welcome to join in. In the summer season, roughly May through September, you can count on being entertained by assorted continuous community "specials"; Native dancing; dramas and melodramas, and salmon derbies galore in southeast Alaska.

All summer in Arctic towns Kotzebue and Barrow, and in Nome in western Alaska, Eskimos perform age-old, story-telling dances in parka and mukluks for visiting tour groups, and for fun. Near Haines, at Port Chilkoot, home of Alaska Indian Arts, Inc., the Chilkoot Indian Dancers put on a fine show, in authentic costumes they have made in the freewheeling "school." Ketchikan romps through the melodrama "Fish Pirate's Daughter" at the Frontier Saloon. Juneau's historical spoof is "Delilah's Dilemma," following a salmon bake near the entrance to the old Alaska-Juneau Gold Mine.

Here are a few annual, typically Alaskan events for starters. (For many more events and festivals and exact dates, write the area Chamber of Commerce, or consult the Alaska Travel Index section of the state's Worlds of Alaska booklet for their current listing of what's going on.)

January: In its landmark old Russian Orthodox church overlooking an arm of Kachemak Bay on Southwestern Kenai Peninsula, *Seldovia* leads off with a Russian New Year celebration. *Tok* is the major highway regrouping point after entering Alaska, and also is noted as the "Dog Capital." They rev up and rally at the Dog Musher Association grounds and track, continuing into February. When the races are over elsewhere, Tok holds the convivial "Race of Champions," open to all who want to compete on their 20-mile racing trail.

February: To banish winter doldrums, *Cordova* holds its Iceworm Festival complete with a 100-foot iceworm winding through the streets. *Homer* holds a Winter Carnival, and plays a baseball game on snowshoes during the first weekend in February. *Kenai* needs at least ten days for its Winter Carnival and Petroleum-150, a 150-mile snow machine race that begins and ends at the Kenai Mall. The largest winter celebration is in *Anchorage*. The Fur Rendezvous features World Championship Sled Dog Races, sportscar races (on ice), and a Miners and Trappers Ball.

March: Racing continues. *Fairbanks* holds more Championship Sled Dog Races. *Nome* sponsors the 1000-mile Iditarod Sled Dog Race. This one takes time and stamina. Racing buffs gather in Nome and wait convivially in bars along the Front Street finish line, for as long as it takes for the teams to mush in—sometimes up to a month. Also: the 200-mile Nome-Golovin Snowmobile Race.

April: A Walrus Carnival at *Savoonga*, on St. Lawrence Island off the Bering Sea Coast, celebrates the end of the season for hunting the ivory-tusked marine mammals.

May: Highlight is *Petersburg's* "Little Norway" Festival, celebrating the first halibut landings and Norwegian Independence Day, May 17.

June: The Midsummer and Midnight Sun Festivals (June 21): *Nome* has a raft race down the Nome River, starting at midnight; *Fairbanks* "Gold

Panners" play a Midnight Sun Baseball Game, at midnight, without artificial lights; Anchorage holds a 2-week Festival of Music, and an Alaska Festival of Native Arts at the Historical and Fine Arts Museum; Kodiak, a King Crab Festival; starting at Fairbanks, the Yukon "800" Marathon winds through a grueling, 3-river round-trip boat race; Palmer goes mad with its Midsummer Festival featuring Woronzoff Horse Show, papier mache "Grotto Lunkers," and Scottish Games. There are whaling festivals at Barrow and Point Hope.

July: The 4th is a bang-up celebration all over Alaska, that might well run into the 5th or 6th! Small towns are choice places to be, with clan get-togethers, and competitions for prizes: Alaska Logging Championships at Sitka; Loggers Rodeo, Ketchikan; horse races, Palmer; foot race up Mt. Marathon, Seward; and at Kotzebue, they give a prize for the biggest beluga (small white whale) brought in since break-up.

Fairbanks "Golden Days," which commemorates the discovery of gold at Fairbanks in 1902, is the biggest summer celebration; the World Eskimo, Indian, Aleut Olympics is probably the most unusual event. The natives play their old games that take strength and endurance—the ear pull, knuckle hop, and high kick—and also demonstrates skills like seal-skinning (a woman's contest, record time, 60 seconds); they also choose a Native Queen.

August–September: Gold Rush Days, at Valdez; Silver Salmon Derbies at Valdez and Seward. Fairs: Southeast Alaska at Haines; Tanana Valley Fair at Fairbanks; Alaska State Fair at Palmer; Buffalo Barbecue, Delta; Spectacular drama "Cry of the Wild Ram" based on Russian-Alaska history in Kodiak's outdoor amphitheatre; and Kodiak's Jaycee Rodeo and State Fair.

October: Alaska Day Festival (Oct. 18) at Sitka, where, in costume, they reenact the ceremony of transfer of Alaska from Russia to the United States. Oktoberfest in Kenai, as you can tell by the spelling, is the real German beer and pretzels: two nights devoted to good German food, dancing, and band music.

November–December: Alaskans are busy with typical Alaskan holiday celebrations. If you are there, join in.

 NATIONAL PARKS AND MONUMENTS. Decisions on how much land to preserve, how much to develop, and how to designate it are still being debated. It's expected that a satisfactory compromise will be reached eventually. It is proving difficult to decide what will remain "wilderness," the most restrictive classification.

There are 375 million acres in Alaska. When the territory became a state, it gained title to 103 million acres. So far the state has taken only 36 million of them, while 44 million acres went to Alaska Natives under the Settlement Act of 1971. A million acres are privately owned, and the federal government has kept the rest frozen. Now an Alaska Lands Bill is supposed to be passed that will resolve such questions as the location and size of areas to become national parks, forests, wilderness and wildlife refuges, and which might be preserves that can be developed and resources that can be used. Most members of the environmental movement, wherever they are, are totally at odds with Alaska industry—oil, mining, timber—that needs to develop in order to survive. Many Alaskans feel they alone should make decisions on their state, and that they are capable of judging how much land should remain pristine.

After an extension on a compromise bill failed in 1978, and time was running out on the federal freeze, Secretary of Interior Andrus acted under the Federal Lands Policy Management Act and withdrew 110 million acres of Alaskan land for three years. He withdrew 13 million more for two years after President Carter designated 56 million of the withdrawn acres as national monuments (seventeen of them), permanently preserved as wilderness under the Antiquities Act of 1906.

Since then proposals and recommendations have included a reduction in the number of total withdrawn acres, a redesignation of the 17 national monuments into new national parks and/or preserves, and an expansion of existing ones. The Secretary's threat that he may invoke the same section (d-2) of the Federal Lands Policy Management Act and keep the land withdrawn for twenty rather than three years, is pressuring legislators to produce and pass a more acceptable bill in Congress. Alaskans don't want more than 100 million acres of their state "locked up" until the next century.

Meanwhile, the wondrous landscapes of Alaska are appreciated and enjoyed by visitors, each in his own way. *McKinley National Park* is certainly one of the continent's outstanding wilderness areas, remote and unspoiled. This striking, scenic park is dominated by the highest peak in North America, 20,320-foot Mt. McKinley. This jagged, bulky mountain rises some 17,000 feet above the surrounding parkland and has two principal peaks. Most of the mountain is covered with ice and snow and provides a powerful spectacle from far away or at the closest approach, which is some 26 miles. The park straddles the Alaska Range southwest of Fairbanks, and it is surrounded on three sides by the new Denali National Monument. Although the mountain dominates the park, it should not overshadow other scenic and wildlife attractions for the visitor. A trip over the more-than-90-mile graveled McKinley Park Road is like a visit to a giant natural-history museum of mountain and tundra and wildlife.

The park can be reached by plane (a 3,000-foot airstrip is maintained for light aircraft); three times a week, by rail, from Anchorage or Fairbanks; by paved road, Alaska 3, from Anchorage or Fairbanks; and by the gravel, summer only Denali Highway, Alaska 8, a 135-mile road, of which some 20 miles leading from Paxson are paved. The road extends from Paxson, on Milepost 185.5 on the Richardson Highway, Alaska 4, to the village of Cantwell, located 1.8 miles beyond the junction of the Denali Highway with the Anchorage-Fairbanks Highway (George Parks Highway). Charter flights are available from Anchorage or Fairbanks. *Alaska-Yukon Motorcoaches* schedule daily bus service between Anchorage and Fairbanks via McKinley Park. There are also other special sightseeing motorcoach tours.

When the historic old part of the hotel inside the park burned, imagination was put to work. The concession was renamed Mt. McKinley Park Station Hotel, and near the entrance to the park you will also find Mt. McKinley Village, a motel, and McKinley Chalet.

An 8-hour Tundra Wildlife Tour, conducted daily by experienced driver-guides, carries tourists to Eielson Visitor Center, 65 miles west, and back. Fare includes a picnic lunch. Frequent stops are made to photograph flowers, birds, mountains, and animals, particularly grizzlies, caribou, Dall sheep, and moose.

On clear days, the north summit of Mt. McKinley, 19,470 feet, is visible 31 miles off, to the southwest. In the foreground is Muldrow Glacier, which drops from the mountain and spreads out over the valley floor.

There are several campgrounds within the park. Beyond Mile 14 at the Savage River Bridge, permits to drive private vehicles are issued only if you have a reservation for one of the 72 campsites available beyond. The motorist should bring a camp stove with plenty of fuel, as well as all the supplies he thinks he will need, the nearest store being many miles away. Free shuttle buses run often along the McKinley Park Road to serve the public. Check at Park Headquarters for schedules and current rules and regulations, or write to Superintendent, Mount McKinley National Park, Box 9, McKinley Park, AK 99755. Phone (907) 683-2294.

North Face Lodge is near Wonder Lake. Farther on is rustic Camp Denali, about 90 miles from park headquarters. Both are now surrounded by the new Denali National Monument (see Wilderness Lodges).

Glacier Bay National Monument is located about 40 miles northwest of Juneau, in the Fairweather Range of the towering St. Elias Mountains. It is the largest unit in the national park system, with 4,381 square miles. The scenery is some of Alaska's most spectacular—deep fjords, tidewater glaciers, jutting icebergs, and ice-capped mountains. The geologically inclined will be deeply impressed by the examples of early stages of postglacial and interglacial forests. Rare species of wildlife abound.

But the "hottest" attractions are those icy glaciers, grown bigger and better in Glacier Bay than anywhere else in the world. It's not that the ice in active glaciers is left over from ancient ice ages. Nor are they a sign of extreme cold climates. The ice is perhaps 200 or 300 years old, depending on how fast the glacier flows—usually a few feet a day. Though prehistoric animals have been found frozen intact in northern tundra, they would never survive the pressure and grinding motion of a glacier.

Glaciers form in areas with a long winter of temperatures generally below freezing and a lot of precipitation. On the coast, temperatures seldom get below zero, but moisture bearing winds and warm ocean currents bring 80–140 inches of rain in a year. A few thousand feet higher in the mountains, this moisture falls as snow. It accumulates to great depths and doesn't have a chance to melt completely during the short summer season. Then the snowfields on mountain slopes turn into moving rivers of ice. At Glacier Bay their downward journey terminates at tidewater, which makes the area a great laboratory for observing them. Everyone from kayak paddlers to passengers on large cruise ships include this ever-changing and fascinating bay in their Inside Passage itineraries.

There has been concern that increased ship traffic in Glacier Bay may be hampering the annual whale migration there. No one wants the whales to stop going there, and so the situation is being monitored. Scientists watch for signs that the whales are nervous, and then they try to reassure them by establishing non-conflicting travel corridors for the ships. The numbers and size of ships entering the Glacier Bay are also being regulated. Some are rerouted to other scenic areas nearby, such as Tracy Arm, a narrow fjord long cherished by boaters.

Glacier Bay is accessible only by plane or boat. From Juneau, *Alaska Airlines* has several flights daily to Gustavus Airport, a 7,500-foot runway, which will handle any private plane, including jets. It is located 10 mi. from Glacier Bay Lodge, with bus connections. Accommodations are available at Glacier Bay Lodge or Gustavus Inn, close to the monument. From the Lodge, the *Thunder Bay* makes daily excursions to the glaciers and the mini-cruise ship *Glacier Bay Explorer* takes tour groups to overnight at a glacier. From Juneau, the M/V *Glacier Seal* specializes in nature-oriented yacht/plane tours in the Bay.

There are no established campgrounds in the monument, but there are plenty of places to camp along the several hundred miles of coastline and on the many islands. Supplies should be obtained in Juneau. Bring appropriate rain gear.

Katmai National Monument is a 2,792,137-acre area on the Alaska Peninsula across from Kodiak Island. There is no highway access to the monument; it is accessible only by air or by charter boat. Katmai consists of over 4,200 square miles of ocean bays, fjords, and lagoons, backed by a range of glacier-covered peaks and volcanic crater lakes. Behind these lies an interior wilderness of forest, lake chains, and the Volcanic Valley of Ten Thousand Smokes. The monument was established in 1918, six years after one of the most violent volcanic eruptions in recorded history gave the valley its name. The monument is a meeting place for two life zones—the Hudsonian, with its spruce forest and dense red grass, and the Arctic, with short grasses and low-lying plants. Most prominent animal is the giant Alaska brown bear, largest land carnivore. Moose are also fairly common. Fish and waterfowl are abundant. Overnight sightseeing tours and first-class fishing accommodations are operated from June 1 through mid-Sept. by *Wien Air Alaska*, 4100 International Airport Road, Anchorage, AK 99502.

Klondike National Historical Park. Commemorating the turn of the century gold rush, this newly developing park extends from Pioneer Square in Seattle to Skagway and beyond, as it follows the route of the gold seekers. A section of downtown Skagway, and segments of the Chilkoot Trail and White Pass Trail are part of the park. Eventually, joined by Canada, the project will take in the route all the way to Dawson City, goal of the Klondike gold rush mob. Then the parks will become Klondike International Historical Park.

Sitka National Historical Park on Baranof Island near Sitka is known for its fine examples of totem poles along a totem-guarded lovers' lane. Most striking of the totems standing at the park's entrance is the towering Governor Brady or Sonny Hat pole. It is surrounded by Tlingit Wolf House posts. The poles were collected for display at the Louisiana Purchase Exposition at St. Louis in 1904 and the Lewis & Clark Centennial Exposition at Portland in 1905. They were then returned to Sitka and placed at the site of a last ditch battle, when the Russians defeated the Tlingit Indians in 1804. Nearby is the site of a Kiksadi Indian Village destroyed by the Russians. The new headquarters building and Indian Cultural Center include observation rooms for watching native craftsmen at work. Conducted tours during the summer.

 NATIONAL FORESTS. The state's two national forests, Chugach and Tongass, comprise a total of over 20 million acres, giving Alaska more national forest land than any other state. The perhaps 500 miles of maintained trails are fewer than elsewhere. Its primitive flavor is further conserved by fewer campgrounds (most still undeveloped) than in any of the western states. Most wilderness enthusiasts consider this adds to the overall experience. Hikers should contact the Forest Service Headquarters for information and maps that pinpoint campgrounds and outlying cabins available. Trips should be planned with great care, and with an awareness of possible hazards lurking far off the beaten paths.

The Russians found Eskimos living in the Prince William Sound area when they called there, descendants of those who had arrived thousands of years ago, according to evidence from archeological diggings. The Natives called themselves a name (picked up by the Russians) that has evolved to the present Chugach, pronounced Chew'gatch. "Tongass" came from the name of the Native Tlingit Indian clan living near the southern end of the forest.

Chugach and Tongass between them cover most of southeast Alaska and much of the coastal area of southcentral Alaska. They either border or are near most of the major coastal cities, offering a magnificent natural recreational area within easy reach of the majority of the state's residents.

Chugach, with 4,726,000 acres, second in size among national forests only to the Tongass, stretches along the coast of the Gulf of Alaska, taking in the islands and most of the land bordering Prince William Sound. Naturalists are aboard the ferries plying the Marine Highway through this watery section of the forest. They interpret the prolific and fascinating sea and bird life and the immense, iceberg calving Columbia Glacier. The Chugach reaches to Seward on the Kenai Peninsula and is just across Turnagain Arm from the state's largest city, Anchorage. To this area is added Afognak Island, first set aside as a reserve in 1891 by President Harrison.

Formerly of considerable importance for its copper deposits, the Chugach area has in recent years been geared to military operations centered around Anchorage, with multiple-use development of commercial fishing, timber, and recreational resources in the forest itself. The fault that brought the disastrous Good Friday earthquake of 1964 just about bisects the forest, and an excellent interpretive program has been established to help the public understand the powerful natural forces that have shaped the rugged landscape. A visitor center is operated during the summer within the Portage Glacier Recreation Area, about 50 miles southeast of Anchorage and in the heart of the area most dramatically affected by the quake. Nearby towns to the forest are Anchorage, Cordova, Kodiak, Seward, Valdez, and Whittier.

Within the forests are Kenai moose, Dall sheep, brown and black bear, mountain goat, and elk, animals among the largest in North America. The forest is also nesting ground for one of the largest concentrations of trumpeter swans, Canadian geese, and other waterfowl and shore birds. Most of the saltwater fishing in Prince William Sound is concentrated in the streams and waters around Valdez and Cordova. Some king salmon are caught in the fall and winter, while silvers are taken in quantity from July into September. Razor clams, Dungeness and king crab are among shellfish found on the forest shores. The lakes and streams of the forest offer an exciting challenge for freshwater fishermen.

By far the largest national forest within the 50 states, the *Tongass* has 16 million acres and covers most of southeast Alaska. It is divided for administrative purposes into two divisions: North, with headquarters at Juneau, and South, with headquarters at Ketchikan.

Sprinkled among these two population centers are the interesting and historic towns of Petersburg, Sitka, Wrangell, Haines-Port Chilkoot, Skagway, and Yakutat. Southeastern Alaska is the site of extensive glacial activity, with 175 named glaciers in the coastal area. By contrast, a profusion of wildflowers greets those who visit the forest during the long summer days. The forest supports wildlife in abundance—black and brown bear, moose, mountain goat, deer, wolves, coyotes, otter, muskrat, beaver, fox, mink, marten, upland game birds, and migratory waterfowl. There is also a variety of fresh- and saltwater fishing on the lakes, streams, and bays of the forest.

There are also these fascinations for tourists: totems, territorial museum and Indian villages, salmon canneries, "Trail of '98" gold mines, the "Ice Cap" back of Juneau, scenic wilderness trails, and mountain climbing.

Within the National Forests are camp and picnic grounds, swimming sites, winter sports areas, and an extensive system of wilderness cabins. Pick up a Forest Service map for locations and capacities and regulations. Many are on or near the highway; some are reached only by plane.

Pribilof Islands, in the Bering Sea, 1,000 miles west of Anchorage, is a seal and otter reserve. The islands are the homeland for the largest northern fur seal herd in the world and sanctuary for over 180 varieties of birds. Protected now by international treaty, the annual harvest of the seals is managed by the U.S. Government. In addition to the sea mammals, the Pribilofs offer a richness of subarctic and alpine flora, thousands of sea birds nesting on cliffs, and the Aleut village of St. Paul. About 500 Aleuts live on St. Paul and practically all of them attend the Old Russian Orthodox Church. Because it is 250 miles to the nearest land, St. Paul has been virtually isolated for about a century, and some vestiges of the Aleut culture may be evident around town. Away from the cliffs and the village, it is not unusual to see Blue Arctic foxes and reindeer herds. Via Reeve Aleutian Airways, Alaska Tour & Marketing Services (see Tours) offers 3-, 4-, and 6-day tours (prices from under $500).

Aleutian Islands. Stretching from the Alaska Peninsula in a deep southwesterly curve across the north Pacific toward Japan, the Aleutians are probably the most remote part of Alaska. The distance from the point nearest the Alaska mainland, Unimak Island, to the most distant island, Attu, is over

1,000 miles. This semivolcanic, treeless archipelago, termed "The Chain," consists of about 20 large islands and several hundred smaller ones. Before the coming of the white man, the islands were dotted with Aleut villages; today there are communities only at Nikolski, on Umnak Island; Unalaska, on Unalaska Island; and Akutan, on Akutan Island. Visitors are not encouraged to visit the complex facilities of the U.S. Navy at Adak and Shemya. No passenger boats reach the Aleutians yet, but legislation is pending to extend once a month service to the Alaska Peninsula and the Aleutian Islands. Meanwhile, the chain is serviced by Reeve Aleutian Airways.

Reeve has one-hour scenic flights (weather permitting) of the Cold Bay Area and the *Izembeck National Wildlife Refuge.*

Bethel, 80 miles from the Bering Sea, was originally an Eskimo village and is the hub of a tundra-villages area. As transportation center and administrative headquarters for the lower Yukon and Kuskokwim delta areas, encompassing about 70 native settlements, Bethel is as important to Alaska as it is little-known to outsiders. With a population of about 3,400, it is a big city in the tundra, with a library, museum, radio and television station, theater, hotel, bank, newspaper, maternity home, child-care center, regional office of the Alaska State Troopers, the largest Alaska Native Service field hospital in the state, an $8.8-million regional high school, and a $3.5-million regional dormitory for boarding students. Around Bethel live moose, wolf, beaver, muskrat, waterfowl, and ptarmigan. The *Clarence Rhode Wildlife Refuge,* to the northwest, encompasses one of the largest waterfowl breeding grounds in the world.

Nunivak Island, home of *Nunivak National Wildlife Refuge,* is noted regionally for its large herd of reindeer, its transplanted herd of musk ox, and its Eskimo settlement of Mekoryuk. This is one of the least-touristed parts of Alaska, and visitors find themselves feeling as though they are a hundred years back in time. Wien makes scheduled flights to the island, and if you want to stay overnight you should arrange with the airline for accommodations, which are limited and not deluxe, at Mekoryuk.

Bristol Bay, less than an hour's flight time southwest of Anchorage, is renowned for its fishing. Most of the world's sockeye, or red salmon, comes out of Bristol Bay waters and is processed there, with fishermen and canneries working round the clock to "make the pack."

The best time to witness this feverish activity is in July, but it is wise to make reservations, for aircraft are booked solid then, carrying cannery crews to the area.

In addition to its sockeye, silver, and King salmon, the Bristol Bay region is famous for its grayling, arctic char, Dolly Varden, northern pike, and rainbow trout. Fishermen who have thrown out their lines around the world say that some of the top sport fishing anywhere is in the major rivers and lakes of the Bristol Bay region.

Wien Air Alaska and/or Kodiak Western Airlines have daily flights to the Bristol Bay area towns of King Salmon and Dillingham. From King Salmon, a road runs to Naknek, on Kvichak Bay, an inlet of Bristol Bay. Kvichak Lodge, at Naknek, and Golden Horn Lodge and Royal Coachman Lodge, near Dillingham, have comfortable accommodations and major in sport fishing.

STATE PARKS. Write to State of Alaska Dept. of Natural Resources, Division of Parks, 619 Warehouse Ave., Suite 210, Anchorage, AK 99501 for an informative folder and map of Alaska's State Park System, America's largest (and youngest). The system includes campgrounds, recreation areas, waysides and historic sites. The largest is Chugach State Park in the wilderness surrounding Anchorage. Others are Denali State Park in the McKinley Park area and Kachemak Bay State Park and Kachemak Wilderness Park on the Kenai Peninsula. Plentiful campgrounds throughout the state offer fishing, hunting, hiking, bird watching, and other outdoor activities. Following are a number of typical such campgrounds. *Bird Creek,* on Seward Highway 26 mi. south of Anchorage. Large site that is fast becoming one of Alaska's most popular recreation areas. Spectacular scenery on the drive along Turnagain Arm to reach the area, and then an inspiring view across the Arm to Hope and Chugach Range from Bird Creek. *Hope,* a once booming gold-rush city, now a small village. Abandoned gold mines can be found up Resurrection Creek Valley. Rainshelter. Picnic units, camping sites. Excellent salmon fishing in Bird Creek. *Eklutna* is nestled in an Alpine canyon, 23 miles north on Glenn Highway, 8 miles east on gravel road. Two landing strips also in use. Freshwater glacial streams with waterfalls. Toe of Eklutna Glacier at far end of canyon. Spruce and cottonwood. Dall sheep and mountain goats often visible on canyon walls. Bear, moose, fox, coyote, ptarmigan, grouse also seen. Picnic area. Campsites.

Fairbanks, *Chatanika River,* 39 miles north on Steese Highway. Located in area of extensive mining operations. Visitors can see where huge gold dredges separated gold from gravel. Gutted creek beds with waves of left-behind gravel make good photo subjects. Even beginners can pan and come up with gold from the streams. Good hunting and fishing in area. Some picnic tables.

Stariski is 22 mi. north of Homer, at Mile 154 on Sterling Highway. Attractive grounds, with grassy areas framed by spruce trees. Bluebells and fireweed bloom in June and July. Excellent views of Mt. Iliamna and other peaks on Alaska Peninsula across Cook Inlet. Rainshelter. Picnic area. Campsites.

Bernice Lake lies 10 miles north of Kenai on North Kenai Rd. Small, lovely lake, popular for swimming, boating, and picnicking. Restful site in stretch with superior scenery. Picnic area. Campsites.

The rules and regulations are standard and insure your maximum pleasure. Follow fire rules; no firearms; leash pets; protect the facilities and natural features; no off-road driving; dispose of waste in the proper places. There's a $10 yearly fee for park use, and you can get your windshield decal as you go through Tok Visitor Center, or from district offices, or from the Park Rangers on duty. You may stay 15 days a year, except in some of the more popular areas such as Eagle River and Bird Creek in the Chugach district, and Fort

Abercrombie on Kodiak Island, where it may be 4 or 7 days. Except at the height of the camping season, you should find space in the roomy recreation areas, though the Alaska State Park System is on a first come, first served basis; no reservations needed for the present.

 CAMPING OUT. Even for those who consider themselves camping veterans, outdoor living in the vast, largely untamed land that is Alaska can be a very unusual experience. It's a good idea to carry water jugs and insect repellent (neither of which you may have to use much of the time), and treat all wild animals as wild animals. In other words, exercise caution in the presence of wild animals and give them a wide berth.

Obviously not all campsites are in the wilds. Many are in or quite close to populated areas. Almost every town has a public campground. And there are many commercial campgrounds in the state.

Driving the Alaska Highway, there will be adequately spaced campgrounds. Everyone should invest in one of the detailed road guides listed under *Recommended Reading.* From Mile 0 at Dawson Creek through the over 1,500 miles to the end at Fairbanks, the Alaska Highway has facilities and supplies, the longest distance between without some "civilization" perhaps 40 or 50 miles. There's a lot of camaraderie along the way as camping families meet up in the campgrounds, and share experiences.

In Yukon Territory the fee is $10 a year to use all Territorial Government campgrounds, which are exceptionally pleasant. Campground stickers are sold at visitor information centers and by campground maintenance offices.

The U.S. Forest Service maintains remote-area cabins reached by trail, boat or plane. Bush charters cost about $155 an hour (1980 prices; they are rising and unpredictable), up to 4 persons in a small plane, in the Tongass National Forest and the Chugach National Forest. All are located on fishing water. The lakeside cabins come equipped with safe boats. They're a bargain, renting for $5 per day per party, maximum stay 7 days. Reservations are necessary. Write to Information Officer, U.S. Forest Service, Tongass National Forest, Juneau, AK 99801; or U.S. Forest Service, Chugach National Forest, Suite 230, 2221 East Northern Lights Blvd., Anchorage, AK 99504.

Don't overlook the camping possibilities in BLM campgrounds in the Gulf of Alaska and Fairbanks areas, and also at Nome and Taylor on the Seward Peninsula jutting into the Bering Sea. No charge, except for the Delta Campground at mile 1414 on the Alaska Highway. It is $2 per day per party.

 TRAILER TIPS. The condition of the Alaska Highway is generally so good that there are few problems in trailer towing, provided both the trailer and tow vehicle are in proper shape. Usually, no difficulty is encountered in towing trailers of up to 15 feet. Trailers of 16 to 30 feet must be towed by a standard-size car. Trailers of more than 30 feet must be towed by a vehicle with a rating at least equal to that of a ¼-ton truck. For trailers of more than 60 feet in length, 8 feet in width, or 14 feet in height, permits must be obtained from Alaska Highway Headquarters, P.O. Box 2706, Whitehorse, Yukon Territory. Weight limits are 18,000 pounds for single axle, 32,000 pounds for tandem axle, and 73,500 for wheel base 55 feet and over. One-wheel luggage trailers are not suitable for the long gravel highway. Bottled gas is available at most towns and many of the smaller stops along the highway. Most of Alaska's many fine roadside campgrounds accommodate trailers, but there are few hookups. Water is available at most stopping spots, but may be limited for trailer use. Other supplies are available at regular intervals along the highway, making it unwise to overload your car and trailer with food and other items. Trailer towing along the highway should be avoided during the spring thaw, when the roadbed is often rough. At Customs, officials may require the listing of all contents. Most small household items carried on trailers may be carried on the regular Tourist Permit. Modern, well-equipped mobile-home camps are located in all major cities, and many accommodate transient or overnight trailers.

LODGING HOUSES. As Alaska's tourist accommodations move toward wall-to-wall carpeting, the number of old-fashioned lodging houses diminishes. Generally, this type of transient housing lacks in-room shower or bath, and many do not have private toilets. Some contain equipment no more modern than a wash basin. Local visitor information centers and Chambers of Commerce will be able to give you suggestions, addresses, and rates of places available.

WILDERNESS LODGES. Two contrasting areas, formed by opposing forces, have notable lodges. *Brooks Lodge,* on Naknek Lake in the Katmai National Monument, features a portion of "baked Alaska." The "Valley of 10,000 Smokes" was sculpted by a violent volcanic eruption in 1912.

Definitely unbaked is Glacier Bay National Monument. From the dock of beautifully architectured *Glacier Bay Lodge,* the main feature is riding out among icebergs decorated with curious seals to reach the faces of glaciers, which carved, and then melted to fill, the spectacular bay.

Small, homey *Gustavus Inn* near the jet airport not far from the Monument is now operated by children of the original 1928 homesteaders, parents of 9. King and silver salmon abound in surrounding waters of Icy Strait and Glacier Bay; Cutthroat and Dolly Varden trout in the Salmon River, a stone's throw from the Inn. Bus transportation is available to nearby Bartlett Cove, headquarters for Glacier Bay National Monument.

Lodges with some of the best all-inclusive fishing packages out of main cities are rounded up in "Fish Our Alaska" by *Alaska Tour & Marketing Services.* (See *Tours.*) And there are many more than mentioned here in the state-compiled Travel Index of their comprehensive "Worlds of Alaska" booklet, most of them reached by air or water only.

In the Southeast "Panhandle" look for excellent possibilities in the vicinity of "Salmon Capital" Ketchikan. *Humpback Lake Chalet* comes with boats and motors; up to 6 people can fly in for trout fishing in this well-stocked glacier-carved lake. (Outdoor Alaska, Box 7814, Ketchikan, AK 99901.) Near an Indian village, Klawock, on Prince of Wales Island, reached by ferry, small plane and boat, both the *Prince of Wales Lodge* and the *Fireweed Inn* have restaurants and rooms with bath. The *Log Cabin Sports Rental, Inc.* is a tenter's lodge. All offer sportfishing and recreational packages. *Waterfall* is a resort recycled from an historic cannery near Hydaburg Totem Park. *Yes Bay Lodge* (The Hack Family, Yes Bay, AK 99950) package rates include all: family-style meals, room, equipment, guide and many activities: hunting, fishing, hiking, photography, as well as services. *Thayer Lake Lodge* (Box 5416, Ketchikan, AK 99901) is on Admiralty Island. It's American Plan, and also has 2 cabins for up to four people with cooking facilities for do-it-yourselvers. *Taku Glacier Lodge* (195 S. Franklin St., Juneau, AK 99801) is 30 air miles from Juneau in mountain and glacier wilderness. The lodge is vintage log, and they opt mostly for day visitors who come for the delicious salmon bake, and for the flightseeing en route over the Juneau Ice Field.

In Central Alaska, Mt. McKinley dominates. The *Mercer Ranch* (Healy, AK 99743) has pack trips in Mt. McKinley National Park. Guests sleep in the bunkhouse before and after trips, and eat in the ranch kitchen with the Mercer family. Two resorts are for live-ins; both now surrounded by the National Park and with grand views of North America's king of the mountains. *Camp Denali* (P.O. Box 67, McKinley Park, AK 99755) is about 90 miles into the Park, in the midst of alpine and sub-Arctic terrain. Its primitive facilities are more than offset by its surroundings, friendly staff of enthusiastic, nature-minded young people and the owners whose individual attention leads toward an in-depth wilderness experience. June through August, the camp offers week-long Sourdough Vacations and Wilderness Workshops. They're all-inclusive: lodging, nutritious meals, guiding, interpretive programs, recreational equipment, and transportation round trip from McKinley Station, a most enlightening and photo-worthy drive. *The North Face Lodge* (P.O. Box 66, McKinley Park, AK 99755) near Wonder Lake has regular plumbing, mountain view, and offers complete wilderness packages including meals and transfers for one or two nights. On the Kenai Peninsula, south of Anchorage, and near its tip at Homer is Willard's *Moose Camp* (Caribou Lake, Homer, AK 99603). Besides assorted outdoor recreation around its log lodge and cabins, the camp has 4- to 14-day hunts for moose, Dall sheep, caribou, goat, elk, and bear. Across Kachemak Bay from Homer the *Kachemak Bay Wilderness Lodge* (China Poot Bay, Homer, AK 99603) is open year-round with complete packages on per day rates, and in summer they offer 4-, 5-, and 8-day packages. From Anchorage, you'll fly to *Alexander Lake Lodge* (P.O. Box 4–212, Anchorage, AK 99509) for nesting waterfowl including trumpeter swans, and many big game animals as well as sport-fishing. But you can drive along mountain-rimmed Turnagain arm to *Alyeska Resort,* about 40 miles from Anchorage (Girdwood, AK 99587). There are restaurants, cocktail lounge, chairlift sightseeing at this year-round ski resort, glacier and wildlife flightseeing tours at the adjacent air service, and gold pans for rent at the nearby Erickson Crow Creek Gold Mine. Rustic *Chulitna Lodge* is on the west side of the Cook Inlet (Box 1452Q, Star Route A, Anchorage, AK 99502). *Evergreen Lodge* (Box 264 Star Rt. C, Palmer, AK 99645) is a complete family resort with marina, boats, fishing, sightseeing, even a campground and trailer park.

In Southwest Alaska, besides *Brooks Lodge* in the Katmai, *Wien Air Alaska* maintains "Angler's Paradise" fly-in fishing camps in the heart of the Bristol Bay fishing area. There is fine trophy fishing out of *Kulik Lodge* and *Grosvenor Camp* plus great activities for the nonfishers: float trips, boat trips, hiking, rockhounding, observing and photographing birds and wildlife—especially bears, who are also avid fishermen. Plus flightseeing tours over the Valley of 10,000 Smokes with Katmai Air Services, as well as other aspects of this fascinating National Monument. For information and reservations contact Wien Air Alaska, 4100 International Airport Rd., Anchorage, AK 99502. *Iliamna Fishing Lodge* (Ketchum Air Service, 2708 Aspen Dr., Anchorage, AK 99503); *Silvertip Lodges* (Box 6389-S, Anchorage, AK 99502); *Iliaska Lodge* (Box 28-S, Iliamna, AK 99606); *Kvichak Lodge* (Box 37, Naknek, AK 99633); and the *Golden Horn Lodge* (P.O. Box 546, Anchorage, AK 99510); all have fine fly-in fishing and overnight or longer packages.

In the far north, *Camp Bendeleben* (P.O. Box 1045–S, Nome, AK 99762) has guided hunting, fishing, sightseeing and photography trips out of an early 1900 goldmining camp at Council, about 75 miles northeast of Nome. Ice fishing in winter.

Silvertip-on-the-Unalakleet River is near the Eskimo town of Unalakleet on Norton Sound of the Bering Sea. They fish for trophy Arctic char and grayling and salmon and have special duck and goose hunts in September.

 HOT SPRINGS. Alaska has no health spas as such, but north country old-timers swear by the health-giving waters of two hot-springs vacation resorts located at opposite ends of the state.

Arctic Circle Hot Springs is the farthest north in the United States. Guests can pan for gold and watch the midnight sun—in mid-June—as well as dip in the mineral waters, which are cooled down from their natural 139 degrees. Besides indulging in two warm indoor pools, an olympic-size outdoor one, and hot mineral baths, visitors also explore Gold Rush sites near the mighty Yukon River. Also offered are cabins, trailer and camper park, dining room, cocktail lounge. The hot springs, 136 mi. from Fairbanks, were first seen by whites in 1893. The Steese Highway leads to within 8 mi. of Circle Hot Springs, and a good branch of road goes the rest of the way. Many persons, however, fly from Fairbanks.

In southeastern Alaska, *Bell Island Hot Springs,* 45 mi. from Ketchikan, is reached by float plane from Ketchikan in approximately 25 min. Observed temperatures of the water range from 125 degrees to 162 degrees. The water is high in mineral content of the sodium chloride type, though sulphate is also present. The hot springs are used for the baseboard heating system and for filling the olympic-size swimming pool. Each cabin has a king-size bathtub, great for taking a hot mineral-water soak. Bell Island Hot Springs caters chiefly to fishermen, but their families are happy there, too. For rates, with and without fishing, write to 131-3rd Ave. N., Edmonds, WA 98020. *Chena Hot Springs,* 62 mi. E. of Fairbanks, is now under extensive development with several modern cabins available. The mineral springs were first found by whites in 1907. *Manley Hot Springs,* about 165 mi. from Fairbanks and at the end of the Elliott Hwy., has hot springs that run to temperatures of 136 degrees. Manley Roadhouse is an old hostelry that has been open since 1910. A public campground is near the bridge in town. Daily air service from and to Fairbanks.

CONVENTION SITES. Alaska handles about 400,000 tourists and conventioneers annually. Because of this the Alaskan cities are well-equipped to offer a variety of activities suitable for programs for wives. These include local sightseeing tours, ranging from wildlife viewing to nightclub visits—even health clubs! It is characteristic for hospitable Alaskans to arrange special treats for ladies, such as visits in Alaskan homes, champagne brunches, and fur fashion shows. Most conventions, especially those of an international or national character, go to Anchorage. The state's second most popular convention city is Fairbanks. Juneau has been for long a noted regional convention site, as has Ketchikan, the city closest to Seattle. Sitka boasts one of the state's finest convention centers. Kodiak is one of the busiest and most picturesque fishing ports in the U.S.A. Kenai is a favorite convention center for oil-related or technical groups.

Mt. McKinley Lodge, Alyeska Ski Lodge, and Glacier Bay Lodge all have convention and meeting facilities. (For further convention information, write the local Convention and Visitors Bureau.)
Visitors Bureaus.)

SPECIAL INTEREST. Local Chambers of Commerce and Visitor Centers are alert to special interests of visitors and can give referrals, gold mining to bird-watching—even square dancing. Fairbanks: *Alaskaland.* Open noon to 8 daily from end of May through summer contains a wealth of Alaskana in and out of doors. Homer: The *Pratt Museum,* maintained by the *Homer Society of Natural History.* Good sea otter display. Nome: The *Carrie McLain Memorial Museum* emphasizes the Gold Rush: the *Arctic Trading Post Museum,* the Eskimo. Kotzebue: *Ootukahkuktuvik* (Place having old things) is the name of a museum containing maska, whaling guns, and items made of ivory. This charming museum is in the process of moving, but it is worth checking to see if it may be reopened. The *Living Museum of the Arctic,* recently completed, has dioramas of the Arctic environment; animals, birds, sea life; also live demonstrations of crafts like skin sewing and ivory carving, and cultural dances in Eskimo native dress. The Eklutna Indian village 25 miles north of Anchorage on the Glenn Highway has old and new Russian Churches and an interesting Indian-Russian graveyard.

HISTORIC SITES. Over a hundred sites and landmarks are listed in the National Register. Here's a sampling: Anchorage: *Earthquake Park* in the Turnagain district provides a visible reminder of a recent violent history. The terrain has been left unchanged since the shattering quake of March 27, 1964, but nature is reducing the once-awesome scars.

Barrow: *Polar Expedition Building,* now a restaurant, was constructed in 1881 for use as headquarters for the First International Polar Expedition and was so occupied until 1883. Memorial where Will Rogers and Wiley Post perished in fatal aircraft in 1935 is 12 mi. S.W. of Barrow and accessible only by boat or plane.

Copper Center: Established in 1896, this is one of oldest white settlements in interior Alaska. Original *log-trading post,* rebuilt and modernized in 1932, is still open for business. First homestead in southcentral Alaska established here.

Eagle: *Amundsen's Cabin* is where Captain Roald Amundsen, the Norwegian explorer, stayed when he reached Eagle on Dec. 6, 1905. From Eagle he telegraphed the news that his ship, the *Gjoa,* had reached Herschel Island, having navigated the Northwest Passage. He had trekked overland from his ship, frozen off Canada's Arctic shore. His house is a few yards from the riverbank.

Fairbanks: *Felix Pedro Monument* stands at site of his famed Pedro Creek Discovery Claim, Mile 17 on the Steese Highway. Here, in 1902, he found gold that started the stampede to the Alaska interior. The S.S. *Nenana,* at Alaskaland, is typical of sternwheelers that plied the waters of Yukon, Tanana, Chena, and other northern rivers during Gold Rush era.

Ft. Yukon: *Restored fort* recalls area's role, in 1847, as farthest-west outpost of Hudson's Bay Co. Located on the banks of the Yukon. Grave markers in Ft. Yukon Cemetery date to 1868.

Kenai: *Ft. Kenay,* restored fort, was established in 1869 by Battery F, 2nd Artillery, U.S. Army. Nearby is site of *Redoubt St. Nicholas,* a fortified Russian fur-trading post established in August 1791 by Russian traders. Kenai is the oldest white settlement on the Alaska mainland, second oldest in the state. *Russian Orthodox Church* (1894) is still in use. *Russian chapel* nearby.

Kodiak: *Ft. Abercrombie State Historic Site,* N.E. of city, is the former site of a World War II installation, contains several bunkers and other evidence of military functions. Erskine House, the oldest in Alaska, in now a museum.

Nome: Mineral-bearing beach facing the Bering Sea still contains gold for the visitor who wants to pan up some "color" where 30,000 stampeders camped and prospected in the early days of the century.

Whitehorse: Sternwheeler S.S. *Klondike* and the *Keno* (in Dawson, Y.T.) represent Yukon River gold rush riverboats.

LIBRARIES. The *Alaska Historical Library,* Juneau, contains more than 15,000 volumes of Alaskana, many of them rare. Included is the famous Wickersham Collection, the most extensive collection of books, documents, and manuscripts relating to Alaska. The five-level *University o Alaska Library,* Fairbanks, has an outstanding collection of Alaskana. Th library is a repository of government documents and is a key resource source receiving 11,000 periodicals. In Anchorage, both the National Bank c Alaska's Heritage Library and the Alaska Pacific University Library hav extensive Alaskana collections. Virtually every town and city maintains public library, many with volumes of historical importance. *Sheldon Jackso College,* Sitka, has an excellent collection of Pacific Northwest exploration

TOURS. Package tours have been proliferating in th last few years, and there are many fine ones. Pick package that highlights places that exude "Alaska," you are a cheechako (newcomer) and your vacatio time is limited. It's possible to see much of big Alaska in only a week if you fl a lot. Most tours aim toward 2 or 3 weeks, though the trend is toward shorter even "minitours," to particular areas. Tours use assorted modes o transportation and allow for some optional tours along the way. If you buy prepaid, pre-packaged tour with definite word on what's covered and wha isn't, your budget won't be shot during the trip, due to inflation, currently world-wide travel worry.

Give or take a few adjectives and glowing terms, and you can believe the brochures put out by airlines, cruise ships, and tour operators pushing escorted and independent tours by land, sea, and air. Invariably, the promotion is liberally laced with colorful photographs, but Alaska's grand-scale scenery does not need any touching up. What's included is spelled out. With great distances to cover, round-trip transportation is a big item. Tours to far out places like the Pribilof Fur Seal Islands, for example, are priced to include a 2,000-mile round-trip flight via Reeve Aleutian Airways, from Anchorage. Generally, hotels, transfers, tips, guide services, and all sightseeing features outlined and described in the itinerary are conscientiously delivered. Meals are not included. Usually, there will be a choice of prices and places to eat. Meals could cost over $25 a day per person; more if you frequent the fanciest places (and drink, too), depending on current inflation rate, of course.

The big question is how to choose among the assorted general tours of varying length, plus an intriguing assortment of "optional tours" off the beaten tour trails. Most tours leave room in larger cities, Anchorage, Fairbanks, and Juneau, to add some optionals. It is advantageous to include them when you plan your trip, especially in summer. Your best friend can be your local travel agent, especially those knowledgeable about Alaska. A good travel agent is hardworking and will know all the time- and money-savers for getting you to Alaska and home again. Using their service won't add to your costs; they work on a commission basis. They may well have been on a "fam" (familiarization) trip to the Great Land, and be able to steer you in the right directions. Or they will know where to get the information.

To start you planning, here are some active firms majoring in Alaska tours. They are known and respected for giving top value and performance.

Some firms have "grown up" with Alaska tourism, and are now reinforced by the second generation. They support DOT (Division of Tourism) and belong to AVA (Alaska Visitors Association), where they socialize in hearty Alaskan style, and also talk over their mutual problems and successes. They work closely with airlines that will get you from home to Alaska direct or from West Coast tour departure points, and with cruise ships, ferries, motorcoaches, railroads, and local Alaskans interested in promoting tourism in their communities.

Atlas World Travel, 4038–128th S.E., Bellevue. WA 98006.

Johansen Royal Alaska Tours, 4th & Blanchard Bldg., Seattle, WA 98121.

Alaska Travel Bureau, Logan Bldg., 1411 4th Ave., Seattle, WA 98101.

Knightly Travel Service Inc., 1200 Westlake Ave. N., Suite 503, Seattle, WA 98109.

Maupintour, 900 Mass., Lawrence, KS 66044.

Leisure Corp., 207 Main St., Ketchikan, AK 99901.

Atlas Travel Tours Ltd. (Gray Line), Travelodge Mall, Box 4206, Whitehorse, Y.T., Canada, handles Yukon Territory.

Continental Trailways, 1512 Commerce St., Dallas, Texas, 75201. Features 20- and 30-day escorted air/bus/steamship tours to Alaska from Los Angeles, San Francisco, Seattle, and Denver.

TravAlaska Tours, 4th & Battery Building, Seattle, WA 98121. Among President Chuck West's many "firsts" in the industry is flying the first tourists to the Arctic in the early 1950s. TravAlaska offers low cost, all-season tours of a week or two on an "independent basis"—no escort, not part of a group. They also design custom tours and have innovated "Cub Coach Service," small well-appointed, 10- to 16-passenger sightseeing vans. Check with *Alaska Sightseeing Co.* offices in Juneau, Anchorage, and Fairbanks.

Kneisel Travel, Inc., 345 N.E. 8th Ave., Portland, Oregon 97232. Norm Kneisel. "Mr. K" himself, led the first motorcoach tour to travel the full length of the Alaska Highway. Today his galaxy of deluxe tours are classic. "Mr. K's Alaska Treasure Chest" has Air/Sea Tours for independent travelers. The "Green Carpet" programs are for those who want to travel in an escorted group. The Kneisel tours, from their founding, are based on Mr. K's philosophy of "the finest in carefree travel arrangements." They allow choices in ferries and cruise ships, but they make a point of including worthwhile extras in the initial tour price. It's part of the "carefree." They *know* you will want an upgraded cabin rather than the simplest one on your cruise ship. And they include the cost of shore excursions in the prepaid price, knowing that you wouldn't want to miss anything at a port-of-call. In fact, the overall price includes complete sightseeing throughout, whether on a Mr. K Independent Alaska or a Green Carpet, just to add to the "carefree." They've learned that tour optionals can add up when they're pay-as-you-go. This way a traveler knows in advance and can compare what the price covers. Moreover, passengers taking a green carpet tour always know where they are going and where they've been. Departure morning they receive a "Travel Log" of their itinerary and interesting sights to watch for, with space to add their own notes and observations.

Westours, 300 Elliott Ave. W., Seattle, WA 98119. (They also have offices in Anchorage, Fairbanks and Juneau.) Long on experience in Alaska travel, this oldest and biggest tour company has at their disposal cruise ships: Holland America's *Statendam;* Cunard's *Princess;* and their own *Fairweather* mini-cruiser specially built for the daytime cruise of Lynn Canal between Juneau and Skagway, described in Southeast Exploring. They also have Gray Line motorcoaches for their "Hyway Tours" through Alaska and Canada, including the Canadian Rockies, and for city sightseeing. Westours hotels, in strategic places for housing their tour groups, are some of the finest. The company works closely with major airlines. The staff, augmented by Alaska enthusiasts in summer, goes all out to look after Westourists. The motorcoach driver-tour guides are exceptional on excursions, such as those out of Anchorage, to the Matanuska Valley and on down to Valdez. Some are "natives," perhaps including a member of a homesteading family, who know the area well. This means the most comprehensive collection of cruises, cruise/tours, and flightours, plus optional tours, available from one company. Altogether, Westours covers thousands of miles. They swear that their "Basic Alaska Tour" has never been equaled. It's all wrapped up in their current picture-enhanced and information-filled Alaska brochures.

Princess Tours, based on the 18th floor of the new Fourth & Blanchard Building, Seattle, WA 98121, has been working at promoting their image as "The Vacation Company." Their attractive Alaska Vacation brochure with its colorful cover is an eye-catcher in any travel agent's rack. Their tours include sailings on the *Sun Princess, Island Princess* and the *Pacific Princess. Princess* offers 12 well-planned Alaska Vacations that combine air/sea/land travel. They have appropriate, descriptive names for the things you'll see the most of: Wilderness Routes, The Klondike Trail, and Gold Rush Country are examples. Leaning toward the trend to shorter tours, they have some that take a week or so: Scenic Treasure, Glacier Bay Grandeur, and Northland Explorer. But they are designed so that it is simple to add special interest optional tours. The longest and most comprehensive Alaska vacation in *Princess's* book is The Best of Alaska, Escorted. They promise travelers (who may be nervous about traveling independently in big Alaska) an intrepid leader, sworn to reveal all things best and beautiful along the way. The trip extends from Vancouver, B.C. to Kotzebue above the Arctic Circle, including such high points on the way as Mt. McKinley Park and the excursion to mammoth Columbia Glacier. Ask about the Fly/Drive program called "Alaska Your Way" for independent travelers. Three 8- and 9-day planned itineraries with hotel reservations en route explore different faces of Alaska—you do the driving.

Western Airlines, P.O. Box 92931, Los Angeles, CA 90009, or 50y W. Third Ave., Anchorage, AK 99502, or your local Western office or travel agent will have the airline's Alaska Blue Book, updated annually. Besides the popular "Magic Weeks," the book lists over 150 tours, hunting and fishing, resorts, and hotels in Alaska. Write the following airlines for information and brochures on the areas they serve, and the tour packages they offer:

Alaska Airlines, Seattle-Tacoma International Airport, Seattle, WA 98158.

They offer a Buy Alaska fare: $10 each to stop over in Ketchikan, Sitka, Juneau, Wrangell, Petersburg, Yakutat, Cordova or Anchorage, if you buy a round trip ticket Seattle to Fairbanks. They also fly to Glacier Bay and to the Arctic.

Northwest Orient Airlines, Minneapolis-St. Paul International Airport, St. Paul, Minnesota, 55111, or your regional sales office.

Wien Air Alaska, 4100 International Airport Rd., Anchorage, AK 99502, features "Best of Alaska" tours to the Arctic, to the Katmai National Monument, and to their Angler's Paradise Camps.

When you come to the end of the road in Alaska, it is often the start of more adventure. Optional tours to more remote places around the fringes of Alaska can be tied in with a general package tour, or purchased by travelers "on their own," in car or camper. It is advantageous cost-wise and for better timing to add optionals at the time you plan your itinerary. There are substantial savings using Tour-Basing Air Fares.

Alaska Tour & Marketing Services, Inc., Suite 312, Park Place Building, 6th & University, Seattle, WA 98101, keeps a finger on the pulse of all Alaska travel and majors in optional Alaska tours. Robert and Lori Giersdorf are president and vice president. Daughter Debbie is also a vice-president, in charge of Glacier Bay. The other vice-president in the family is son David, who with his wife Melanie, operate *Alaska Tour Center* Anchorage branch of ATMS, at 838 W. 4th. "Working teams," from a string of huskies to husbands and wives and whole families, are common throughout the Alaskan scene, as you'll discover as you travel up there.

Working with Alaska Airlines, ATMS packages tours to southeastern Alaska points including former Russian capital Sitka in its lovely island setting, and Glacier Bay. The daily sightseeing trip via the Lodge's *Thunder Bay* cruiser is for the birds, sea life, and watching mighty glacier faces "calve" huge chunks of ice. Likewise, on the *Glacier Bay Explorer,* with the added thrill of overnighting within sight and sound of a glacier. But the Bay is also famous as a "hot spot" for fishing trout, salmon, and halibut. The sportfishing packages are all wrapped up in a 16-page brochure called "Fish Our Alaska." The newest innovations at ATMS are fly-drive packages and many minitours, described in their expanded "Best of Alaska Destinations" brochure.

Flying with Alaska Airlines and Wien Air Alaska, ATMS packages the Arctic and western Alaska. Tours include hotels, and the choice of overnighting at Barrow, at the top of the continent, or Kotzebue, above the Arctic Circle (both Eskimo towns) in the Deadhorse Hotel at Prudhoe Bay, or gold-rush-founded Nome on the Bering Sea. The "Great Arctic Adventure" overnights at both Kotzebue and Nome; 3 days/2 nights.

Several packages are based on savoring Alaska's prime commodity, vast, unspoiled wilderness, as found in the Katmai National Monument, where volcanic heat created the remarkable "Valley of 10,000 Smokes," and in top-of-them-all Mount McKinley (20,320 feet) National Park.

Special for travelers who have but one day to give to wandering off their general tour itinerary are jaunts to first Russian capital Kodiak on its island in the Gulf of Alaska; to Sitka, Russian-American capital; to Juneau, today's state capital; and even the Arctic. You can fly in the morning, rub noses with Eskimos as they go about their summer fishing and seal and whale meat drying chores, watch them carve ivory, blanket toss, and dance, and return to your hotel by night, clutching your Arctic Circle Certificate to prove it.

Alaska Sightseeing Company, American Sightseeing and *Gray Line* offer sightseeing in and around main cities: Anchorage, Fairbanks, and Juneau. Their information desks are usually in the hotel lobby or nearby. They'll sell you what's available, gold dredges to nightlife tours.

If you are traveling on your own, what do you do with your camper and gear? There are safe places to leave them at departure points. Look in the yellow pages of directories in Anchorage, Fairbanks, and Juneau, if you are wondering what to do with your pet. There are many listings.

To sum up the tour situation:

Over a century ago, Russia sold Alaska to the U.S. in one big bargain package. Now it's being resold in smaller packages, to tourists. Alaska-covering tours, in general, travel in the best of—but similar—circles around the state. The optionals are planned out of the main cities on the itinerary. However, if you have a yen to see some special place—even Siberia—chances are there's a way. When in Nome, check bush airline *Munz Northern,* at th airport. Besides their scheduled milk runs to deliver people and goods to small far west coastal communities, they flightsee near the International Boundary and Date Line, where you can peek into the Soviet Union—and "tomorrow."

SPECIAL INTEREST TOURS. The Division of Tourism's comprehensive "Worlds of Alaska" travel booklet has some pages devoted to What to Do in Alaska. They list a couple of hundred operations that cater to people who want to pan for gold, go on photo safaris, run rivers, fish, hunt (over a hundred licensed big game guides), backpack; trail ride, go dogsledding, mountaineering, skiing, and flightseeing. Write D.O.T., Pouch E, Juneau, AK 99811. Some tours take river routes, rafting the Tatshenshini, or the Alsek, that cut through mountains and glaciers north of Glacier Bay. Some head for trekking in Mt. McKinley Park, the Katmai, Prince William Sound, and trips out of wilderness base camps to Misty Fjords and the North Slope. Many groups are geared to people who have never tried a "backwoods" experience, but have always wanted to. The following outfits majoring in such Alaska wilderness expeditions might have what you are seeking. *Alaska Campout Adventures,* 6458 Citadel Lane, Anchorage, AK 99504. Alaska Raft adventures, from McKinley Village, offer 2½- and 4-hour floats on the Nenana River whitewater. *Mountain Travel,* 1398 Solano Ave., Albany, CA 94706; *Sobeck Expeditions,* P.O. Box 67, Angels Camp, CA 95222 and *Western River Expeditions,* 7258 Racquet Club Drive, Salt Lake City, Utah 84121 offer longer river-running trips. *Questers Tours & Travel,* 257 Park Ave. So., N.Y. 10010, concentrate on bird and plant life. *Alaska Travel Specialists, Inc.,* 499 Hamilton Ave., Suite 212, Palo Alto, CA 94301, aim their wilderness adventures, graded according to difficulty, to small groups and families.

Westours, largest tour wholesalers (and retailers), and long involved in Alaska travel, has been collecting optional tours to suit a variety of interests. They're available out of main Alaska cities and Whitehorse, Y.T. under their subsidiary, *Alaska Hyway* Tours (Gray Line motorcoaches). They annually update their "Sightseeing Alaska" brochure, available at regional Westours travel desks and from the main headquarters at 300 Elliott Ave. W., Seattle, WA 98119. They feature such diverse excursions as a Matanuska River Float Trip (from Anchorage), a Taku Flightseeing/Salmon Bake (from Juneau), a motorcoach trip on the newly opened, scenic Carcross Highway connecting Skagway and Whitehorse. While overnighting in Valdez during the Columbia Glacier excursion from Anchorage, there's time for an informative "End of the Pipeline" tour.

For a roundup of several tours that accent wilderness, Russian-American history, gold-rush remainders, and native cultures, contact *ATMS,* Suite 312, Park Place Building, 6th & University, Seattle, WA 98101. Their "Best of Alaska" pamphlet describes and gives prices for some choice ones, among them: The *Pribilof Seal Islands and Bird Rookeries; Land of Katmai and Valley of 10,000 Smokes;* and both fishing and sightseeing tours in *Glacier Bay National Monument.* The firm has also compiled some companion pieces: "Fish Our Alaska" rounds up all the best sportfishing, the "hot spots" and yacht charters. Especially for the potential, independent, "on-your-own" travelers is their "Fly/Drive Alaska and the Yukon" brochure with a number of driving itineraries featuring guaranteed overnight accommodations throughout.

 GARDENS. Several communities boast attractive gardens, but there are no formal gardens on the scale of the "lower 48," probably due to the short growing season. At *Arctic Circle Hot Springs,* water piped underground from the hot springs has produced some of the best state-grown vegetables in this very interesting garden. In *Fairbanks,* there are more than 400 privately owned greenhouses. Many residents are proud to show visitors through their private produce plants. The U. of Alaska's experimental farms are outstanding, and efforts show up in the brightly landscaped campus grounds. The jumbo products of garden plots can be seen on display at fairs throughout the state in late summer. *Skagway* has several attractive flower gardens, which visitors find impressive. The city of Anchorage has a greenhouse with tropical plants, birds, and fish at 5200 DeBarr Road. The Centennial Rose Garden, claimed to be the northernmost municipal one, is between 9th and 10th and M and N in the west end of the park strip near the bandstand.

 MUSIC. With a population approaching half a million scattered over a vast area, it may be surprising to the visitor to find strong support for cultural activity in the 49th state.

Anchorage: The major music festival of the state each year is the *Alaska Festival of Music.* The *Anchorage Symphony Orchestra* has a full season, as does the *Anchorage Community Chorus.* The *Anchorage Concert Association*

brings world-renowned artists and groups to the city.

Fairbanks: *University of Alaska* music groups provide excellent periodic presentations. The *University-Fairbanks Symphony* presents winter concerts. The *Fairbanks Light Opera Company* performs in fall and winter. The *Fairbanks Concert Association* brings outstanding performers to the city.

Juneau: The *St. Paul Singers* present an annual Christmas concert.

In small communities, cruise ship arrivals may be greeted by the spirited high school band.

In late fall, winter, and early spring, most Alaska communities of any size are entertained by visiting artists or groups. Some, such as that in Haines, have rather full schedules, considering the relatively low population.

 STAGE AND REVUES. Many communities put on local shows and bring in talent from the outside. For example, at Kenai, the *Central Peninsula Concert Association* contracts with well-known performers, and the Haines schedule has included the Heiken Puppet Theater, Lola Montez and her Spanish Dancers—even a harpsichordist. The *Alaska Repertory Theater,* based in Anchorage, presents a season of full-spectrum fare and "goes on the road" between seasons.

In the larger cities (Anchorage and Fairbanks), performances are at professional level. Elsewhere, especially in the hinterland towns what is lacking in finesse is made up for by enthusiasm and vigor. Usually there is an admission charge.

Anchorage: *Theater 1* stages excellently executed productions. Bard of Alaska Larry Beck reviews gold rush days with Robert W. Service poems, songs, and audio visuals in the Alaska Room at the Anchorage Westward Hilton. *The Alaska Story* plays at the Captain Cook Hotel.

Dawson City: *The Gaslight Follies,* with local talent, is presented at the Palace Grand Theater in summer, nightly, except on Mon. *Diamond Tooth Gertie's, at the Community Hall, features a 1900 gambling hall, complete with faro and can-can girls.*

Fairbanks: *Fairbanks Light Opera Company* presents such contemporary musicals as *Oklahoma!* At the Fairbanks Inn they serve up Alaskana with their Dinner Theater.

Haines: Special for their city centennial celebrations lasting through 1981, the *Lynn Canal Players* present a revue of melodrama ("Lust for Dust!") and vaudeville.

Nome: Don't miss the "Frivolous Front Street Follies" at the *Fort Davis Roadhouse.*

Whitehorse: A local talent show, *Frantic Follies,* based on the Gold Rush era, is staged from mid-June through Aug., nightly, except Monday.

 BARS AND NIGHTCLUBS. Anchorage: *Top of the World* at the Anchorage-Westward Hilton Hotel is high above Alaska's largest city. The cocktail lounge of *Anchorage TraveLodge* is a favorite meeting place of the cosmopolitans. Entertainment nightly in the cocktail lounge of *Holiday*

Inn. Captain Cook Hotel has *Whale's Tail* on the ground floor and *Crow's Nest* on top, *Upper 1*, at Anchorage International Airport, has a clear view of planes flying in from and taking off for distant lands. *Penthouse Lounge* in Sheffield House, high as you can get. Great floor-to-ceiling window on Mt. McKinley and Cook Inlet. *Simon & Seafort's Saloon*, 420 L, has old-time decor. *Donovan's*, 101 Benson Blvd., is a well-stocked, convivial Irish pub. *Monkey Wharf*, 529 C St. Live monkey business behind the bar; on-stage entertainment, and dancing. *Peanut Farm*, 4 miles out of the Seward Highway has ice-skating, too, in winter. *The Bird House* at Bird Creek about 20 miles further is a leftover from Alaska R.R. construction days. It's jerry-built so crooked that when things start to look straight it's time to call it quits.

Circle: The bar at *Yukon Trading Post* is Alaska in the bush. Excepting the Haul Road, Circle (or Circle City) is the northernmost point you can drive to from the interconnecting highway system on the continent. If you started from Mexico City, this is as far north as you could go.

Copper Center: The lounge in famed *Copper Center Lodge* has a historical atmosphere.

Fairbanks: *Palace Saloon*, at Alaskaland, dips into the past for pioneer flavor. Live music nightly at the *Piano Bar* of The Switzerland, at 3-Mile Airport Way. Also *Club 11* and *The Ranch*, and for all-round family fun, the *Malemute Saloon* at Cripple Creek Resort, 12 miles past the U. of Alaska. Don Pearson recites Robert W. Service ballads superbly in summer. The *Pump House Saloon* is 1.3 miles on Chena Pump Road (see restaurants).

Homer: *Waterfront Bar* is a fishermen's favorite, with gusty nautical color. *Salty Dawg Saloon*, at the end of Homer Spit, has a lot of old-fashioned atmosphere plus super views of boats and glaciers.

Kodiak: *The B & B* (for Beer & Booze), handy for fishermen, opposite boat harbor and *Solly's Office*, on the Mall.

Nome: *The Gold Dust Saloon* in the Nugget Inn where tour groups stay overlooks the Bering Sea. The *Bering Sea Saloon*, and the *Board of Trade Saloon* on Front St. exude the rugged north. Out of town a short distance, the specialties of the *Ft. Davis Roadhouse* are Tanglefoot and Bering Ball cocktails and the lively Frivolous Front Street Follies.

Sunrise Inn, 45 miles from Seward, on Kenai Lake and in the Chugach National Forest, has a friendly bar. Look out the window and you might see Dall sheep.

In addition, there are many unique, highly colorful bars in small towns and inns tucked along side roads. Explore—and ye shall find.

DRINKING LAW. Warning. Bars close only between 5 A.M. and 8 A.M., so if you're lodging near one—and it's hard not to in this well-salooned land—it may get a bit noisy outside at about six in the morning.

SUMMER SPORTS. *Hunting:* Just as the brochures describe it, Alaska is truly a hunter's paradise, though guides are crying that the re-designation of land and curtailing of areas is ruining business. The interior forests and mountains provide shelter—diminishing as civilization marches on—for black, brown, and grizzly *bear, moose, caribou, Dall sheep,* and other game. *Deer, black bear, brown bear, moose,* and *mountain goat* are shot in southeastern Alaska. Some of the most spectacular hunting is provided in western Alaska, where many of the best-known guides and outfitters accommodate visiting shooters. The most-prized *Kodiak,* or *Alaska brown bear,* the largest land carnivore, is taken on Kodiak Island and on the Alaska Peninsula. The world's largest *moose* are found on the Kenai Peninsula. *Grizzly bear* are most often taken in the interior. Aside from spring hunting, August through November is generally considered the open season on most game—but dates are not rigorous. There are many closed areas and restricted species, such as the Arctic's polar bear and walrus, and the musk ox.

No hunting or trapping license is required of a resident of Alaska under the age of 16. Hunting license, $12; hunting and trapping license, $15; hunting and sport-fishing license, $22; hunting, trapping, and sport-fishing license, $25.

All nonresidents, regardless of age, must have a valid hunting license and tag(s) in their possession while taking or attempting to take game.

Guides are required by law for nonresidents hunting brown bear, grizzly bear, and Dall sheep. Their services are highly recommended for hunting other species as well. (A list of registered guides is available from the Dept. of Commerce, Division of Occupational Licensing, State of Alaska, Pouch D, Juneau, AK 99811.) Nonresident fees are: Hunting license, $60; hunting and fishing license, $90; hunting and trapping license, $200; "Trophy Fee" or Locking Tags are these: Brown or grizzly bear, $250 each; black bear, $100 each; bison, $250; moose, $200 each; sheep, $250 each; caribou, $20 each; elk, goat, $125 each; musk ox, $1,000 each; wolf, $50 each; wolverine, $50 each.

(It would be very wise, before embarking on a hunting trip, to write the Alaska Department of Fish and Game, Subport Building, Juneau, AK 99811, or regional Fish and Game offices, for up-to-date rules and regulations.) To hunt some protected species you may have to draw for it, requiring an additional fee of $5 or $10.

Fishing: With its miles of jagged coastline, rushing mountain streams, and many interior lakes, Alaska provides an exciting variety of both salt- and freshwater fishing. The season is literally year-round, with some closed areas and times, especially on salmon. Many fishing tours are offered by tour operators and private guides and the Alaska Department of Fish and Game issues information listing the best fishing spots along the Alaska Highway and other major routes. *Salmon* are found in most coastal waters and in some streams. Various *trout* are taken from the streams, and the Arctic provides a special challenge in the exotic *sheefish,* which is a cousin to the salmon, and more delicious! Another visitor favorite is the *grayling* of southcentral and interior waters. Non-resident sport fishing licenses: one day, $5; 10 days, $15; one year, $30. None needed for non-residents under 16 years of age.

For a roundup of the best in sportfishing lodges through Alaska and the package prices and yacht charters out of Ketchikan and Juneau, write for the "Fish Our Alaska" brochure, Alaska Tour & Marketing Services, Inc., Suite 312, Park Place Building, 6th & University, Seattle, WA 98101.

Major salmon derbies are at Petersburg (Jan. through Sept.), Ketchikan, Juneau (mid-May to mid-July), Haines (last weekend in May and first weekend in June), Sitka (late June), Juneau (late July), Seward and Valdez (in August).

Boating: There are all kinds of rivers and lakes for kayaking, canoeing and rafting expeditions with wildernesswise leaders; food and gear often furnished. Local charters and rentals may be available. McKinley Village–based Alaska Rafting Adventures has been planning new tours combining fishing and rafting and including more wilderness areas. Write Gary Kroll at Box 66, McKinley, AK 99755 for information on trips on the Talchulitna River and stays at a wilderness lodge. Another top fishing river they'll be floating is the Karluk, out of Kodiak, reached now by direct flight from Seattle. And then there's the Arctic, a run on the Kelly River, out of Kotzebue by bush flight to a point on a gravel bar.

Scuba and skin diving: Underwater diving is popular along the coast, especially around Sitka, Ketchikan, Juneau, Kodiak, and Anchorage. Equipment can be rented in these cities. Alaska divers wear no less than quarter-inch wet suits. *Spearfishing* is fair, but the principal diving trophy is the king crab.

Swimming: If you like to swim, don't leave your suit when you pack for your Alaska vacation. Coastal waters can be somewhat chilly, but lakes are warm enough, thanks to nearly 24 hours of daylight. Some towns have community swimming pools, and besides hot-springs resorts, hotels and motels are leaning toward putting in pools.

Footracing, spectator or participant: A grueling contest that has been staged each July 4 in Seward for many decades is the Mt. Marathon footrace, which sends the hardy and the hopeful up the 3,022-foot peak behind the city and back, with the best racers completing the run in less than an hour. Long-distance runners vie in the 26-mile, 385-yard Equinox Marathon at the University of Alaska campus, near Fairbanks.

Golf: You can tee off almost to midnight at the Fairbanks Golf & Country Club and at nearby Arctic Acres. Anchorage: 18-hole Moose Run Golf Course at Fort Richardson, and four 9-holers in vicinity; another at Elmendorf Air Force Base, an hour away in the Matanuska Valley. The greens offer more than golf, such as super scenery and glimpses of wild life. At Soldotna on the Kenai Peninsula, you can alternate teeing and driving at the Birch Ridge Course with salmon fishing in the Kenai River.

Hiking: The state and federal governments have cleared hundreds of miles of trails in scores of Alaska forests and mountain areas. There are about 500 miles of trails alone in the national forests. The most famous hiking trail is the Chilkoot Pass Trail of '98, part of the International (Canada and U.S.) Klondike Gold Rush Historical Park. Guides conduct trail tours from Skagway. For many, it is the outstanding adventure in Alaska, combining scenery, history, legend, and outdoor camping.

Mountain climbing: Alaska's mountains offer variety ranging from afternoon rock ascents to climbing the highest peak in North America. But be prepared in every respect—and have guides on any extended climb. And *skiing* goes on well into summer, above Alyeska Resort. Glaciers are reached by Alyeska Air Service planes. They also offer flightseeing tours.

 WINTER SPORTS. *Skiing:* Alaska's powder snow offers an exciting challenge for skiing, but development of the state's many natural slopes has been slow. There is only one large, well-developed ski resort in the state—*Mt. Alyeska Ski Resort,* about 40 mi. from Anchorage. It features 5 double chairlifts, poma lift, 2 rope tows, ski school, rental equipment, accommodations, dining room, cocktail lounge, day lodge with sundeck and snackbar, and Skyride Restaurant at top of chairlifts #1 and #4. Alyeska Resort starts weekend lift operations early. By mid-December, the action is daily, and continues through May on the upper slopes. National and International competitions are held here. Besides skiing (including heli-skiing) there are dogsled rides and horse-drawn sleigh rides, plus lively "aprés-ski" entertainment. For complete information on the resort and some super seasonal ski packages and reservations, write General Manager, Alyeska Resort, Girdwood, AK 99587. Fairbanks has two easily accessible ski slopes near the city. There are ski runs and ski tows near Homer. Across the bridge on Douglas Island at Juneau's *Eaglecrest* ski area, there is a chairlift, 2 rope tows, and a day lodge. *Turnagain Pass Area,* 59 mi. from Anchorage on the Seward Hwy., is popular with cross-country skiers and snowmobilers; snowfall here is often over 12 feet. If you want to ski on glaciers, try those adjoining Juneau Ice Field; you can get there by helicopter.

Dog Sledding: Bear Bros. Whole Wilderness Experience, Box 4-2969, Anchorage, AK 99509, offers dog sledding, cross-country skiing and summer kayaking. Some others: Chugach Express Dog Sled Tours, Box 261, Girdwood, AK 99587; Denali Dog Tours & Wilderness Freighters, Box 1, McKinley Park, AK 99755.

Ice Skating: Although Alaska is really deficient in commercial rinks, ice skating on frozen lakes is popular in almost every community during the months of Dec. through Mar.

Curling: This old Scottish favorite is played avidly in wintertime in Anchorage, Fairbanks, and in Whitehorse, Yukon Territory.

 SPECTATOR SPORTS. In mid-Jan., there is the annual 200-mi. cross-country snow-machine race, Kenai to Homer and return. In late Jan., there is the annual Midnight Sun "600" snowmobile race, Anchorage to Fairbanks and return. In early Feb., Anchorage stages the 3-day North American Ice Racing Championship at Sand Lake. In mid-Feb., Anchorage is at it again, this time with the World Championship Sled Dog Races. In late Feb., Fairbanks puts on a 5-day Fairbanks curling Club International Bonspiel. In early Mar. Fairbanks stages the Junior North American Championship Sled Dog Races, Women's North American Championship Sled Dog Race, and Cleary Summit Cup Ski Race. In mid-Mar., Fairbanks is host to the Old

Man's Sled Dog Race, invitational, and the 3-day North American Championship Sled Dog Races. Also in mid-Mar., there is the Snowmobile Race, Nome to Teller and return. Winter sports are closed out with the Motor Mushers Snowmobile Point Race at Anchorage in early Apr. At the end of May Kotzebue holds snow machine races along with Eskimo games.

For indoor spectator sports, the University of Alaska plays college cagers from the "lower 48." In mid-Feb., Juneau stages a 6-day Gold Medal Basketball Tournament.

Anchorage, Fairbanks, Palmer, and Kenai field good independent baseball teams. On June 21, Fairbanks has its Midnight Sun Baseball Game with the local Gold Panners, one of the top non-professional teams in the country, playing at midnight at the Growden Memorial Stadium without artificial light. Two days later Fairbanks stages its Yukon 800 Riverboat Race to Galena and return.

On July 4, Seward runs the Mt. Marathon Race. Late in July, Fairbanks stages the 3-day World Eskimo Indian Aleut Olympic Games. In mid-Aug., Dawson holds a raft race on the Klondike River, as part of its Annual Discovery Day celebrations. On Sept. 22, the Equinox Marathon is run at the University of Alaska, at Fairbanks. During Christmas week, at Kotzebue, Eskimo men and women compete in dog-team racing, snowshoeing, snow-machine racing, wrestling, finger-pulling and other native and not-so-native sports.

 SHOPPING. The best buys in Alaska are products of native materials made by Natives and other artists and craftsmen living in the state. Look for carvings out of ivory, soapstone, jade, and wood, and items made from fur. You'll find a wide choice of jewelry, mukluks, masks, totem poles, paintings, baskets, and even food items that *look* Alaskan. But how does one know that an item was produced in Alaska and is an authentic souvenir?

The state has adopted two symbols that guarantee authenticity of crafts made in Alaska by its people, and it supplies them with tags and stickers to put on their work. If the piece you covet has a hand symbol, it was made by one of the Native peoples. A dipper-shaped flag symbolizes that it was made in Alaska, by a resident, of materials which can be found in the state (though they may have been imported, as well, to be crafted here). If some items with these emblems seem more expensive than you expected, examine them and you'll probably see that they are one of a kind and have been made by hand. There are many more shops than those listed here, but part of the fun of shopping is discovering for yourself!

Alyeska Resort: *Kobuk Valley Jade Co.* and *Nugget Inn* lobby gift shop.

Between Anchorage & Fairbanks: *Tatlanika Gift Shop*, Mile 276 on the Parks Hwy. Alaska-made arts and crafts.

Anchorage: *Anchorage Historical and Fine Arts Museum Gift Shop*, 121 W. 7th. Native Alaskan arts, posters, note cards, and other Alaskan items for sale. *Bering Sea Originals*, 636 E. 15th. Handcrafted ceramics, candles. *Alaska*

Native Arts and Crafts Cooperative, 3rd and E. Wood, horn, ivory, woven reeds, and leather items made by Alaska natives. *Anchorage Fur Factory,* 120 E. 5th, *David Green Furriers,* 130 W. 4th, and *Martin Victor Furs,* 428 W. 4th (and also in Fairbanks at 3rd and Lacey). *Carlquist Anchorage Jewelers,* 543 W. 4th. Soapstone, ivory, nugget and jade jewelry. *The Gilded Cage,* 715 W. 4th, benefits the handicapped; *Laura Wright Parkys,* 326 E. St.; both offer very Alaskan souvenirs. *Trading Post,* Anchorage Westward Hilton Hotel. Carved ivory, jade, Alaska black diamond. The *Alaskan Food Cache,* 726 E St., garners delectable provisions from America's Last Frontier, and packs them cleverly. Also sends them by mail. Send for catalog with prices.

Barrow: Eskimo handicrafts that can be purchased at the world's largest Eskimo village include native yo-yos, baleen baskets, mukluks, dolls, and ivory and bone carvings.

Chugiak: *Chief Chugiak Gifts,* Mile 21 on the New Glenn Hwy. at the North Birchwood Loop intersection on Jayhawk Dr. Gold-nugget, jade, hematite, and ivory jewelry; carvings and seal-skin items.

Copper Center: *Grizzly Gift Shop,* Mile 93 on the Richardson Hwy. Jade, ivory, hematite, goldstone.

Dawson City, Yukon Territory: *Dawson Hardware Museum and Dawson Boutique.* Gold Rush relics and old bottles. *Klondike Nugget & Ivory Shop.* Nugget and ivory souvenirs.

Eagle: Items made here from local woods include dog sleds, cache, and fish wheel kits.

Fairbanks: *Alaska House-Alaska Art Gallery,* 1003 Cushman. Eskimo ivory, soapstone, painting by Alaskan artists. *Eskimo Museum and Gift Shop,* 7 Mile Richardson Hwy. Eskimo arts and crafts, ivory, jade, and hematite. *Gold Pan Trading Post;* in the lobby of Fairbanks Inn, 1550 Cushman. Native handicrafts, Alaska jewelry. *Mukluk Shop,* 545 2nd Ave. Summer parkas, mukluks, locally handcrafted in Alaskan homes. *Alaska Jade Cache,* 2450 Ravenwood, has finished art pieces and also rough jade direct from the mine. The *Gold Mine,* 402 5th Ave., has it "by the piece or poke." Driving the "Freeway" about 14 mi. from Fairbanks at Mile 1506, it would be hard to miss *Con Miller's Santa Claus House Gift Shop* at North Pole, Alaska. It's noted for a special stamp and the volume of mail handled every Christmas!

Ft. Yukon: Beadwork, craftwork, furs at local store.

Gakona: *Little Alaska Cache.* Wide range of Alaskan-made items. *Posty's.* Athabascan baskets, moccasins, and mittens; diamond willow and burl, jewelry and beadwork.

Homer: *Alaska Wild Berry Products* (delicious). *Homer Artists Gallery* features local paintings, arts and crafts. The *8x10 Art Gallery,* native-landscaped log cabin, full of art and the artist full of wildflower information.

Kodiak: *Baranof House Museum.* Antique Russian samovars and trays, seal-oil candles, handcrafted silver jewelry, handwoven Aleut basketry. Some items may be for sale. Check out *Norman's* and other shops "on the Mall."

Kotzebue: *Walsh's long-time store and Arctic Rivers Trading Co.* sell Eskimo crafts work: masks, furs, skin paintings, jade jewelry, raw jade, jade and ivory carvings.

Nome: *Arctic Trading Post*. Most extensive stock of authentic Eskimo ivory carvings in Alaska.

Tok: *Farren's* advertises Alaska-smoked salmon and "squaw candy." By the cache, the *Burnt Paw* features "Northland Specialties"—a wide assortment.

WHAT TO DO WITH THE CHILDREN. *Around And About Anchorage with Children,* by the Anchorage Volunteer Service League, is full of ideas for family fun. $6.50 brings it postpaid from P.O. Box 3762-S, Downtown Station, Anchorage, AK 99510. Or ask at the Log Cabin where it's available for $5.95 if you are in Anchorage. *Mt. McKinley National Park,* with its wildlife, birds, and flora, will amaze, excite, and instruct. At various places the children will see animals in the open; for animals for close-up viewing there is the *Alaska Children's Zoo,* 7 mi. from Anchorage. *Alaskaland,* at Fairbanks, seems designed for children of all ages. A ride on the sternwheeler *Discovery* out of Fairbanks will be a trip long remembered; so will a trip on the narrow-gauge *White Pass & Yukon Route,* between Skagway and Whitehorse. Fishing streams, especially those with *salmon spawning,* draw interest. *Indians, Aleuts, and Eskimos* and all the products they craft, will leave indelible impressions. *Skagway,* a living page out of the past, will appeal to kids with a taste for history and color. Local shows: the *Chilkat Dancers* at Port Chilkoot; the *Fish Pirate's Daughter* in a bar, at Ketchikan; Skagway's *In the Days of '98;* Kodiak's *Cry of the Wild Ram;* and Juneau's *Delilah's Dilemma* may be highlights of a vacation for some youngsters. Gold mines, gold panning, ghost towns, old forts, museums, gift ships, sled dogs, totem poles, a trip on the Alaska Railroad, sawdust-floor saloons where popcorn and soda pop are served, ferry boats, glaciers, fishing boats, baseball games at night without lights, nights without darkness, chair lifts to high places, riverboat races, sourdough breakfasts—these and a list that could extend for pages more will keep kids alert, cheerful, and responsive to the environment.

INDIANS, ESKIMOS, AND ALEUTS. Descendants of the prewhite inhabitants of Alaska now number about 70,000. They live in widely separated villages scattered along the 25,000-mile coastline and the great rivers of the 49th state, of which the population generally ranges from about 30 to about 500. The villages, some 200 of them, rather than the tribes, are, as a rule, considered to be the basic social units. The so-called tribe name usually denotes the language group, not the nation. The Native Land Claims Settlement Act was passed in 1971. This allowed for $900 million in cash plus 40 million acres of land to be paid to the natives for their rightful historic lands—a landmark settlement. To administer this, 12 Native Regional Corporations have been formed in Alaska; the 13th is for all Alaska Natives residing "outside." The Indians, Eskimos and Aleuts are citizens of the United States, naturalized collectively by the Citizenship Act of 1924. They are not wards of the government, though the Bureau of Indian Affairs and other federal agencies do perform functions aimed at meeting the special needs of these first families of the largest state. That there have been and remain bitter other federal agencies is no secret. Though some of the native peoples still hunt and fish for part of their food, many have moved to Alaska's larger cities, such as Fairbanks and Anchorage, and a few have gone as far as the "lower 48." Visitors are sometimes surprised to learn that there are no reservations and that Alaskan Eskimos never did live in igloos, as did their Canadian cousins. In the remote north, where building material is scarce and freight high, houses are usually built from driftwood and salvage. Modest frame homes predominate elsewhere. Native clothing is still seen, but store-bought jackets and boots are gradually taking over from the famed fur parkas and mukluks. The ubiquitous tennis shoes and sweat-shirts are now making appearances on the smaller set. On the surface, the smiling Eskimos appear happy in their changed way of life, but serious social studies indicate the transition has been traumatic and has left deep scars. But they are still exceptionally friendly with visitors and appear to enjoy putting on an entertaining show, built around their cultural past, for expectant tourists.

Along the Alexander Archipelago is the home of three southeastern groups: Tsimpshians, now living mostly in Metlakatla on Annette Island, just south of Ketchikan; Haidas, on the south end of Prince of Wales Island at the village of Hydaburg; and the Tlingits. In the interior of Alaska are the formerly nomadic northern Athapascans, closely related to the Navajos, Apaches, and Hopi of the southwestern states. They live along wide river-valleys bordered by high mountains—a land of short summers and severe winters.

On the Alaska Peninsula, extending down the Aleutian Chain, are the Aleuts, related to the Eskimos. Some of the finest basketry in the world was formerly produced by the Aleut women of Attu Island. Today the Aleuts generally live in well-constructed frame houses. Many are members of the Russian Orthodox Church.

And on the western and northern coasts are the Eskimos—famed in photograph and travel brochure. This harsh habitat, generally treeless with short summers and long, cold winters, was able to sustain a rich culture, which evidence indicates flourished 2,000 years ago. Even today, in remote places, while the Eskimo moves more and more into the money-economy of the white man, the Eskimo male still hunts walrus, whale, and seal, and his wife retains her fur-sewing skills. His boat, powered by an outboard engine, is covered with walrus skin. An interesting, up-to-date, and in-depth summing up is provided by *Alaska Native People*. This Alaska Geographic book, available from Northwest Publishing Company (address below) for $19.95, is full of color photographs.

 RECOMMENDED READING. Maybe it's due to those long winter nights that Alaskans are well educated and avid readers. Book stores, all dealing in Alaskana, are rampant, with most always an airport branch; all great for browsing. Some favorites are the *Book Cache* in Anchorage; the *Baranof Book Store* in Juneau. Highway and other independent travelers would do well to invest in one of the almost mile-by-mile guides like *The Milepost,*

well to invest in one of the almost mile-by-mile guides like *The Milepost*, Alaska Northwest Publishing Co., Box 4 EEE, Anchorage, AK 99503 ($7.95, plus $1.00 postage—or plus $2.75 postage if you want it sent first class); it's long revered and useful. The same company publishes *Alaska* Magazine and a wealth of books about the state, including recent guides on fishing and hunting. Send for their catalog with prices. Among them, for cooks: long-time Alaskan Ruth Allman's handwritten *Alaska Sourdough* recipes ($4.95); and *Lowbush Moose* (rabbit!), a collection of retired Alaska State Trooper Gordon Nelson's favorite recipes and anecdotes ($5.95). Larry Lake's *Alaska Travel Guide*, Box 21038, Salt Lake City, Utah 84121 ($4.95 plus 75¢ postage) includes a hotel directory and a small but attractive color section. He updates it himself, annually, and it's glove-compartment size. *Alaska Travel Publications, Inc.*, Box 4-2031, Anchorage, AK 99509 has books on specific areas: They explore the *Katmai* ($8.50), *Mount McKinley National Park* ($8.95), and *Prince William Sound* ($8.50). State legislator Mike Miller's *Alaskabooks*, Box 1494, Juneau, AK 99802, are small, inexpensive, but full of accurate, useful information—particularly *Camping and Trailering* and *Off the Beaten Path*. Each sells for $2.00. His newest local guide, on Juneau, sells for $3.50. It is most useful to have in hand while you are in the capital city. The official, free travel book *World of Alaska*, edited by Mrs. Diana Murphy, State Information Officer, is updated annually. It's available by writing Alaska State Division of Tourism, Pouch E, Juneau, AK 98111.

 HOTELS AND MOTELS. As you might expect, accommodations in Alaska frequently carry the tang of the frontier, but there'll be no lack of modern conveniences now. You'll recognize some familiar chain names: Great Western, Hilton, Sheraton, and the recurring Sheffield Houses, an Alaskan chain that has hotels in Fairbanks, Juneau, Kenai, Kodiak, Sitka, Valdez, Whitehorse, Y.T. Canada, and three in Anchorage. Some mix the older mood of turn-of-the-century Gold Rush grandeur with the decor. Prices are generally a notch higher than in the "lower 48's" Northwestern states. But, as almost everywhere in the world, prices are hard to predict because of inflation. In smaller cities, especially in Southeast Alaska, prices will be lower. While the larger cities have many hotels and motels, summer travel is heavy in our 49th state, and space is blocked in advance by tour groups. The price is included in the package tour, an overall saving because rooms are based on group rates. There are also lower rates during "thrift season," early spring, late fall, and winter. Reserve ahead, unless you are self-sufficient with camper, trailer, or tent. Stop by visitor information centers and Chambers of Commerce, wherever you are, for local lodging leads, and prices. Accommodations are listed in order of their price category. Prices are based on double occupancy. *Deluxe:* over $60; *Expensive:* $45-60; *Moderate:* $35-$45; and *Inexpensive:* under $35. For a more complete explanation of hotel and motel categories see *Facts At Your Fingertips* at the front of this volume. In the Arctic space may be limited or non existent unless you are with an Arctic tour. Then you will stay in the finest, which is probably the only hotel with all the comforts.

BARROW

Top of the World Hotel. *Deluxe.* Open year-round, over $100 double buys amazing luxury on Arctic Ocean edge. 40 rooms, coffee shop, restaurant. Polar bears (stuffed) highlight lobby. You may find space all booked by oil prospectors.

BETHEL

The Kuskokwim Inn. *Expensive.* Open year-round. Coffee shop and dining room. (No bar, town is currently dry.) Box 218, Bethel, AK 99559.

CORDOVA

Prince William Motel. *Moderate.* Small motel in downtown Cordova, with café and cocktail lounge. TV. Box 848. Cordova, AK 99574.

Reluctant Fisherman. *Moderate.* Coffee shop, restaurant, bar with live entertainment. Hunting and fishing trips. By boat harbor. Box 1309, Cordova, AK 99574.

DILLINGHAM

New Dillingham Hotel. *Expensive.* With annex, can handle over a hundred in 19 rooms with music and carpeting. Both room and board available. Box 194, Dillingham, AK 99576.

Dillingham Inn. *Moderate.* Nine rooms with bath. Box 217, Dillingham, AK 99576.

FAIRBANKS

Fairbanks Inn. *Deluxe.* Large, two-story motor inn, with inviting rooms. No pets. Winter plug-ins available. Dining room, cocktail lounge, beauty salon, laundry, valet service. Seasonal rates. 1521 Cushman St.

Golden Nugget Motel. *Deluxe.* Two-story motel with comfortable, attractive rooms. Steam bath. No pets. Restaurant, cocktail lounge. 900 Noble St.

Captain Bartlett Inn. *Deluxe.* 205 rooms. Spruce-log lobby, Alaska decor, and "largest fireplace in Alaska." Jacuzzi and sauna. Near Alaskaland Centennial Park. Restaurant, lounge. 1411 Airport Way.

Traveler's Inn. *Deluxe.* Huge, multi-story motor inn, with many different types of units, some studio rooms, some suites. No pets. Coffee shop, cocktail lounge, excellent restaurant. 813 Noble St.

Chena View. *Expensive.* Downtown. Spacious and new. Restaurant and bar.

Golden North Motel. *Moderate.* Near the International Airport. In-room coffee. Restaurant and cocktail lounge nearby. Seasonal rates. 4888 Airport Rd.

Roaring 20's Hotel. *Expensive.* 100 rooms near downtown. Restaurant and lounge, plus meeting and banquet rooms, pool, entertainment, liquor store, travel desk, barber and beauty shop, courtesy limo. Cushman at 11th.

Polaris Hotel. *Expensive.* Large hotel conveniently located in town, with restaurant and cocktail lounge. 427 First Ave.

Towne House Motel. *Expensive.* Medium-size motel near downtown. Attended pets OK. 1010 Cushman.

Alaska Motel. *Moderate.* New with wall-to-wall carpets, kitchenettes, and laundry facilities. 1546 Cushman.

Fairbanks Hotel. *Moderate.* Modest-size, clean, downtown hotel, convenient location, comfortable, pleasant atmosphere. 517 Third Ave.

Klondike Inn. *Moderate.* Large rooms with kitchen facilities. Laundry, lounge, and courtesy car. 1316 Rewak Dr.

Tamarac Inn Motel. *Moderate.* Smaller motel with 20 units. 252 Minnie St.

Aurora Motel. *Inexpensive.* Modern cabin units near university campus. Kitchenettes available at extra cost. 2016 College Rd.

Cripple Creek Resort. *Inexpensive.* Recycled buildings of ghost mining camp. Open summers. Full of atmosphere. Family entertainment and fun in Malemute Saloon. Two dining rooms, one mining-camp style. 11 miles out College Road at Ester. Open late May to Labor Day.

GLENN & RICHARDSON HIGHWAY JUNCTIONS

Ahtna Lodge. *Deluxe.* Locally owned by "People of the Copper River." 30 rooms, restaurant, bar, gift shop.

Hub of Alaska. *Moderate.* South Junction, open 24 hours, motel restaurant, garage, services.

Along the Alaska Highway: Try the **Talbot Arm Motel** with many services at Mile 1083, open year round and new; and the large **AlasKon Border Lodge** at Mile 1202, Beaver Creek, where the food is excellent and you can even play peewee golf.

HOMER

Anchor River Inn. *Inexpensive.* Hospitable hosts offer many services: motel, campground, restaurant, home bakery, plus the latest news on salmon fishing. Sterling Highway, Mile 156.9, about 15 miles north of Homer.

Baycrest Motel. *Moderate.* Recently expanded, and with great mountain-water view. Some units with kitchens. Boat for charter. Mile 170 Sterling Highway.

Heady Hotel. *Moderate.* 46-room log hotel in downtown area is landmark, recently expanded and renovated. Some kitchenettes, open year-round. A favorite with Alaskans. Café next door. On Sterling Hwy.

Land's End. *Moderate.* Open Memorial to Labor Day. Fascinating location at end of Homer Spit, recreational area 6½ miles from town. Bunk rooms to suites. Restaurant, bar. Activities arranged; fishing, hunting, sightseeing.

Inlet Inn. *Inexpensive.* 11 rooms. Limo from airport and ferry.

Seafair Motel. *Inexpensive.* Located across from Homer High School, and affording view of Kachmak Bay, this motel offers rooms and apartments with private baths, some cooking units. Pets welcome.

KENAI

Sheffield House. *Expensive.* Medium-size two-story motel, centrally located. TV, 24-hour direct-dial phones. Coffee shop, dining room, bar. On Willow St.

The Place Motel. *Moderate.* 15 rooms. Café and bar.

Katmai Motel. *Inexpensive.* Restaurant, lounge.

KODIAK

Kodiak Sheffield House. *Deluxe.* Across from fascinating fishing boat harbor. 50 rooms, plus 40 more in new addition. Regional giant, Kodiak Bear (stuffed) on display. Coffee shop, dining room, bar.

Shelikof Lodge. *Expensive.* Recently remodeled two-story building downtown. Restaurant and cocktail lounge. Alaskan artifacts featured in gift shop.

Kodiak Star Motel. *Moderate.* 26 rooms, some with kitchenettes. Laundry facilities.

KOTZEBUE

Nul-luk-vik Hotel. *Deluxe.* A prefabricated, flown- and barged-in native-corporation-built hotel. 85 rooms with phones, restaurant, bar, gift shop. Very well managed and decorated. Overlooking Kotzebue Sound of Arctic Ocean. Fine midnight sun viewing rooms on each floor. Houses tours.

MT. McKINLEY

Mt. McKinley Park Station Hotel. *Deluxe.* Large inn near railroad depot and airstrip, 1¼ miles beyond park entrance. Variety of accommodations available, including some in renovated railroad cars. Audio-visual presentations, naturalist lectures, hiking trails. Sightseeing trips at extra charge. Snack shop, saloon, dining room, gift shop. Open in summer. Store, gas stations, parking lot.

McKinley Chalet. *Deluxe.* Suites. A few miles from Station Hotel, and overlooking Nenana River.

Mt. McKinley Village. *Expensive.* 6¼ mi. S. of park entrance. Coin laundry. Gas station, groceries, campground, café and bar. Open May 15 through Sept. At Mile 154.8, Denali Hwy.

Carlo Creek Lodge. *Moderate.* Rustic log cabins and modern trailers with bath, 15 miles south of Park entrance.

McKinley KOA Kampground. Groceries, laundromat, restaurant nearby. 10 miles north of Park entrance. Free transportation to Park Station and Visitor Center. Optional Hills of Fire tour to coal fields. Open in summer. (Some other fine KOA campgrounds are at Tok on the Alaska Highway, and at Sunrise, 7½ miles along the Hope Road off the Anchorage–Seward Highway.)

NOME

Nugget Inn. *Deluxe.* Arctic tours stay here. Otherwise on space-available basis. Some rooms overlook restless Bering Sea. Attractive Gold Rush decor and spacious lobby, restaurant, bar. On Front St.

Polaris Hotel. *Inexpensive.* Bar and liquor store. 24 rooms, but baths are mostly down the hall. Space may be scarce because of renewed interest in gold prospecting.

SEWARD

Breeze Inn. *Moderate-Expensive.* At small boat harbor.

Marina Motel; Murphy's Motel, both *moderate* and not far from small boat harbor.

New Seward Hotel and Gift Shop. *Moderate.* Handy to bus and ferry terminals. Round-the-clock courtesy coffee. Half a block to food and drink.

Van Gilder Hotel. *Inexpensive.* Vintage look and old-fashioned charm and hospitality.

SOLDOTNA

International Hotel. *Expensive.* Two-story motor inn on Kenai River. Comfortable rooms, attractive furnishings. TV. Direct-dial phones. Fishing (license required). Golf. Dining room, bar. At Mile 95, Sterling Hwy.

4 Royle Parkers. *Moderate.* Small motel with gas, liquor, lounge and restaurant. On Kenai Spur road, mile 98.

River Terrace Motel. *Inexpensive.* Small motel with pleasant rooms, TV, radios, car plugs. Restaurant, beer and wine. At Mile 95.2, Sterling Hwy.

Soldotna Inn. *Moderate.* This motel offers units with private baths, some kitchenettes. Free TV and coffee. At Kenai Jct.

TOK

Golden Bear Motel. *Moderate.* Sixteen rustic log units, with private baths, kitchenettes or full kitchens. Coin laundry. Gift shop. Campground, trailer park, and free picnic area. Small wildlife museum. Open Mar.–Oct. 15. Seasonal rates. On Glenn Hwy., ¼ mi. S of jct. Alaska Hwy. (P.O. Box 276).

Tundra Lodge. *Expensive.* 45 new deluxe rooms bring the total to 78. Large restaurant, separate cocktail lounge, gift store, liquor store, and laundromat. KOA campground also remodeled and enlarged to 54 sites—full hookup, many drive-thru sites. Tenting area with fire pits. Campground facilities: shower house, car/truck wash, sanitary dump, and ice machines. Tundra Lodge and KOA are the largest, most modern on the Alaska Highway between Whitehorse and Fairbanks. At Mile 1315 (P.O. Box 336).

Alaskan Parker House Motel. *Moderate.* Open year-round. Restaurant, bar, gift shop, gas station, and liquor store.

Tok Lodge (pronounced Toke). *Moderate.* 16 rooms with bath. Restaurant, bar, game room, liquor store.

VALDEZ

Lamplighter Hotel. *Deluxe.* 50 rooms, restaurant, bar. Close to shopping.

Sheffield House. *Deluxe.* 100 units with full bath and shower. Dining room and bar. Marina, dock, boat and motor rentals. Fishing Tackle & bait shop. Daily custom smoking and canning service. No pets. At Valdez' small-boat harbor.

Totem Inn. *Expensive.* Alaskan touches in lobby include mounted wild game and cheery fireplace. Restaurant and lounge. Richardson Hwy. and Meals Ave.

Valdez Motel. *Moderate.* With assorted singles, doubles, and family units among its 27 rooms. Features "Pipeline Club."

Village Motel. *Moderate.* Family cottages with kitchenettes. Children, pets O.K.

WASILLA

Eskimotel. *Moderate.* 10 modern units, gourmet dining room, bar. Banquet room for 100, and a dorm that sleeps 8 at $10 each.

  YOUTH HOSTELS. In Ketchikan and Nome contact the Methodist Church. The *Juneau Youth Hostel* is in the Northern Light Church. In Sitka it is in the Presbyterian Church. At McKinley Park, there's one near the Station Hotel. Ask around for location of Cordova's. The *Whitehorse, Y.T. Youth Hostel* is on the Alaska Highway in the Recreation Center at the Whitehorse International Airport. In Yukon Territory, along the highway before Kluane Lake, the Mountain View Lodge is now a hostel; Minto on the Yukon River also has one. Write the National Offices, American Youth Hostels, Delaplane, VA 22025 for listings. As in the Pacific Northwest states to the south, state and federal campgrounds are logical stopping spots for young people trying to travel inexpensively through the 49th state. In Anchorage, the *YMCA,* at 6th and F, offers inexpensive accommodations for servicemen and civilians. At Fairbanks, the *University of Alaska* makes rooms available in summer for students attending workshops and campus conventions. (For inexpensive commercial accommodations, see section on *Lodgings.*) Still, with the high cost of transient housing in most parts of Alaska, camping gear with warm sleeping bags is top-priority equipment for any budget-conscious youth.

DINING OUT in Alaska means a wide variety of exciting and unusual foods for the traveler. Reindeer steak or stew, sourdough bread and sourdough pancakes, and sheefish are only a few Alaskan specialties that visitors like to try. Not to be missed here, of course, is seafood—the king crab, fresh salmon, halibut, or tiny Alaskan shrimp, and scallops. You may be offered "moose milk," but unless you see it produced from the animal before your very eyes, it will probably be ordinary milk laced with cinnamon and (likely) some whiskey. Check the hotel listings for the city you are visiting. Often hotel or inn dining rooms are the best in town, or the only place. Sometimes eating at the "only place in town" turns out to be a delightful, friendly, and often delicious experience. Don't hesitate to ask the "natives" where they eat, when they want to splurge, and when they want to eat inexpensively—but well. Food in Alaska won't seem cheap, and the farther from the source of supply, the costlier it gets. Except in the big cities, the following categories won't mean much, other than give you a clue to the tab. Generally, budget about $35 per day per person for restaurants other than the fast food kind. Breakfast or lunch may run $4 to $8; dinners $8–$30. Restaurants are listed according to their price category. Categories and ranges for a complete dinner are: *Deluxe:* $20–$30; *Expensive:* $15–$20; *Moderate:* $9–14; and *Inexpensive:* about $8. A la carte meals would cost a bit more. For a more complete explanation of restaurant categories see *Facts At Your Fingertips* at the front of this volume.

CORDOVA

The Reluctant Fisherman. *Moderate.* Takes full advantage of Cordova's jewel-like setting in lovely harbor bordered by mountains.

DELTA JUNCTION

Meals for the traveler are available in the "moderate" price range in Delta Junction at **Evergreen Inn** (highly recommended).

FAIRBANKS

Bear and Seal Restaurant. *Deluxe.* Fine food, elegant surroundings. Bar. In Travelers Inn, 8th & Noble.

Sourdough Dining Room. *Deluxe.* Rustic, but elegant: warm wood finish and fireplace, with nearby Dogsled Saloon (lady bartenders). Captain Bartlett Inn, 1411 Airport Way, near Alaskaland.

The Switzerland. *Expensive.* "A bit of the Old World" with specialties from Switzerland, Austria, Germany, France, Belgium, Spain, and Italy. American special is New York steaks for two, served with a bottle of champagne or sparkling burgundy. Bar. On Airport Rd. at Mile 3.

Club 11. *Expensive-Moderate.* Warm atmosphere with fireside dining. Prime ribs and steaks are the specialties, also chicken and seafood. Bar, with music and dancing. At Mile 11, Richardson Hwy.

Husky Dining Room. *Expensive-Moderate.* In Fairbanks Inn. Alaskana decor features mural in copper of a husky team racing up the wall. Tasty food comes in husky-size portions. Also a Dinner Theater with Alaskan entertainment. Ask at hotel desk. Bar adjacent. 1521 Cushman.

Ivory Jack's. *Expensive-Moderate.* Goldstream Road. Restaurant with salad bar 2nd floor, above bar with music and lots of locals.

Mine Room. *Expensive-Moderate.* "Lodes" of atmosphere in cozy, dim mineshaft decor. Alaskan food featured, including reindeer. Also family bunkhouse dining in larger room, and nightly entertainment at nearby Malemute Saloon of the Cripple Creek Resort. At Ester, 12 miles west on Nenana Highway.

The Ranch Dinner House. *Expensive-Moderate.* Everything, plus fine Mexican food. 2223 South Cushman.

Kobuk Kettle Traveler's Inn. *Moderate.* Coffee shop open 6 A.M. to midnight. 8th & Noble.

Sandbar Restaurant. *Moderate.* Nostalgic dining aboard the old river queen *Nenana,* drydocked now at Alaskaland.

Tiki Cove. *Moderate.* Popular downtown restaurant featuring well-cooked food, good service. Chinese and American dishes. Charming Oriental-Polynesian atmosphere. At 546 3rd Ave.

The Pumphouse. *Inexpensive-Moderate.* Don't miss the atmosphere and antiques in this historic Old Chena Pumping Station on the Chena River. Now a restaurant and saloon, it's about 2 miles on the Chena Pump Road. They'll make you welcome whether you come by boat, float plane, car, or bicycle. (You may need a map to find the Pump Road. It takes off where the Geist Road, the Chena Ridge Road, and Highway #3 headed for McKinley come together, a short distance out of town.)

Arctic Pancake House. *Inexpensive.* Pancakes come in assorted nationalities with Alaskan sourdoughs the specialty. Across from the Log Cabin Visitor Center.

Star of the North Bakery. *Inexpensive.* Good meals, and where they bake the delicious doughnuts for the sternwheeler *Discovery* cruise refreshments.

Also good bets *(inexpensive)* for family meals: **H. Salt, Esq.** for fish 'n' chips; **Kentucky Fried Chicken** for fingerlickin' plus Country Style Ribs; and terrific **Tio Taco's,** for burritos and enchiladas.

HOMER

Porpoise Room. *Moderate.* Located on the Homer Spit and overlooking the small-boat basin and Kachemak Bay, this dining room specializes in fine steaks and Homer seafood. Bar.

Sterling Café. *Moderate.* Grade-A meats and seafood, homemade pies. By Heady Hotel.

Waterfront Bar and Dining. *Moderate.* Dinners only at this cozy dining room. In downtown Homer.

Acropolis. *Moderate.* A Greek restaurant with Pizza Bar and other Italian food. Grecian decor features painting of namesake.

The Ebbtide Dinner House. *Moderate.* In the middle of town.

Putter Inn. *Moderate.* 5 miles out east road, overlooking Kachemak Bay. Name kept, though "putting green" never developed. Very popular. The locals head there for good food and dancing.

Land's End. *Moderate.* At the end of the Spit. Seafood specialties. Open Memorial Day to Labor Day only.
   Inexpensive. **The Parfait Shoppe** for hamburgers, milk shakes, and soft ice cream; the **Reel House** for soup, sandwiches and movies; and the **Soup Bowl** at the Lakeside Mall.

KODIAK

Sheffield House Dining Room. *Expensive.* Overlooks fishboat harbor.

Copper Corner. *Moderate.* Steak House, but Kodiak's seafoods served, too.

Harbor Room. *Moderate.* Shelikof Lodge.

Rendezvous Inn. *Moderate-Expensive.* At Middle Bay, this Ocean View Roadhouse has dining and cocktails from 12 noon to 12 midnite.

Sollie's Office on the Mall. *Moderate.* Bar and restaurant, also serving Country Rock music.

Harvester Food Cache. *Inexpensive.* Homebaked goodies; home-style cooking; accent on fish and clam strips and chips.

NOME

Colo's Place in the Bering Sea. *Expensive.* Seafood and steak.

The Roadhouse. *Expensive.* 3 miles out of town. Reindeer steaks a specialty. Newly expanded, it's a place to meet convivial locals. Nome's ex-mayor may be tending the bar. Order his concoctions, a "Tanglefoot" or a "Bering Ball" while watching the "Frivolous Front Street Follies" in the Starlight Room.

The Polar Cub. *Moderate.* Serves breakfast and lunch, then the staff moves to the Roadhouse for serving dinners. Behind Front St., next to sea wall.

SEWARD

Apollo Restaurant. *Moderate.* Italian-Alaskan, and delicious.

Harbor Dinner Club. *Moderate.* Seats 100 for local seafood and choice steak specialties. Also cocktails.

Captain's Table. *Moderate.* Next to the Breeze Inn. Overlooking the beautiful Seward small-boat harbor, rebuilt after 1964 earthquake.

SOLDOTNA

Riverside House. *Moderate.* Adjoins International Motor Hotel, specializes in steaks and Alaska seafoods.

TOK

Tok Lodge. *Moderate.* Hearty Alaskan meals, cocktail bar, and pool room.

VALDEZ

Pipeline Club. *Expensive.* In Valdez Motel. Salmon is so fresh it may not be on the menu yet—ask the waitress.

Sheffield House. *Expensive.* Restaurant overlooks picturesque boat harbor. Drinks iced with chunks of the Columbia Glacier.

Hangar 9. *Moderate.* At airport.

Organic Grubstake. *Moderate.* Across from the small boat harbor. Features natural foods.

Meals in the *Moderate* category can also be found in the restaurants in the Lamplighter Hotel and the Totem Inn.

Pizza Plaza. *Moderate.* View of pipeline terminal site from Harbor Club Bar. Plus ravioli, spaghetti, lasagna.

Valdez Café. *Moderate.* Chinese-American. Downtown.

INDEX

(The letters **H** and **R** indicate hotel and restaurant listings.)